Thomas Rawson Birks

The Companion Psalter

Or four hundred and fifty versions of the Psalms, selected and original, for public or private worship

Thomas Rawson Birks

The Companion Psalter
Or four hundred and fifty versions of the Psalms, selected and original, for public or private worship

ISBN/EAN: 9783337290566

Printed in Europe, USA, Canada, Australia, Japan

Cover: Foto ©Lupo / pixelio.de

More available books at **www.hansebooks.com**

The Companion Psalter:

or

FOUR HUNDRED AND FIFTY

VERSIONS OF THE PSALMS,

SELECTED AND ORIGINAL,

For Public or Private Worship.

"*Sing Psalms unto Him.*"—1 CHRON. XVI. 9.

LONDON:
SEELEYS AND CO., 1874.

[All rights reserved.]

LONDON:
PRINTED AT THE OPERATIVE JEWISH CONVERTS' INSTITUTION,
PALESTINE PLACE, CAMBRIDGE HEATH.

PREFACE.

THE COMPANION PSALTER, as its name implies, is not designed or adapted to displace any Hymn-book now in use, but to supply a want, occasioned by recent changes in our Church Psalmody.

The Church of England for a long time made provision for singing in the congregation only by the Old and New versions of the Book of Psalms. But when spiritual life revived in the last century, and the hymnal stores of our language were largely increased, private zeal supplied, to some extent, this great defect in the public liturgy. Many collections were prepared, and came into use in many churches, composed of selected versions of the Psalms, and a larger number of hymns by modern writers.

Of late the change has proceeded further. The great increase of the materials from which a selection can be made, with other reasons, have led recent compilers to omit the Psalter entirely, except a few versions blended with the general series of hymns, and thus to depart entirely from the earlier usage of the Church of England.

This change, though a great improvement on the whole, is attended with a partial danger and loss. For metrical versions of the Psalms fulfil a double purpose. They supply a directly Scriptural basis for modern hymnody, by association with that inspired book, which has been the fountain head of worship to the Church for three thousand years. They bring the sacred book into closer contact with the present experience and wants of Christians, and hereby lessen the risk of divergence from the Scriptural standard of piety into a sensational or mediæval style of worship; while the reading or chanting of the Psalms, as appointed in the Prayer-book, is thus brought into nearer connection, by an intermediate link, with the whole range of the hymnal treasures of the Church of Christ in these latter days.

The present Psalter is designed to supply the want which has thus recently arisen. It contains about 450 versions, or an average of fifteen for each day of the month. Nearly one hundred are taken from Dr. Watts, but with considerable license of needful alteration, and many from other sources of the last century. The psalms or hymns of deceased writers, when published forty years, seem to me also to rank as the public property of the Church of Christ, and those which have appeared without reserve of rights in three or four collections. I am indebted to Dr. Kennedy for liberty to use his own versions in the "Cambridge Psalter," and "Hymnologia Christiana," and to the Rev. W. Balfour for a similar use of the "Aston Collection;" to the Rev. H. Downton for Ps. 101.2 and 102.5; and to the Rev. E. H. Bickersteth for Ps. 90 and 84.8. One-fourth of the whole are original. To retain the character of a supplement to other collections, about fifty of the best versions are omitted, being found in so many hymn-books, and a list of these with some references is given. The peculiar metres are also expressed by a new and simple notation, and a second index is given of the answering tunes in six well-known books of Church music.

I now commend this humble effort to assist English Christians in their service of domestic or public psalmody to the blessing of Him, who inspired long ago the sweet Psalmist of Israel, and who renews and varies His manifold gifts to His church from age to age.

T. R. BIRKS.

TRINITY PARSONAGE, CAMBRIDGE,
    August 24, 1874.

INDEX OF FIRST LINES.

Above these heavens' created rounds	*Watts*	36.2
All creatures wait upon Thy will	*Balfour ?*	104.4
All hail! victorious Lord	*Goode.a.*	110.3
All power and grace to God belong	*Pratt's Coll.*	118.4
All ye nations, praise the Lord	*Montgomery*	117.2
Almighty Father, wise and just	*T.R.B.*	86
Ancient of mercies, as of days	*Lyte ?*	89.4
Arise, O King of grace, arise	*Watts*	132
As pants the hart for cooling springs	*Lowth.a.*	42
Awake, our souls! to bless our King	*Watts.a.*	135
Before thy mercy-seat, O Lord	*Bathurst*	119.2
Behold, the lofty sky	*Watts*	19.3
Behold, the morning sun	*Watts*	19.4
Behold the sure Foundation Stone	*Watts*	118.2
Bless, O my soul, the living God	*Watts*	103
Blest are the sons of peace	*Watts*	133
Blest are the souls that hear and know	*Watts*	39.3
Blest be the Lord, who heard my prayer	*Dwight*	28.2
Blest is the man, for ever blest	*Watts.a.*	32.3
Blest is the man who fears the Lord	*T.R.B.*	112
Call Jehovah thy salvation	*Montgomery*	91.2
Come, O come, in sacred lays	*Sandys*	148.2
Come, sound his praise abroad	*Watts.a.*	95.2
Creator of the world, to Thee	*Coffin.a.*	137.4
Day of light, all days excelling	*Hymnol.a.*	118.5
Earlier than the star of morning	*Hymnol.a.*	143.3
Early, my God, without delay	*Watts*	63.2
Earth, with all thy thousand voices	*Hymnol.*	66.4
Eternal Lord, thy deeds of might	*T.R.B.*	111.2
Except the Lord do build the house	*T.R.B.*	127
Except the Lord the city keep	*Mason.a.*	127.2
Extol the Lord, the Lord most high	*Balf. Coll.*	47
Fall down, ye nations, and adore	*Montgomery*	72.4
Far as the isles extend	*Goode*	72.3
Far as thy name is known	*Watts*	48.2
Far from the world, O Lord, I flee	*Cowper*	55.3
Father, I bless thy gracious hand	*Watts*	119.7
Father, I sing thy wondrous grace	*Watts*	69
For ever blessed be the Lord	*Watts*	144
For ever, Lord, thy faithful word	*Hymnol.a.*	119.11
Founded in the holy mountains	*T.R.B.*	87.2
From age to age exalt His name	*Watts.a.*	107.2
From depths of woe to God I cry	*Lyte*	130.2
From heaven, O Lord, thy holy eyes	*T.R.B.*	14
From lowest depths of woe	*N.V.*	130

Gently, gently lay Thy rod	*Lyte*	6.2
Gird on Thy conquering sword	*Doddridge*	45.6
Give ear, O Lord, unto my voice	*T.R.B.*	5.3
Give glory to the Lord	*Lyte*	29.4
Give thanks to God, he reigns above	*Watts*	107
Give thanks to God most high	*Watts.a.*	136.5
Give to our God immortal praise	*Watts*	136.2
Give to the Lord, ye sons of might	*T.R.B.*	29
Glad was my heart to hear	*Montgomery*	122.2
God in his temple let us meet	*Montgomery*	132.3
God is my strong salvation	*Montgomery*	27.4
God is our Help, when ills abound	*Gilpin.a.*	46.2
God is our sure defence, our aid	*Kennedy?*	46.3
God is the refuge of His saints	*Watts*	46
God of glory, God of might	*Lyte*	101.2
God of grace, in hours of sadness	*T.R.B.*	42.2
God of my life, look gently down	*Watts.a.*	39.2
God of the morning, at whose voice	*Watts*	19.2
God rules in realms of light	*Hymnol.a.*	93.4
Great God! create my heart anew	*Watts.a.*	51.2
Great God! how oft did Israel prove	*Watts.a.*	78
Great God! indulge my humble claim	*Watts*	63
Great High Priest, in glory seated	*T.R.B.*	110.5
Great is the Lord, O let us raise	*Hymnol.*	48.4
Great is the Lord our God	*Watts*	48
Green pastures and clear streams	*Montgomery*	23.7
Hail, gracious Source of every good	*Auber*	61.2
Hail to the Lord's Anointed!	*Montgomery*	72
Hallelujah! raise, O raise	*Conder*	113.3
Haste, O Lord! my soul deliver	*T.R.B.*	70
Hasten, Lord, the glorious time	*Auber*	72.5
Have mercy on me, Lord!	*T.R.B.*	51
Have mercy on me, Lord, my soul is weary	*T R.B.*	6
He reigns, the Lord the Saviour reigns	*Watts*	97
He that hath made his refuge God	*Watts*	91.3
Hear me, O God of righteousness	*T.R.B.*	4
Hear me, O Lord, attend my cry	*T.R.B.*	39
Hear me, O Lord, in my distress	*T.R.B.*	143
Hear my prayer, O God of Love	*T.R.B.*	64
Heavenly Father, I will praise Thee	*T.R.B.*	30
Help, Lord! the godly ceaseth	*T.R.B.*	12
Help me, Lord, I trust in Thee		56.2
High above created things	*Lyte*	93.3
High in the heavens, eternal God	*Watts*	36
High on the bending willows hung	*Pratt'sColl.a.*	137.4
Hills of the North, rejoice!	*Oakley*	98.3
How are thy servants blest, O Lord!	*Addison.a.*	107.4
How beautiful the sight	*Half. Coll.*	133.4
How blest is he who fears the Lord	*T.R.B.*	128
How blest, O Lord, are they	*T.R.B.*	1.2
How blest the man, with mercy crowned	*Goode*	32
How blest the souls, O Lord, who stand	*Watts.a.*	92.2
How blest Thy creature is, O Lord!	*Cowper*	112.2
How did my heart rejoice to hear	*Watts*	122
How excellent, O Lord, thy name	*Montgomery.a*	8.4

INDEX.

How faithful, Lord, thy loving word!	Kennedy.a.	85.4
How good and upright is the Lord	T.R.B.	25.2
How good, how faithful, Lord, art thou	Lyte	78.3
How good to praise thee, glorious Lord	Kennedy.a.	92.2
How great a being, Lord, is thine	Mason.a.	36.3
How honoured is the holy place	Watts.a.	48.3
How long, O heavenly Father!	T.R.B.	13
How long wilt thou forget me, Lord?	N.V.	13.2
How lovely, how beloved is Thine abode	Bickersteth	84.8
How lovely, how divinely sweet	Simeon's Coll.	84
How near is thy salvation, Lord!	T.R.B.	85.5
How pleasant, how divinely fair	Watts	84.3
How pleasant, Lord of hosts, how dear	Hymnol.	84.7
How precious is the book divine	Fawcett	119.10
How shall I sing that Majesty?	Mason.a.	103.4
How shall the young secure their hearts?	Watts	119.3
How sweet, how heavenly is the sight	Balf. Coll.	133.3
How terrible in power art Thou	T.R.B.	66
I lift my soul to Thee	Watts.a.	25
I love the Lord, for he hath heard		116
I love the Lord, his gracious ear	Steele	116.2
I praise the Lord, my heart was faint	Kennedy.a.	30.3
I thirst, but not as once I did	Cowper	42.3
I waited meekly for the Lord	T.R.B.	40
I will extol thee, O Most High	T.R.B.	32.2
I'll praise my Maker with my breath	Watts	146
In all my vast concerns with Thee	Watts	139.3
In anger, Lord, rebuke no more	T.R.B.	38
In Judah, Lord, thy name was known	T.R.B.	76
In my distress to God I cried	T.R.B.	120
In silent wonder, Lord, I stand	Watts.a.	139.5
In this wide, weary world of care	Lyte	132.2
In time of tribulation	Montgomery	77
In vain the powers of darkness try	Lyte	52.2
Incarnate God! the soul that knows	Newton	91.4
It is the Lord the Saviour's hand	Watts	102.3
Jehovah reigns, let all the earth	T.R.B.	97.4
Jesus, ascend thy throne	Goode	110.2
Jesus, Lord, to thee we sing	Auber	110.4
Joy to the world, the Lord is come	Watts	98.2
Judge me, Lord, in righteousness	Montgomery	43.5
Judge me, O Lord, in thee I trust	T.R.B.	26
Judge me, O Lord, my cause maintain	T.R.B.	43
Judge me, O Lord, to thee I fly	Lyte	43.2
Keep silence, Lord, no longer	T.R.B.	83
Let God arise, and all his foes	T.R.B.	68
Let us, with a gladsome mind	Milton	136
Let Zion from the dust arise	T.R.B.	102.2
Long as I live, I'll bless Thy name	Watts.a.	145.3
Lord, before thy throne we bend	Montgomery	123
Lord, end not thou my mortal life	N.V.	102.4
Lord, for ever at thy side	Montgomery	131

Lord God of my salvation...	*Lyte*	88
Lord, I am Thine, but Thou wilt prove...	*Watts.a.*	17
Lord, I daily call on Thee...	*Beaumont*	141.2
Lord, I have made Thy word my choice	*Watts*	119.13
Lord, I have sinned, but O forgive	*Lyte*	51.4
Lord, I will bless thee all my days...	*Watts*	34
Lord, I would stand with thoughtful eye	*Lyte*	69.2
Lord, let me know mine end...	*Balfour*	39.3
Lord my God, in thee I trust...	*Lyte*	7.2
Lord of earth, Thy forming hand...	*Hymnol.a.*	73.4
Lord of hosts, how blest is he...	*Lyte*	91.5
Lord of hosts, how lovely fair...	*Turner*	84.2
Lord, thou art Love divine	*Lyte*	85.3
Lord, thou hast been Thy people's rest...	*Montgomery*	90.5
Lord, thou hast heard Thy servant's cry	*Watts.a.*	118.3
Lord, thou hast searched and seen me through	*Watts*	139.2
Lord, thou wilt hear me when I pray...	*Watts.a.*	4.2
Lord, thy heart in love hath yearned...	*Keble.a.*	85.2
Lord, to us our sires have told...	*S.P.C.K.a.*	44.2
Lord, when I count Thy mercies o'er...	*Watts*	139.7
Lord, where shall guilty sinners flee? ...	*Watts*	139.4
Lord, who shall in Thy courts abide? ...	*T.R.B.*	15
Mid stately halls of royal power...	*T.R.B.*	82
Mine eyes and my desire...	*Watts*	25.3
My God, in whom are all the springs...	*Watts*	57
My God, my everlasting Hope!	*Watts*	71
My God, my King, thy various praise...	*Watts*	145
My heart is full, and I must sing...	*Kennedy.a.*	45.8
My heart, with zeal o'erflowing...	*T.R.B.*	45
My never ceasing song shall show...	*Watts.a.*	89
My Saviour and my King...	*Watts*	45.2
My Saviour, my almighty Friend...	*Watts*	71.2
My Shepherd is the Lord, I know...	*Keble*	23.6
My Shepherd will supply my need...	*Watts*	23.2
My song shall be of mercy...	*Downton*	101.2
My soul, inspired with sacred love...	*N.V.a.*	103.3
My soul lies cleaving to the dust...	*Watts*	119.4
My soul, praise the Lord, speak good &c.	*O.V.*	104
My spirit on Thy care...	*Lyte*	31.4
My times of sorrow and of joy...	*Beddome*	31.2
My trust is in the Lord...	*Lyte*	11.2
No change of times shall ever shock...	*N.V.a.*	18
Not to ourselves, who are but dust...	*Watts.a.*	115
Not unto us, almighty Lord!...	*Lyte*	115.3
Not unto us, but Thee alone...	*Cennick*	115.2
Now let the Church in strains of praise...	*Kemble'sColl.*	146.3
O all ye lands, rejoice in God...	*Auber*	66.3
O bless the Lord from day to day...	*Watts.a.*	34.2
O bless the Lord, my soul (2)...	*Watts*	103.2
O bless the Lord, the Only Wise...	*T.R.B.*	32.4
O blessed souls are they...	*Watts*	32.2
O blessed souls, who fear to stray...	*T.R.B.*	1
O cast thy burden on the Lord...	*T.R.B.*	55.4

INDEX.

O cease, my wandering soul	Unknown.a.	116.6
O Christ, thy work completed	T.R.B.	110
O Christ, whose intercession	T.R.B.	20.3
O come, let us sing to the Lord	T.R.B.	95.3
O come, loud anthems let us sing	N.V.	95
O comfort to the weary	T.R.B.	89.7
O fairest bowers of Eden	T.R.B.	119
O for a shout of sacred joy	Watts.a.	47.2
O fret not in the evil day	T.R.B.	37
O give thanks unto the Lord	T.R.B.	136.3
O God, my heart is fully bent	N.V.	108
O God of glory, God of grace	Lyte	90.4
O God of hosts, our King and Lord	T.R.B.	89.2
O God of love, how blest are they	Lyte	37.2
O God of love, my God thou art	Lyte	63.4
O God of mercy, hear my call	Watts.a.	51.5
O God of mercy, hear my cry	Lyte	55
O God of truth and grace	Lyte	18.3
O God, our fathers oft have told	T.R.B.	44
O God our strength, to Thee the song	Auber	81.2
O God, the King of nations	T.R.B.	79
O God, the Lord of heavenly grace	T.R.B.	60
O God, the Rock of ages	Bickersteth	90
O God, thou art my God alone	Montgomery	63.5
O God, thy mercy, vast and free	Unknown	119.8
O God, when thou didst lead the way	T.R.B.	68.3
O gracious God, when troubles lower	Auber	41.2
O had I pinions like a dove	Watts.a.	55.2
O had I the wings of a dove	Kelly.a.	55.5
O happy state on earth to see	Hymnol.	133.5
O how blest, with holy song	T.R.B.	45.7
O how I love Thy holy law!	Watts.a.	119.10
O Israel's Shepherd, Joseph's Guide!	N.V.a.	80
O keep me, Lord, from shame	N.V.a.	31
O King of earth, and air, and sea	Heber	147.3
O King of mercy, from thy throne on high	T.R.B.	80.6
O King of saints, supremely fair	Watts.a.	45.3
O Lord, defend us! as of old	Bathurst	74
O Lord, from Salem's ruined walls	Downton	102.5
O Lord, in might excelling	T.R.B.	91
O Lord, in trouble hear us	T.R.B.a.	20
O Lord my Rock, I cry to thee	T.R.B.	28
O Lord of hosts, my soul cries out	Kennedy	84.6
O Lord, of life the Fountain	T.R.B.	11
O Lord our God, how great thy name	T.R.B.	8.3
O Lord our God, thy light and truth	Montgomery.a	43.4
O Lord, our heavenly King	Watts	8
O Lord, the everlasting God	Balf. Coll.	104.3
O Lord, the King of Zion	T.R.B.	7
O Lord, the night of woe is past	T.R.B.	85
O Lord, thy mercy from above	Montgomery.a	43.6
O Lord, to thy deep wisdom blind	Kennedy.a	73
O Lord, what foes abounding	T.R.B.	3
O Lord, within thy sacred gates	Wesley	63.3
O may the Spirit from on high	Chr. Psalm	45.5
O my soul, thy powers combining	Balfour?a.	103.5

O plead my cause, thou God of grace	T.R.B.	85
O praise our great and gracious Lord	Auber	78.2
O praise the Lord, and thou, my soul	N.V.	146.2
O praise the Lord, for he is Love	Hymnol.	136.6
O praise the Lord, his greatness sing	T.R.B.	147
O praise the Lord in that blest place	N.V.a.	150.3
O praise the Lord, the God of love	Hymnol.a.	113.4
O praise the Lord, ye hosts above	S.P.C.K.a.	148.4
O praise ye the Lord, prepare your glad voice	O.V.	149.2
O save us, heavenly Lord	T.R.B.	124
O Saviour, Shield and Hiding-place	T.R.B.	22
O serve the Lord with gladness	Balf. Coll.a.	100.3
O sing to God, ye heathen lands	T.R.B.	68.6
O solemn joy of righteous souls	T.R.B.	58
O Son of God, ascended high	T.R.B.	68.4
O taste and see that He is good	T.R.B.	34.3
O teach us, Lord, with tender care	T.R.B.	41
O thank and bless Jehovah's name	T.R.B.	105
O that in the congregation	T.R.B.	107.6
O that the Lord would guide my ways	Watts	119.5
O that the Lord's salvation	Lyte	14.2
O thou God, who hearest prayer	Kennedy.a.	65.4
O thou great Fountain, full and free	Chr. Psalm.	36.4
O Thou most holy, just, and true	Watts.a.	56
O Thou, our hearts' delightful choice	T.R.B.	20.2
O Thou, that hear'st when sinners cry	Watts	51.3
O Thou, who art my only Stay	N.V.	43.2
O Thou, who to our humble prayer	N.V.a.	65.3
O Thou, whom thoughtless men despise	Lyte.a.	36.5
O vineyard of the Lord, how blest	T.R.B.	80.5
O when from all the ends of earth	T.R.B.	14.3
O when will sinners understand?	T.R.B.	94
O who can tell the countless ills	T.R.B.	52
O why should sinners madly rave	T.R.B.	2.2
O Zion, glorious things to come	Unknown	87
O Zion, when I think on thee	Kelly	137.3
Of mercy and of judgment, Lord	T.R.B.	101
Oft from youth have sorrows tried me	T.R.B.	129
On God I cried in trouble's hour	Lyte	120.2
On thee, O God of purity	Wesley	5.2
One thing with all my heart's desire	Balf. Coll.	27.2
Our guilty deeds, O Lord	Hymnol.a.	90.3
Our Lord is risen from the dead	Wesley	24.2
Out of the depths of guilt and fear	Gilpin.a.	130.3
Out of the depths to thee I cry	Kennedy	130.5
Praise, Lord, for thee in Zion waits	Lyte	65
Praise, O my soul, the Lord! how great	Kennedy.a.	104.5
Praise, O praise the name divine	Merrick.a.	150
Praise the Lord, who reigns above	Wesley	150.2
Praise the Lord, whose mighty wonders	Hymnol.a.	148.5
Praise the Lord, ye hosts on high	Balf. Coll.	148.3
Praise the Lord, ye saints, adore him	T.R.B.	149
Praise to God on high be given	Lyte	134
Praise ye Jehovah! praise the Lord &c.	M.C.C.	149.3
Praise ye the Lord! in joyful lays	T.R.B.	113.2

Praise ye the Lord! ye tribes of earth, &c... *T.R.B.*	...	100.4
Preserve me, Lord, from those ... ... *Lyte*	...	140
Preserve me, Lord, I trust in Thee ... ... *T.R.B.a.*	...	16
Preserve me, Lord, in time of need ... ... *Watts.a.*	...	16.2
Quiet, Lord, my froward heart ... ... *Newton*	...	131.2
Raise the psalm, let earth adoring... ... ... *Hymnol.*	...	96.3
Redeemed from guilt, redeemed from fears... *Lyte*	...	116.5
Rejoice, ye righteous, in the Lord ... ... *T.R.B.*	...	33
Repulsed, dispersed, chastised by Thee ... *Fawcett?*	...	60.2
Return, my soul, unto thy rest ... ... *Montgomery*		116.4
Return, O God of love, return ... ... *Watts.a.*	...	90.2
Return, O Lord of hosts, return ... ... *Watts.a.*	...	80.2
Rise, gracious God, and shine ... ... *Goode*	...	67.2
Save me, Lord, from every foe ... ... *T.R.B.*	...	59
Save me, O God, and by thy name... ... *T.R.B.*	...	54
Searcher of hearts, to Thee are known... ... *Montgomery*		139.9
See the vineyard early planted ... ... *Kelly.a.*	...	80.4
Send out thy light and truth, O God ... *Montgomery.a*		43.7
Shepherd of Israel, God of grace ... ... *Lyte*	...	80.3
Shepherd of the ransomed flock ... ... *S.P.C.K.*	...	23.6
Shine, mighty God, on Britain shine ... *Watts.a.*	...	67
Shine in our souls, O King of grace ... ... *Doddridge.a.*		67.3
Sing the great Jehovah's praise ... ... *Sandys*	...	66.2
Sing to the Lord a new-made song ... ... *N.V.*	...	98
Sing to the Lord a noble song ... ... *T.R.B.*	...	96
Sing to the Lord aloud ... ... *T.R.B.*	...	81
Sing to the Lord our Might ... ... *Lyte*	...	81.3
Sing to the Lord with joyful voice... ... *Watts.a.*	...	100.2
Sing to the Lord, ye distant lands ... ... *Watts.a.*	...	96.2
Sing, ye sons of night, O sing ! ... ... *Lyte?*	...	29.2
Songs of immortal praise belong ... ... *Watts*	...	111
Sovereign Ruler of the skies ! ... ... *Ryland...*	...	31.3
Sweet is the memory of thy grace ... ... *Watts*	...	145.3
Thank and praise Jehovah's name ... ... *Montgomery*	.	107.4
That thou, O Lord, art ever nigh ... ... *Auber.a.*	...	75
Th' Almighty reigns, exalted high ... ... *Watts*	...	97.3
The earth is thine, O Lord most high ... *N.V.a....*		24
The festal morn, my God, is come ... ... *Merrick*	...	122.3
The great Jehovah reigns ... ... *Watts*	...	92.2
The heavenly spheres to thee, O God ... *Hymnol.a.*		145.4
The heavens are telling, high and wide... *Keble*	...	19.3
The heavens declare Thy glory ... ... *T.R.B.*	...	19
The heavens declare thy glory, Lord ! ... *Watts*	...	19.6
The heavens declare Thy wondrous fame ... *Kennedy.a.*		89.5
The heavens reveal thy greatness, Lord ! ... *T.R.B.a.*		19.7
The King shall in thy strength, O Lord ! ... *T.R.B.*		21
The Lord ascendeth up on high ... ... *Moravian*		47.4
The Lord, from heaven His lofty throne ... *T.R.B.*	...	16.3
The Lord himself my Portion is ... ... *T.R.B.*	...	53
The Lord himself, the mighty Lord ... *N.V.*	...	23
The Lord is come, the heavens proclaim ... *Watts*	...	97.2
The Lord is King of kings, he reigneth ... *T.R.B.*	...	93
The Lord Jehovah reigns ... ... *Watts*	...	93.3

The Lord my Shepherd is	*Conder*	23.2
The Lord my Shepherd is, no want I know...	*Montgomery.a.*	23.4
The Lord my strong salvation is	*Lyte*	27.5
The Lord of glory is my Light...	*T.R.B.*	27
The Lord our God is full of might	*Kirke White* ...	29.4
The Lord unto his Christ hath said	*Kennedy.a.*...	110.5
The mighty God, the Lord, hath spoken ...	*T.R.B.*	50
The Spirit breathes upon the word	*Cowper*... ...	119.12
The steps of all the just, O God !	*T.R.B.*	37.4
The tempter to my soul hath said	*Montgomery.a.*	3.2
There is a safe and secret place	*Lyte*	91.6
There's not a bird with lonely nest... ...	*Noel*	139.6
Thou art gone up on high (2)	*T.R.B*	47.3
Thou gracious God and kind	*Goode.a.* ...	79.2
Thou, gracious God, hast saved our souls ...	*Auber.a.* ...	31.5
Thou, Lord, by strictest search hast known .	*N.V.a.*	139
Thou, Lord, in heavenly glory...	*T.R.B.*	99
Thou, Lord, my glory and defence... ...	*Watts.a.* ...	3.3
Thou who art enthroned above	*Sandys*... ...	92
Through foes and dangers, sin and death ...	*Lyte*	60.3
Thy earthly dwellings, Lord, are fair ...	*Lyte*	84.5
Thy mercies fill the earth, O Lord	*Watts*	119.6
Thy mercies, O my God and King	*Lyte*	89.6
Thy name, almighty Lord.	*Watts*	117
Thy way, O God, is in the sea	... ...	77.2
'Tis a pleasant thing to see	*Lyte*	133.2
'Tis by Thy strength the mountains stand ...	*Watts.a.* ...	65.2
To God the great, the ever blest	*Watts.a.* ...	106
To God, the mighty Lord	*N.V.a.*	136.4
To God with earnest cry	*T.R.B.*	142
To God your voice in anthems raise	*N.V.a.*	68.2
To heaven I lift my waiting eyes	*Watts*	121.2
To the everlasting mountains	*Isl. Coll.* ...	121.3
To the God of all creation	*Hymnol.* ...	95.4
To Thee before the dawning light	*Watts*	119.15
To Thee, O Lord, my spirit flies	*T.R.B.*	141
To Thee, O Lord. our hearts we raise ...	*S.P.C.K.a.* ...	65.5
Truly, Lord, my soul doth wait	*T.R.B.*	62
Try us, O God, and search the ground	*Wesley*... ...	139.8
Unshaken as the sacred hills	*Watts.a.* ...	125
Up to the hills I lift mine eyes	*Watts*	121
Voice unto voice is telling...	*Lyte ?*	84.4
Wait, O my soul, thy Maker's will	*Beddome* ...	27.3
We bless the Lord, the just, the good ...	*Watts*	68.4
What grace, O Lord, and beauty shine ! ...	*Hymnol.* ...	109
What is our life ? 'tis but a span	*Montgomery.a.*	39.4
What shall I render to the Lord ?	*Watts*	116.3
When dangers press, and fears invade ...	*Auber*	62.2
When I pour out my soul in prayer	*N.V.*	102
When Israel forth from Egypt came ...	*T.R.B.*... ...	114
When overwhelmed with grief	*Watts*	61
When tempests round us gather	*Kennedy* ...	130.3
When we, our wearied limbs to rest	*Lowth*	137

INDEX.

When Zion from her bonds arose	T.R.B.	126
Whene'er the morning lights the skies	Unknown	143.2
While passing through the wilderness	Chr. Psal.	37.3
Who in the Lord confide	Wesley.a.	125.2
Who, O Lord, with favour blest?	Goode.a.	15.2
Whom have I, Lord, in heaven but Thee?	T.R.B.	73.2
Whom have we, Lord, in heaven but Thee?	Auber	73.3
Whom should we love like Thee?	Lyte	18.2
Why do the troubled nations?	T.R.B.	2
Why should I fear in days of ill?	T.R.B.	49
Wilt thou not, O Shepherd true?	Mercer's.a.	119.16
With all my powers of heart and tongue	Watts.a.	138
With glory clad, with strength arrayed	N.V.a.	93.2
With hearts in love abounding	Auber.a.	45.4
With my whole heart I seek thy face	Watts	119.14
With my whole heart, O God our King	T.R.B.	9
With my whole heart, O heavenly King	T.R.B.	138.2
With one consent let all the earth	N.V.	100
With songs and honours sounding loud	Watts.a.	147.2
With songs of grateful praise	Goode	107.3
Ye boundless realms of joy	N.V.	148
Ye holy souls, in God rejoice	Watts.a.	33.2
Ye saints and servants of the Lord	N.V.a.	113
Ye servants of God, your Master proclaim	Wesley	93.5
Ye that obey the immortal King	Watts	134.2
Your harps, ye trembling saints	Toplady	137.2
Zion stands by hills surrounded	Kelly	125.3

OMITTED VERSIONS AND REFERENCES.

A. *Hymns Ancient and Modern*; B. *Barry's Hymn Book*; C.Ch. *Christian Knowledge*, 1st and 2nd; H. *Hymnal Companion*; K. *Kemble's New Church Hymn Book*; Ps. *Bickersteth's Christian Psalmody*.

- 8 O thou to whom all creatures bow B C, H 196
- 18 Thee will I love, my Strength ... B 286, H 224
- 19 The spacious firmament on high B C, H 362, K 368, Ps. 33
- 23 The Lord my pasture shall prepare BC, 217, H 239, K 100, Ps. 143
  The King of love my Shepherd is A 330, Ch. 512
- 26 We love the place, O God! ... A 164, C 436, Ch. 540, K 52
- 31 My times are in thy hand ... B 252, H 68, K 215
- 34 Through all the changing scenes C A, 310, Ch. 334, H 102, K 392
- 36 O Lord, thy mercy, my sure hope B C, K 241, Ps. 25
- 42 As pants the hart for cooling streams ... B C, A 310, Ch. 334, H 102 K 392
  Affliction is a stormy deep ... B, K. 391, Ps. 118
- 47 Thou art gone up on high (1) ... A124, C73, Ch.525, H157, K160
  Christ is gone up with a joyful C 72, H 156
- 51 Have mercy, Lord, on me ... B C, A 81, K 114, Hy. 220
  Show pity, Lord, O Lord, forgive B, K 113, Ps. 110
  A broken heart, my God, my King B H 104, K 112

xiv OMITTED VERSIONS AND REFERENCES.

55 O had I, my Saviour, the wings . B H 243, K 426, S 67
65 Eternal source of every joy... ... B 178, H 37, K 90, Ps. 492
   Fountain of mercy, God of love... A 225, C 144, H 41, K 236
67 To bless thy chosen race ... ... B C, H 79, K 290, Ps.191
   God of mercy, God of grace ... B A 63, C 251, Ch. 373, K 273
69 God of my life, to thee I call ... B A 234, C 135, H 329, K 178
71 When all thy mercies, O my God B C 270, H 363, K 223, Ps. 38
72 Jesus shall reign where'er the sun A 196, C159, Ch.407, H85, K110
77 God moves in a mysterious way... B A 192, Ch. 257, H 211, K 257
84 O God of hosts, the mighty Lord! B C, Ch. 443, Ps. 385
   Lord of the worlds above ... ... B C 147, Ch. 423, H 186, K 42
   Pleasant are thy courts above ... A 307, C 486, Ch. 483, H 184
87 Glorious things of thee are spoken B C 230, Ch.368, H 214, K401
90 O God, our help in ages past ... C266, Ch.446, H201, K99, Ps.14
92 Sweet is the work, my God, ... B C 294, Ch.50, H 150, K 23
96 The Lord will come, the earth B 102, C7, H 50, K 105, Ps.543
97 The Lord is King, lift up the voice C 288, Ch. 513, K 184
100 All people that on earth do dwell A 156, C490, Ch.331, H357, K26
    Before Jehovah's awful throne ... B C 143, H 35, K 28, Ps. 9
103 O bless the Lord, my soul! (1) ... B H 354, K 344, Ps. 225
    Praise, my soul, the King of heaven B A 198, C 241, Ch.484, H 383
    My soul, repeat His praise... ... H 372, K 264   [K 176
104 O worship the King, all-glorious A156, C245, Ch.477, H 381, K47
106 For mercies countless as the sands B H 366, K 288, Ps. 203
117 From all that dwell below the ... C 271, Ch. 366, H 360, K 377
118 This is the day the Lord hath ... B Ch. 48, H 147, Ps. 287
119 Father of mercies, in Thy word... B C 289, H 198, K 203
    O Word of God incarnate ... ... C 435, Ch. 462, H 200, K 350
    Lord, thy word abideth ... ... A 201, B 380, Ch. 426
135 Praise, O praise our God and King A 224, H 39
137 Far from my heavenly home ... A 176, Ch. 358, H 112, K 202
139 O thou to whose all searching ... B 263, Ch. 460, H 106, K 222
148 Praise the Lord, ye heavens ... A 174, Ch. 486, H 384, K 97
150 Praise the Lord, his glories show B C 482, Ch. 485, H 376, K 48

INDEX OF TUNES.

A. *Hymns Ancient and Modern.* C. *Christian Knowledge Society Tune-book (Sulivan.)* H. *Hymnal Companion (Bickersteth.)* M. *Mercer's Psalter and Hymn-book.* P. *Parish Tune-book (Chambers.)* Hy. *Hymnary (Barnby.)*

A.M., B.M., Four Eights, Alternate Rhymes, and Couplets. All Long Metre Tunes.
A2.M. 8884, Ps. 19.7; A. 274, 370; C. 16, 205, 400, 432, 531; H. 271; P. 155; Hy. 90, 267, 282, 368, 420.2, 569.
A3.M. 8888,88; Ps. 139.9.
   A. 17, 171, 331, 353, 369, C. 30, 255, 456; H. 18, 190; M. 41, 65, 229, 235; P. 26; Hy. 45, 85, 103.2, 133, 217, 272, 328, 382, 455, 582.2.
A4.M. 9898, Ps. 50, 93.
   C. 32, 179, 204; H. 280.
B2.M., Double Long, or Four Couplets.
   A. 53; C. 18, 37, 498; H. 32, 362; M. 14, 142; P. 94, 96, 98. Hy. 46, 369.

C2.M., Double C.M. Ps. 31.5, 63.3, 78, 84.7, 119.9, 145.4.
  A. 167, 263, 295, 317, 319, 373 ; C. 53, 82, 99, 142, 184, 300,
  388, 389, 392, 514 ; H. 28, 203, 225, 259; M. 80, 183, 196, 253, 272.
  Hy. 167, 171, 212, 224, 227, 265, 300, 404, 621.3, 641, 642.

C3.M., 8686,88, Ps. 104.5. H. 285; M. 363; P. 223. Hy. 345.

C4.M., Ps. 84.6. P. 144.

**D.M., 7676 Double, Ps. 2, 3, 7, 11, 12, 13, 14.2, 19, 20, 20.3,
  27.4, 45, 45.4, 72, 77, 79, 83, 84.3, 88, 89.7, 90, 91,
  99.2, 110, 119.**
  A. 25, 66, 86, 97, 142, 245, 282, 290, 291, 298, 328, 340, 844, 366 ;
  C. 40, 45, 63? 98, 113, 135, 137, 157, 159, 167, 173? 176, 195,
  218, 239, 290, 301, 317, 340, 351, 395, 451, 578, 580 ; H. 63,
  88, 89, 90, 120, 122, 132, 165.2, 255, 295, ; M. 5, 92, 161 ; P. 182,
  183, 185. Hy. 20, 35, 109, 117, 225, 285, 378, 512.2, 518, 579,
  592, 600, 620.

D2 (7676). Hy. 99, 143, 199, 462, 612, 622.

E.M., 886886, Ps. 9, 36.5, 39.4, 53, 75, 89.5, 90.4.
  A. 72, 77, 116, 199, 346 ; C. 452, 455, 461 ; H. 222 ; M. 28, 109,
  274 ; P. 163. Hy. 8, 256, 394, 396, 413, 503.

E2.M., 887887, Ps. 47 4, 48 4. H 387 ?; M. 401 ; P. 234.

E3.M., 888,889, Ps. 33.2, 113, 146.
  A. 114? 134? 193 ; H. 361 ; M. 191, 293 ; P. 224. Hy 42, 434.

**F.M., 666688, Ps. 11.2, 18 2, 23.2, 45.6. 67.2, 72.2, 93.3 & 4,
  98.3, 110.2 & 3, 133.4, 136.4 & 5, 148.**
  A. 251, 296, 306, 323 ; C. 39, 169, 289, 344, 394, 423, 483, 492, 510 ;
  H. 92, 136.7, 177, 186 ; M. 102, 126, 158, 387 ; P. 174, 177.
  Hy. 363, 507, 564, 607.

G.M., 8787,887, Ps. 46.3, 90.5, 110.5.   A. 37, 294.
  C. 148, 155, 375, 505 ; H. 54, 55; M. 26, 482; P. 154, 158. Hy. 116.

G2.M., 8787,8877 Ps. 45.7. Same, with last line repeated.

G3.M., 8787 Double, Ps. 65.5, 85.4, 130.4.
  A. 330; C. 177, 281 ; M. 278. Hy. 21, 132, 250, 297, 305, 314,
  341, 379, 398, 411, 430, 548.

H.M. ⎱ **Four Sevens, Alt and Couplets, Ps.107.4,117.2,131; Ps. 6.2,**
I.M. ⎰ **15.2, 23.5, 29.2, 31.3. 66.2, 84.4. 113.3, 136, 150.**
  A. 20, 21, 24, 78, 96, 107! 112, 121? 126, 160, 175, 308, 316; H. 25,
  38, 39, 66, 72, 138, 151, 152, 183*, 185, 223, 286, 304,
  313, 323 ; C. 3, 36*, 55, 60, 64, 73, 89*, 101, 107, 134, 143,
  230, 233, 266, 342*, 549; M. 6*, 58*, 78*, 162*, 220, 248;
  P. 100-105*, 107, 108, 109*, 121, 123 127*, 235 ; Hy. 51, 54,
  157, 162.2, 254, 255, 316, 320, 321, 331, 386, 388, 467,
  468, 491 2, 577, 610.

H2.M. ⎱ **Eight Sevens, Ps. 65.4, 72.4. 85.2; Ps. 7.2, 45.7,**
I2.M. ⎰ **56.2, 59, 62, 64, 91.8, 92, 104.2, 110.4, 123, 134,**
  141.2, 148.2 & 3.
  A. 43.2, 104, 110, 113, 179, 284, 307, 381 ; C. 80*, 128,
  144, 149, 243, 396, 427, 431, 483, 494, 527, 573 ; H. 24,
  61*, 42*, 91*, 116*, 376* ; M. 37*, 90, 98*, 215*, 450;
  P. 118, 119, 124, 128, 130 ; Hy. 149, 249.2, 266, 278, 402,
  495, 562, 585.2, 605.

H3.M. ⎱ **Six Sevens, Ps. 131.2, 43.4, 44.2, 73, 133.2.**
I3.M. ⎰ A. 5, 63, 64, 89, 103, 105, 128 ; C. 4, 94, 119, 123 ? 203, 243,
  267, 280 ; H. 6, 26, 73. 126, 281 ; M. 49, 88, 100; P. 111-113,
  115-117, 120, 231, 232. Hy. 43, 50, 57, 257, 312, 350, 458,
  499, 514, 556.

INDEX OF TUNES.

I5.M., Ten Sevens, C. 20; H. 21, 133, 328; P. 132.
I6.M., Ps. 73.4. Tunes for I.M.
K.M., Tro. 8787, Ps. 30, 42.2, 107.6, 143.3, 148.5, 149.
    A. 33, 59, 95, 174, 303, 374; C. 96, 225, 237, 265, 404, 568;
    H. 31, 63, 77, 82, 131, 195, 302; M. 221; P. 134, 141, 143, 155,
    245. Hy. 27, 80, 108, 166, 219, 271, 322, 373, 374, 383,
    400, 470, 551, 652.
K2.M., 8787 Double, Ps. 66.4, 91.2, 93.4, 96.3, 112.4, 118.5.
    A. 292, 293.2, 350, 356, 372, 378, 379; C. 28, 67, 87, 90, 147, 190,
    199, 294, 306, 308, 311, 334, 491, 555; P. 138, 140, 145-147;
    H. 17, 23, 43, 76, 135, 214, 221, 269, 321; M. 16, 136, 269, 313,
    364, 374, 404. Hy. 132, 250, 297, 305, 314, 341, 379, 398, 411,
    430, 544.
K3.M., 878787, Ps. 125.3.
    A. 39, 52, 94.2, 168, 243, 246, 289.2, 304, 322.2, 359, 365;
    M. 19, 40, 54, 91; C. 69, 117, 164, 168, 352, 372, 484, 570;
    H. 52.2, 53, 62, 83, 134, 194; P. 142, 149-153. Hy. 29, 36, 243,
    310, 384, 426, 428-9, 431, 450, 456, 464.2, 529, 534, 614.
K4.M., 8787,77, Ps. 70, 80.4, 87.2, 103.5, 110.6, 129.
    A. 16, 90, 252, 255, 361; C. 34, 38.2, 554, 576; H. 20, 260;
    M. 107, 183? 404? P. 211. Hy. 91.2, 58, 106, 188, 235, 290, 401.
K5.M., Tr. 7878,77, Ps. 119.16.
    A. 117? 358; C. 249; M. 106, 461; P. 199?
L.M., Four Tens, Ps. 23.4, 84.8.
    A. 14.2, 206, 279, 286, 321, 343; C. 27.2, 66, 91, 97, 105, 329;
    H. 9, 10, 193; M. 12, 348; P. 190, 238; Hy. 32, 47, 101, 185,
    228, 377, 439.2, 444, 590.
L2.M., 11.10.11.10, Ps. 6, 100.4, 149.3.
    A. 325.2?; C. 15, 175. Hy. 53.
M2.M., Ps. 80.6.   A. 348; C. 207.
N2.M., Anap. 8888 D., Ps. 55.5, 95.3. H. 264; P. 186.
P.M., 7676,7776, Ps. 150.2.   M. 134; Dartford, (Calcott's Coll.)
O.M., An. 10.10.11.11., Ps. 93.5, 104, 149,2, 150.3.
    H. 337, 381; M. 10, 25, 57; P. 165, 166. Hy. 542.
S2.M., Double Short, Ps. 90.3.
    A. 124, 318, 332; C. 328, 354, 363, 525; H. 48, 49, 117, 157, 322,
    353; M. 30, 138, 275?; P. 15. Hy. 92, 315, 407, 535, 641.

PSALMS.

1   Day 1.   Psalms 1—8.   A.M.

O BLESSED souls, who fear to stray,
   Nor tread the sinner's downward road!
O happy men, who keep the way
That leads the wanderer home to God!

2 How blest, who in his law delight!
In those green pastures I would rove,
And muse with gladness, day and night,
On the deep wonders of his love.

3 Safe planted by my Father's hands,
In faith and hope my soul shall grow,
Like some fair tree, that rooted stands
Where peaceful rivers gently flow.

4 How rich the fruit, the leaf how fair
Of souls that prize his holy word!
Rivers of love and mercy there
New life to weary hearts afford.

5 O plant us, Lord of heavenly grace,
Near to these fountains of thy love!
Until we reach a nobler place,
Trees in thy Paradise above.

1. S.M.

How blest, O Lord, are they
 Who in thy law delight;
Who love to read thy word by day,
 And meditate by night!

2 Fair trees of righteousness!
 Where life's pure waters flow,
Refreshed and cheered by heavenly grace,
 Their souls in beauty grow.

3 Success and constant joy
 Shall all their course attend;
Praise shall their hearts and lives employ,
 Love crown their journey's end.

4 O how unlike their doom,
 From God's commands who stray!
Light as the chaff that flames consume,
 Or tempest drives away.

5 They who despise thy grace
 In judgment shall not stand,
Nor find among thy saints a place,
 To dwell at thy right hand.

6 But righteous souls are dear,
 O righteous Lord, to Thee!
Shall soon before thy face appear,
 And all thy glory see.

2. D.M.

Why do the troubled nations
 In angry tumult rage;
And, filled with fierce impatience,
 A hopeless warfare wage?

Against the Lord's Anointed
　The princes strive in vain:
The King, of God appointed,
　The kings of earth disdain.

2 Thou, Lord, from heaven thy palace
　　Dost mark each vain design,
　And quell their mighty malice
　　With mightier voice divine:
　Thy Son for ever reigneth
　　On Zion's sacred hill;
　And firm his throne remaineth,
　　Thy counsels to fulfil.

3 His mighty intercession
　　Receives a full reward:
　All worlds are his possession;
　　He reigns, eternal Lord:
　See, broken into shivers,
　　Earth's potsherds ruined lie:
　Life, peace, and joy, like rivers,
　　Stream from the upper sky.

4 Be wise, ye kings, and render
　　Due worship at his throne:
　Chiefs, lords, in all your splendour
　　The Prince of princes own:
　Thy foes, O Christ, shall perish;
　　Thy wrath is burning flame:
　Thy tender love will cherish
　　The souls that trust thy name.

2.2　　　　　　　　　　　　A.M.

O WHY do sinners madly rave
　　Against the anointed King of heaven?
From heaven He stooped, our souls to save;
　　The sceptre now to Him is given.

2 Why seek the rulers, in their pride,
   His easy yoke to cast away?
High seated at the Father's side,
   He speaks, and angel hosts obey.

3 Enthroned in majesty art Thou,
   O Christ, on Zion's sacred hill:
Ye kings of earth, with reverence bow!
   Ye stormy waters, peace, be still!

4 The Lord proclaims his high decree,
   The Father, on the eternal throne:
"O Son beloved, ask of Me,
   And claim the kingdoms for thine own."

5 He asks, and all the heathen lands
   Are given him for his large reward:
That firm decree unshaken stands;
   He reigns, their everlasting Lord.

6 Be wise, ye kings! with fear obey;
   Ye princes! bow before his throne:
Thrice blest they are, and only they,
   Who build their hopes on Christ alone!

3
                    D.M.

O LORD, what foes, abounding
   In malice, proudly say,
My troubled soul surrounding,
   His help has passed away!
But Thou, my hope, my glory,
   Dost all my footsteps guide,
Behind me and before me,
   A shield on every side.

2 To God I cried, complaining,
   And from his holy hill

He heard, my soul sustaining
  With heavenly comfort still:
I laid me down, and sleeping
  Was safe from every foe;
For He, my spirit keeping,
  Did rest and peace bestow.

3 Arise, O Lord, and render
    Thy help in danger's hour;
  Still shield me and defend me
    From sin and Satan's power:
  O hear our supplication,
    Thou holy, wise, and just!
  To Thee belongs salvation,
    In Thee thy children trust.

3.2 A.M.

THE tempter to my soul hath said,
  "There is no help in God for thee:"
Lord, lift Thou up thy servant's head,
My glory, shield, and solace be!

2 Thus to the Lord I raised my cry;
  He heard me from his holy hill:
  At his command the waves rolled by;
  He beckoned, and the winds were still.

3 I laid me down, and slept, I woke;
  Thou, Lord, my spirit didst sustain:
  Bright from the east the morning broke;
  Thy comforts rose on me again.

4 I will not fear, though armed throngs
  Mine ears with threatening clamour fill:
  Salvation, Lord, to thee belongs;
  Blessings surround thy people still.

3.3 C.M.

THOU, Lord, my glory and my strength,
  Wilt on the tempter tread;
Wilt silence all my threatening guilt,
  And raise my drooping head.

2 I cried, and from his holy hill
    He bowed a listening ear:
  I called, "My Father and my God,"
    And He subdued my fear.

3 He shed soft slumber on mine eyes,
    In spite of all my foes:
  I woke, and wondered at the grace
    That guarded my repose.

4 Arise, O Lord! fulfil thy grace,
    While I thy goodness sing:
  Thy Son hath crushed the serpent's head,
    And death hath lost his sting.

5 Salvation to the Lord belongs,
    His arm alone can save:
  Blessings attend his people here,
    And reach beyond the grave.

4 A.M.

HEAR me, O God of righteousness!
  In patient love attend my cry!
Thou, who hast saved in all distress,
Renew thy mercies from on high.

2 How long shall sinful men despise
    Thy great and ever-blessed Name?
  How long shall scorners trust in lies,
    And turn my glory into shame?

3 Thou, gracious God, my portion art;
  The men of faith to Thee are dear:
  O Hope of every contrite heart!
  On thee I call, and Thou wilt hear.

4 In silent watches of the night,
  How turns my lonesome heart to Thee!
  No joy of earth hath such delight,
  As when thy gladdening smile I see.

5 In peace I lay me down, and sleep;
  Thy sleepless love surrounds me still:
  Thy watchful eyes my soul shall keep,
  And bring me safe to Zion's hill.

4.2   C.M.

LORD, thou wilt hear me when I pray;
  I am for ever Thine:
I fear before thee all the day,
  My life to Thee resign.

2 At night I rest my weary head,
    From cares and business free:
  'Tis sweet, conversing on my bed
    With my own heart, and Thee.

3 I pay this evening sacrifice,
    And when my work is done,
  Great God! my faith and hope relies
    Upon thy grace alone.

4 With peaceful thoughts and voice of praise
    I'll give mine eyes to sleep:
  Thy hand in safety keeps my days,
    And will my slumbers keep.

5 C.M.

LORD, in the morning Thou shalt hear
  My voice ascending high:
To Thee will I direct my prayer,
  To Thee lift up mine eye.

2 Up to the hills, where Christ is gone
  To plead for all his saints;
Presenting at his Father's throne
  Our songs and our complaints.

3 Oft to thy house will I resort,
  To taste thy mercies there:
I will frequent thy holy court,
  And worship in thy fear.

4 O may thy Spirit guide my feet
  In ways of righteousness;
Make every path of duty straight
  And plain before my face!

5 Lord, crush the serpent in the dust,
  And all his plots destroy;
Let those, who in thy mercy trust,
  For ever shout for joy.

6 The souls, that love and fear Thy name,
  Shall see their hope fulfilled;
Almighty love their wall of flame,
  And never-failing shield.

5.2 C.M.

ON thee, O God of purity,
  I wait for hallowing grace:
None without holiness shall see
  The glories of thy face.

2 In souls unholy and unclean
    Thou never canst delight;
  Nor shall they, if enslaved by sin,
    Appear before Thy sight.

3 But as for me, with humble fear
    I will approach thy gate;
  Though most unworthy to draw near,
    Or in thy courts to wait.

4 I trust in thine unbounded grace,
    To all so freely given;
  And worship in thy holy place,
    And lift my soul to heaven.

5 Lead me in all thy righteous ways,
    Nor suffer me to slide:
  Point out my path before my face;
    My God, be Thou my guide!

6 O may I ne'er to evil yield,
    Defended from above;
  And kept and covered with the shield
    Of thine almighty love!

5.3 C.M.

GIVE ear, O Lord, unto my voice,
    Receive my morning prayer:
  In thee, my King, will I rejoice,
    To Thee for help repair.

2 Thou, Lord, art holy, just, and wise;
    No evil dwells with Thee:
  The sons of malice, pride, and lies
    Far from thy presence flee.

3 But I will haste, with holy fear,
    To worship at thy feet;
And gladly in thy house appear
    Before thy mercy seat.

4 O lead me onward, day by day,
    In all thy righteous ways;
Assist my wandering heart to pray,
    And fill my lips with praise.

5 Amidst the toils and snares of life
    Thy heavenly peace bestow:
And still rebuke the sounds of strife,
    And lay the tempter low.

6 O let the souls, that trust in Thee,
    Their joys aloud proclaim!
And pour thy blessing, large and free,
    On all who love Thy name.

6   L4.M.

HAVE mercy on me, Lord! for I am weary;
    Deep waves of anguish o'er my spirit roll:
Be thou my Comforter, when life is dreary;
    Thy healing balm can make the wounded whole.

Who shall remember thee in hopeless sorrow?
    Or give thee thanks, when sinking in despair?
Return, O Lord! and let a brighter morrow
    Dawn on the midnight gloom of woe and care.

Sad is my life; my days are spent in weeping,
    My couch by night is watered with my tears:
O still encircle me with love unsleeping,
    And heal my wounds, and banish all my fears.

Mine eyes are dim with grief, my strength is
    failing;
  My foes are strong, and cares and fears in-
    crease:
O let not all my prayers be unavailing;
  Speak gently to my heart, and give me peace.

The Lord is good, He hears my supplication,
  My prayers and tears have reached his throne
    on high:
In hours of anguish, sorrow, and temptation,
  He waits to bless, his mercy still is nigh.

No more I faint, though skies be dark around
    me,
  Though deep the waterfloods that o'er me roll;
For Thou, my God, with tender love hast crowned
    me,
  Thy touch hath healed my wounds, and made
    me whole.

6.2   I.M.

GENTLY, gently lay thy rod
  On my sinful head, O God;
Stay thy wrath, in mercy stay,
Lest I sink before its sway.

2 Heal me, for my flesh is weak;
Heal me, for thy grace I seek:
This my only plea I make,
Heal me for thy mercy's sake.

3 Who within the silent grave
Shall proclaim thy power to save?
Lord, my sinking soul reprieve;
Speak, and I shall rise and live.

4 Lo! He comes, He heeds my plea!
  Lo! He comes, the shadows flee!
  Glory round me dawns once more;
  Rise, my spirit, and adore!

7   D.M.

O LORD, the King of Zion!
  On Thee my hope is stayed:
Save Thou from the fierce lion,
  That makes me sore afraid;
From men of heart ungrateful,
  From bitter scorn and wrong,
From malice deep and hateful,
  And slander's poisonous tongue.

2 Arise, O Lord, and banish
  The fears that haunt my soul;
Let foes before thee vanish,
  And make the wounded whole:
So shall thy congregation
  Surround thee still with praise;
Shall own thy great salvation,
  And joyful anthems raise.

3 Thou, O my Father, triest
  The hearts and reins of all,
And timely aid suppliest
  To keep us, lest we fall:
O let the days of sadness
  Be like a midnight dream,
And peace and heavenly gladness
  Around our spirit beam!

4 The evil and the malice,
  Wherewith the wicked burn,
Shall, like a poisoned chalice,
  To their own lips return:

But I will praise for ever
  Thy righteousness divine;
Thy love that changeth never,
  The grace that seals me Thine!

7.2   12.M.

LORD my God, in Thee I trust!
  Save, O save thy trembling dust
From the roaring lion's power,
Seeking whom he may devour;
From a thousand waves, that roll
Shipwreck o'er my sinking soul:
God omnipotent, I flee
From them all to Thee, to Thee!

2 Thou my inmost wish canst read,
Thou canst help my utmost need:
Let the world thy goodness see,
Let them mark thy grace in me!
Lay the wicked in the dust,
Raise the feeble, guide the just:
Searcher of the heart, I flee
From myself to Thee, to Thee!

8   S.M.

O LORD, our heavenly King!
  Thy name is all divine:
Thy glories round the earth are spread,
  And o'er the heavens they shine.

2 When to thy works on high
    I raise my wondering eyes,
  And see the moon, complete in light,
    Adorn the darksome skies;

3 Lord, what is worthless man,
    That Thou should'st love him so?

  Next to thine angels he is placed,
   And lord of all below.

4 How rich thy bounties are!
   And wondrous are thy ways:
  Of dust and worms thy power can frame
   A monument of praise.

5 O Lord, our heavenly King!
   Thy name is all divine:
  Thy glories round the earth are spread,
   And o'er the heavens they shine.

8.2   C.M.

O LORD, how good, how great art Thou,
  In heaven and earth the same!
There angels at thy footstool bow,
  Here babes thy grace proclaim.

2 When glorious in the nightly sky
   Thy countless worlds I see,
  O what is man, I wondering cry,
   To be so loved by Thee!

3 To him thou hourly deign'st to give
   New mercies from on high!
  Didst quit thy throne, with him to live,
   For him in pain to die.

4 Close to thine own bright seraphim
   His favoured path is trod;
  And all beside are serving him,
   That he may serve his God.

5 O Lord, how good, how great art Thou;
   In heaven and earth the same!
  There angels at thy footstool bow,
   Here babes thy grace proclaim.

8.3   C.M.

O LORD our God, how great thy name
   Through all the world below!
Above the heavens thy matchless fame
   The glorious angels show.

2 At midnight hour when I behold
   Thy wondrous works on high,
The moon and stars, ordained of old,
   Bright wanderers of the sky;

3 Lord, what is man, that thou should'st care,
   With deep and tender love,
To raise him from the dust, to share
   Thy Paradise above!

4 How near thy angels he is placed,
   Made lord of earth below;
With gifts of richest mercy graced,
   Redeemed from sin and woe.

5 How near to Thee, the angels' Lord,
   O wonder passing thought!
In Christ thy Son, th' incarnate Word,
   Our sinful race are brought!

6 O Lord our God, how great thy name
   In earth, and sea, and sky!
May we thy boundless grace proclaim
   Among thy saints on high!

8.4   C.M.

HOW excellent, O Lord, Thy name
   In all creation's lines!
Spread through eternity, thy fame
   With rising lustre shines.

2 These lower works, that swell thy praise,
   High as our thought can tower,
Are but a portion of thy ways,
   The hiding of thy power.

3 O should'st thou rend aside the veil,
   And show thy dwelling-place,
The souls which thou hast made would fail,
   'Twere death to see thy face.

4 Can none behold that face, and live?
   Yea, sinners may draw near:
The Lord is kind, and will forgive,
   His love shall cast out fear.

5 O may we soon before thee stand,
   And find, while we adore,
Fulness of joy at thy right hand,
   And pleasures evermore!

9   Day 2.   Psalms 9—14.   E.M.

WITH my whole heart, O God our King!
   The wonders of thy grace I'll sing,
Thy mighty works proclaim:
Thy praise shall tune my grateful voice;
In Thee aloud will I rejoice,
   And bless thy holy name.

2 When doubts and fears and sins prevail,
When powers of hell thy Church assail,
   Thy help is always nigh:
Thy arm will lay the tyrants low,
Will save from every threat'ning foe,
   And lift thy saints on high.

3 Thou art our refuge in distress,
 Thy throne, O God, in righteousness
  Shall evermore endure:
 O greatest, wisest, holiest, best!
 The men, who know Thy name, shall rest
  Beneath thy wings secure.

4 Arise to judgment, mighty King!
 To humble souls deliverance bring,
  And put their foes to shame:
 The trembling nations then shall own
 The Lord our God is God alone,
  And fear thy glorious name.

10   A.M.

WHY dost thou stand, O Lord, afar?
  Why in dark hours thy presence hide?
 While scornful foes in open war
 Assail thy Church on every side!

2 Arise, O King of heaven, arise!
 And lift the mourners from the dust:
 Thy calm and ever-watchful eyes
 Observe the sufferings of the just.

3 Why should the proud blasphemer say,
 No judge beholds us from on high?
 Almighty God! thy power display,
 And hear thy people's earnest cry.

4 O bid the tempter's awful power,
 The reign of sin and darkness, cease!
 In gloomy skies, when tempests lower,
 Reveal thy promised bow of peace.

5 Lord, thou hast heard the prayer, the sigh
 Of humble souls in their distress;

And secret grace thou wilt supply,
When powers of hell thy saints oppress.

6 O come and reign, our Saviour King!
Through heaven and earth beloved, adored:
Ye saints, rejoice! ye mourners, sing!
Let every creature praise the Lord.

11 D.M.

O LORD, of life the Fountain,
  Why should the scorner say,
"Like startled dove to mountain,
  Flee, trembler, flee away!"
See how the troubled nations
  In Satan's bondage groan!
Faith's old and firm foundations
  Seem almost overthrown.

2 But Thou, O God, remainest
  Enthroned in light on high;
All creatures Thou sustainest,
  Thy temple is the sky:
Though foes in countless numbers
  Stand marshalled in the field,
Thine eye, that never slumbers,
  To me is sun and shield.

3 Thy wrath in fiery vials
  Shall on the proud be poured;
But saints in sorest trials
  Will trust thy faithful word:
For God, the high, the holy,
  Delights, with love unknown,
To bless the meek and lowly,
  And raise them near his throne.

11.2   F.M.

MY trust is in the Lord,
    What foe can injure me?
Why bid me, like a bird
    Before the fowler, flee?
The Lord is on his heavenly throne
Omnipotent to save his own.

2   The wicked may assail,
        The tempter sorely try;
    All earth's foundations fail,
        All nature's springs be dry:
Yet God is in his holy shrine,
And I am strong, while He is mine.

3   His flock to him is dear,
        He guards them from on high;
    He sends them trials here,
        To fit them for the sky:
But safely will he tend and keep
The humblest, feeblest of his sheep.

4   His foes a season here
        May triumph and prevail;
    But, ah! the hour is near,
        When all their hopes must fail;
While like the sun his saints shall rise,
And shine with Him above the skies.

12   D.M.

HELP, Lord! the godly ceaseth,
    The faithful remnant fail;
The might of foes increaseth,
    The lips of pride prevail:

With flattering words unholy,
  And dark deceit, they trust
To snare the meek and lowly,
  And trample down the just.

2 Arise, O thou most blessed
    And glorious Prince of peace!
  To save the poor oppressed,
    And make their sighing cease:
  Thy words, O Lord, securely
    In spotless truth abide:
  Not silver shines so purely,
    In sevenfold furnace tried.

3 What though the proud oppressors
    A moment may prevail,
  And hosts of bold transgressors
    Thy feeble Church assail?
  The powers of darkness never
    Thy covenant can remove:
  Thou wilt preserve for ever
    The children of thy love.

13   D.M.

HOW long, O heavenly Father,
  Wilt Thou thy presence hide,
While foes around us gather,
  And fears on every side?
How long with sorest anguish,
  Temptation, grief, and pain,
Shall our vexed spirit languish,
  And look for help in vain?

2 Have mercy, Lord, and hear us,
    Nor suffer us to die:

2 In love still watching near us,
    Thy hourly aid supply:
O let thy goodness brighten
    The path thy children tread!
Our tearful eyes enlighten,
    With joy anoint our head.

3 So, patiently abiding
    Beneath thy sheltering wing,
And in thy love confiding,
    Our lips thy praise shall sing:
Our souls, redeemed from sadness,
    From sins and sorrows free,
And filled with hope and gladness,
    Shall find their rest in Thee.

13.2

HOW long wilt thou forget me, Lord?
    Must I for ever mourn?
How long wilt thou withdraw from me,
    Oh, never to return?

2 How long shall darkness vex my soul,
    And fears my heart oppress?
My grief how long shall scornful foes
    Insult without redress?

3 O hear! and to my longing eyes
    Restore thy wonted light!
And suddenly, nor let me sleep
    In everlasting night.

4 Then shall my song, with praise inspired,
    To thee, my God, ascend;
Who to thy servants in distress
    Such bounty dost extend.

5 O come! and change my sighs to songs,
   My grief to lasting joy:
And save my life, and bid me still
   That life for Thee employ.

14   C.M.

FROM heaven, O Lord, thy holy eyes
   Survey the world below:
When will the prodigals be wise,
   And seek thy name to know?

2 When shall the pride of foolish men,
   Their guilty terrors, cease?
And earth grow bright and pure again,
   A world of love and peace?

3 O King of heaven, awake, arise!
   Bid thy salvation come:
Look down and hearken from the skies,
   And bring thy wanderers home.

4 Let Zion's sons in Thee rejoice,
   Her ruined walls restore;
Till every tribe with heart and voice
   Thy holy name adore.

14.2   D.M.

O THAT the Lord's salvation
   Were out of Zion come,
To heal his ancient nation,
   To lead his outcasts home!
How long the holy city
   Shall heathen feet profane?
Return, O Lord, in pity,
   Rebuild her walls again.

2 Let fall thy rod of terror,
    Thy saving grace impart:
Roll back the veil of error,
    Release the fettered heart:
Let Israel, home returning,
    Her lost Messiah see:
Give oil of joy for mourning,
    And bring thy church to Thee!

14.3   A.M.

O WHEN from all the ends of earth
   Shall Abraham's seed be gathered home?
Joy in their new, their holier birth,
With weeping, yet with rapture, come?

2 Art they not still thy people, Lord,
Though sorely wandering from thy ways?
Where is the promise of thy word,
And where the fulness of thy grace?

3 Thy promise, Lord, is large and free,
And lasts for ever firm and sure:
Thy grace is boundless as the sea,
And shall from age to age endure.

4 Jehovah! haste the glorious time;
Think on thy mighty deeds of old;
And from the earth's remotest clime
Call home the wanderers to thy fold.

5 The fulness of the Gentiles then
Shall come, and worship at thy throne;
And earth be Paradise again,
Where thou, O God, shalt reign alone.

15 Day 3. Psalms 15—18.   A.M.

LORD, who shall in thy courts abide,
On Zion's hill a welcome guest?
Where saints and angels, near thy side,
Enjoy their everlasting rest.

2 O Christ, the Life, the Truth, the Way!
Lead in the path Thyself hast trod:
Thee may we follow day by day,
To reach the sacred courts of God.

3 Thy lips how free from words of guile!
How full Thy heart of tender love!
How patient, when thy foes revile!
How stern, the scorners to reprove!

4 O wondrous was thy oath, and strange,
To bear the curse for men below!
Our faithful Surety would not change,
He drained the cup of deepest woe.

5 We bless thee for thy deeds of grace:
How bright the pattern Thou hast given!
Thy footsteps, Lord, our souls would trace,
And seek through Thee our rest in heaven.

15.2   I.M.

WHO, O Lord, with favour blest,
Shall within thy temple rest?
Who, protected by thy love,
Dwell on Zion's mount above?

2 He who walks with heart sincere,
Filled with love and holy fear:
Heavenly fruits of grace divine
Daily in his practice shine.

3 Ne'er from truth his lips depart,
  Sacred held within his heart:
  Free from slander is his tongue,
  Pure his hands from fraud and wrong.

4 He the scorners will despise,
  Pride is hateful in his eyes;
  While his choicest love is given
  To the meek, the heirs of heaven.

5 He, great God, a welcome guest,
  On thy holy hill shall rest:
  Saviour, thou our Pattern be;
  Teach us, Lord, to follow Thee!

16   C.M.

PRESERVE me, Lord! I trust in Thee,
   For help on Thee depend;
To Thee in want and danger flee,
   My everlasting Friend!

2 My King, my God! to Thee I pray,
   All help but thine disown;
  No deeds of mine can e'er repay
   The goodness thou hast shown.

3 How shall their sorrows be increased,
   Who idol gods adore!
  I will not share their guilty feast,
   Their madness I deplore.

4 The Lord is mine inheritance,
   Who over all doth reign:
  My lot, secure from all mischance,
   His mercy will maintain.

5 I strive each action to approve
 To his all-seeing eye:
No danger shall my hope remove,
 For thou, my God, art nigh.

6 Therefore my heart all grief defies,
 My glory doth rejoice:
My flesh shall rest, in hope to rise,
 Waked by thy powerful voice.

7 Thou wilt the paths of life display,
 That lead to worlds on high;
Where pleasures dwell that ne'er decay,
 Where joy shall never die.

16.2   A.M.

PRESERVE me, Lord, in time of need!
 For succour to thy throne I flee:
I have no merits there to plead,
My goodness cannot reach to Thee.

2 Oft have my heart and tongue confessed
 How empty and how poor I am:
My praise can never make Thee blessed,
Nor add new glory to thy name.

3 Yet surely, Lord, thy saints below
Some fruits of blessing may receive:
These are the choicest friends I know,
For them, in Thee, I fain would live.

4 Far from the haunts of noisy mirth,
 A nobler portion, Lord, be mine!
Among the men of heavenly birth,
Whose thoughts and language are divine.

16.3   C.M.

THE Lord himself my Portion is,
    My lot he doth maintain :
O what a Paradise is this!
    How measureless my gain!

2 Fair is the portion I receive,
    A heritage divine :
The God, in whom I move and live,
    Is mine, for ever mine!

3 I bless the Father, who hath taught
    My soul his secret will;
Whose love and wisdom, passing thought,
    Surround my pathway still.

4 I bless the Son, whose wondrous grace
    Hath brought him from on high,
With joy to take the sinner's place,
    In grief for him to die.

5 I bless the Spirit, Source of life,
    The Lord of peace and love,
Who leads us through this world of strife
    To happier homes above.

6 O guide us, Lord, to that fair land
    Of pleasures all unknown;
Where countless saints with joy shall stand
    Around their Father's throne!

17   B.M.

LORD, I am thine; but thou wilt prove
    My faith, my patience, and my love:
When men of strife in malice join,
    They are the sword, the hand is Thine.

2 Their hope and portion lie below,
　Their prosperous hours in pleasures flow:
　With hoarded gain they feast their eyes,
　And leave to heirs the wealth they prize.

3 What sinners value I resign;
　Lord, 'tis enough that Thou art mine:
　I shall behold thy blissful face,
　And stand complete in righteousness.

4 This life's a dream, an empty show;
　But the bright world to which I go
　Hath joys substantial and sincere:
　When shall I wake, and find me there?

5 O glorious hour! O blest abode!
　I shall be near and like my God;
　And flesh and sin no more control
　The sacred pleasures of the soul.

6 My flesh shall slumber in the ground,
　Till the last trumpet's joyful sound;
　Then burst the chains with sweet surprise,
　And in my Saviour's image rise.

18   A.M.

NO change of times shall ever shock
　　My firm affection, Lord, to thee;
For thou hast always been my Rock,
A fortress and defence to me.

2 Thou my Deliverer art, O God!
　My trust is in Thy mighty power:
　Thou art my shield from foes abroad,
　At home my safeguard and my tower.

3 By floods of evil sore distressed,
With seas of sorrow compassed round,
I sank, with bitter pangs oppressed,
I lay, in deadly fetters bound.

4 To heaven I made my mournful prayer,
To God addressed my humble moan:
He graciously inclined his ear,
And heard me from his lofty throne.

5 He left the beauteous realms of light,
The trembling earth his presence knew:
Beneath his feet was gloomy night,
On stormy winds he swiftly flew.

6 From every snare, that closed me round,
He brought me forth, and set me free:
O goodness vast, without a bound,
That moved Him to delight in me!

7 Now let th' eternal Lord be praised,
The Rock, on whose defence I rest:
O'er highest heaven his name be raised,
The King of grace, for ever blest!

18.2   F.M.

WHOM should we love like Thee,
    Our God, our Guide, our King?
The Tower to which we flee,
    The Rock to which we cling:
O for a thousand tongues, to show
The debt that we to mercy owe!

2   The storm upon us fell,
        The floods around us rose;
    The depths of death and hell
        Seemed on our souls to close:

To God we cried in strong despair,
And God was nigh to hear our prayer.

3   Above the storm He stood,
    And awed it to repose:
  He drew us from the flood,
    And scattered all our foes:
He sets us in a wealthy place,
And there upholds us by his grace.

4   Whom should we love but Thee
    Our God, our Guide, our King?
  The Tower to which we flee,
    The Rock to which we cling:
O for a thousand tongues to show
The debt that we to mercy owe!

18.3   S.M.

O GOD of truth and grace
    My Saviour and my Guide!
Be with me in my earthly race,
    And lead me to thy side.

2   Strength to the weak Thou art;
    O send me health divine!
  And on my feeble, sinking heart
    With beams of mercy shine.

3   Thy way is good and just,
    Thy word is tried and true:
  Yet tremblers, in your Saviour trust!
    His arm will bear you through.

4   He lives! for ever blest
    My Rock and Refuge be!
  He lives, to give his people rest;
    He lives, to rescue me.

19   Day 4. Psalms 19—23.   D.M.

THE heavens declare Thy glory,
    The firmament Thy power;
Day unto day the story
    Repeats from hour to hour:
Night unto night, replying,
    Proclaims in every land,
O Lord, with voice undying
    The wonders of Thy hand!

2 The sun with royal splendour
    Goes forth to chant Thy praise;
Stars, moonbeams soft and tender
    Their gentler anthem raise:
O'er every tribe and nation
    That music strange is poured;
The song of all creation
    To Thee, creation's Lord.

3 How perfect, just, and holy
    The precepts Thou hast given!
Still making wise the lowly,
    They lift the thoughts to heaven:
How pure, how soul-restoring
    Thy gospel's heavenly ray!
A brighter radiance pouring
    Than noon of brightest day.

4 Thy statutes, Lord, with gladness
    Rejoice the humble heart;
And guilty fear and sadness
    From contrite souls depart:
Thy word hath richer treasure
    Than dwells within the mine,
And sweetness beyond measure
    Attends Thy voice divine.

5 O who can make confession
    Of every secret sin?
Or keep from all transgression
    His spirit pure within?
But let me never boldly
    From thy commands depart;
Or render to thee coldly
    The service of my heart.

6 All heaven on high rejoices
    To do its Maker's will;
The stars, with solemn voices,
    Resound thy praises still:
So let my whole behaviour,
    Thoughts, words, and actions be,
O Lord, my Strength, my Saviour,
    One ceaseless song to Thee!

19.2   A.M.

GOD of the morning, at whose voice
    The cheerful sun makes haste to rise;
And like a giant doth rejoice
To run his journey through the skies;

2 O, like the sun, may I fulfil
The appointed duties of the day!
With ready mind, and active will,
March on, and keep my heavenly way.

3 Lord, thy commands are clean and pure,
Enlightening our beclouded eyes;
Thy threatenings just, thy promise sure,
Thy gospel makes the simple wise.

4 Give me thy counsel for my guide,
And then receive me to thy bliss:
All my desires and hopes beside
Are faint and cold compared with this!

19.3   C.M.

THE heavens are telling, high and wide,
   The glory of the Lord:
The firmament and deeps of air
   His handywork record.

2 Day speaks to day, a gushing fount
   Of praise, that cannot fail:
Day unto day, and night to night,
   Tells out the wondrous tale.

3 No sound, no converse, all unheard
   The solemn voice they send:
Their line goes out o'er all the earth,
   Their words to the world's end.

4 God's law is perfect and entire,
   The wandering mind to win:
God's witness is for ever sure,
   To cleanse the heart from sin.

5 More precious they than finest gold,
   That needs no fire's assay:
The honey and the honeycomb
   Not half so sweet as they.

6 But who can count, most holy Lord,
   His wanderings and his sin?
O cleanse me from my secret faults,
   And make me pure within!

7 So may the musings of my heart,
   And every breathed word,
Accepted rise to thee, my Rock,
   And my redeeming Lord!

19.4 S.M.

BEHOLD, the lofty sky
  Declares its Maker, God;
And all his starry works on high
  Proclaim his power abroad.

2 The darkness and the light
     Still keep their course the same;
   While night to day, and day to night
     Divinely teach his name.

3 Ye British lands, rejoice!
     Here he reveals his word:
   We are not left to nature's voice
     To bid us know the Lord.

4 His statutes and commands
     Are set before our eyes:
   He puts his gospel in our hands,
     Where our salvation lies.

5 Not honey to the taste
     Affords so much delight;
   Nor gold, that has the furnace passed,
     So much allures the sight.

6 While of thy works I sing,
     Thy glory to proclaim,
   Accept the praise, my God, my King!
     In my Redeemer's name.

19.5 S.M

BEHOLD, the morning sun
  Begins his glorious way:
His beams through all the nations run,
  And life and light convey.

2   But where the gospel comes,
      It spreads diviner light;
   It calls dead sinners from their tombs,
      And gives the blind their sight.

3   How perfect is Thy word,
      And all thy judgments just!
   For ever sure thy promise, Lord!
      And men securely trust.

4   My gracious God, how plain
      Are thy directions given!
   O may I never read in vain,
      But find the path to heaven!

5   I hear thy word with love,
      And I would fain obey:
   Send thy good Spirit from above,
      To guide me, lest I stray.

6   While with my heart and tongue
      I spread thy praise abroad;
   Accept the worship and the song,
      My Saviour and my God!

19.6   A.M.

THE heavens declare thy glory, Lord!
   In every star thy wisdom shines;
But when our eyes behold thy word,
We read thy name in fairer lines.

2 The rolling sun, the changing light,
   And nights and days thy power confess;
But the blest volume Thou hast writ
Reveals thy justice and thy grace.

3 Sun, moon, and stars convey thy praise
  Round the whole earth, and never stand:
  So, when thy truth began its race,
  It touched and glanced on every land.

4 Nor shall thy spreading gospel rest,
  Till through the world thy truth has run;
  Till Christ has all the nations blessed,
  That see the light, or feel the sun.

5 Great Sun of righteousness, arise!
  Bless the dark world with heavenly light:
  Thy gospel makes the simple wise,
  Thy laws are pure, thy judgments right.

6 Thy noblest wonders here we view
  In souls renewed, and sins forgiven:
  Lord, cleanse my sins, my soul renew,
  And make thy word my guide to heaven.

19.7   A2.M

THE heavens reveal thy greatness, Lord!
   Sun, moon, and stars proclaim thy skill;
Yet shine they in thy perfect word
                   More brightly still!

Day unto day, and night to night
Thy wisdom speaks, thy power divine:
But in thy word with clearest light
                   Thy glories shine.

O Saviour! let that word go forth
As freely as the circling sun;
Till all who walk this fallen earth
                   To thee are won!

Great Sun of righteousness, arise!
Arise, and bid the darkness flee;
Make sinful hearts divinely wise,
    And homes for Thee.

Where earth's dim shadows deepest fall,
And wandering souls in darkness stray,
Rise, Light of life! and bring to all
    Celestial day.

20   D.M.

O LORD, in trouble hear us,
 And help from Zion send!
O God of grace, be near us,
 To comfort and befriend!
Our mortal weakness strengthen,
 Our earthly wants supply;
Our fleeting moments lengthen
 To endless life on high.

2 Above Thine own anointed
 Thy banner bright shall wave;
Our times are all appointed,
 The Lord his flock will save:
Through life's deceitful mazes
 Thou wilt our path prepare;
Accept our humble praises,
 And hear our whispered prayer.

3 Some trust in armed forces,
 Where kings their power display;
In chariots, spears, and horses,
 And warriors' proud array:
How vain their boasted numbers!
 They fall, but we shall rise;
Our Captain never slumbers,
 Our Saviour never dies.

20.2   C.M.

O THOU, our heart's delightful choice,
  Jesus, for evermore the same!
In Thy salvation we rejoice,
  And triumph in thy conquering name.

2 Th' Almighty Father hears thy prayer,
  And answers from his holy heaven:
New blessings still thy people share,
  And saving strength to thee is given.

3 Vain is the trust in earthly power,
  In horse and chariot's proud array;
Thy name in every threatening hour,
  O Lord, shall be our constant stay.

4 Safe shall we stand, triumphant rise,
  When hostile powers before thee fall;
Save, Lord! and hear us from the skies,
  Almighty Saviour, when we call.

20.3   D.M.

O CHRIST, whose intercession
  Is daily heard on high,
To save from all transgression
  Thy people, when they cry;
The Father hears thee, pleading
  Before the sapphire throne;
As once he heard thee, bleeding
  In agonies unknown.

2 Thy offering of sweet savour
  Is precious in his eyes;
He views with perfect favour
  Thy finished sacrifice:

Now from the heavenly Zion
    All help He will bestow;
The might of Judah's Lion
    Shall vanquish every foe.

3 We joy in thy salvation,
    Thy glories we proclaim;
With songs of exultation
    We triumph in thy name:
Thy prayer with God availeth,
    Blest Advocate above!
Thy counsel never faileth,
    Thy thoughts of perfect love.

21   C.M.

THE King shall in thy strength, O Lord!
    Exult with heart and voice;
The Prince of life, from death restored,
    Shall in thy name rejoice.

2 How soon, to grant his heart's desire,
    Thy goodness was displayed!
When steeped in woe, baptized with fire,
    To Thee the sufferer prayed.

3 He asked for life, and life was given,
    Eternal and divine;
Around his brow the crowns of heaven,
    All bright with glory, shine.

4 How bright his royal diadem!
    His jewels rich and rare:
Each ransomed saint, a costly gem
    Of beauty passing fair.

5 Honour, and majesty, and might,
    O Christ, are laid on Thee;
And angel hosts with deep delight
    Thy perfect beauty see.

6 We praise and bless thee, glorious King,
    Beloved of God most high!
O raise our souls from earth, to sing
    The anthems of the sky!

22   C.M.B.

O SAVIOUR, Shield and Hiding-place!
    Thy wounds our life supplied;
The meek shall feast upon thy grace,
    And there be satisfied.

2 Earth's distant tribes to thee shall come,
    To worship at thy feet;
And weary wanderers find a home
    Beneath thy mercy seat.

3 Thine is the kingdom, and thy sway
    Shall all the nations own;
Earth's mightiest princes homage pay,
    And kneel before thy throne.

4 The countless sleepers in the dust
    By thee to life restored,
Shall own thee mighty, wise, and just,
    Redeemer, King, and Lord.

5 A chosen seed, the sons of grace,
    Thy sceptre shall adorn,
And loud proclaim thy righteousness
    Through ages yet unborn.

23 C.M.

THE Lord himself, the mighty Lord
  Vouchsafes to be my guide;
The Shepherd, by whose constant care
  My wants are all supplied.

2 In tender grass He makes me feed,
    And gently there repose;
  Then leads me to cool shades, and where
    Refreshing water flows.

3 He does my wandering soul reclaim,
    And to his endless praise
  Instruct with humble zeal to walk
    In his most righteous ways.

4 I pass the gloomy vale of death,
    From fear and danger free;
  For there his aiding rod and staff
    Defend and comfort me.

5 In presence of my spiteful foes
    He does my table spread;
  He crowns my cup with cheerful wine,
    With oil anoints my head.

6 O God, who dost thy wondrous love
    Through all my life extend,
  That life to Thee I will devote
    And in thy temple spend.

23.2 C.M.

MY Shepherd will supply my need;
  Jehovah is his name:
In pastures fresh he makes me feed
  Beside the living stream.

2 He brings my wandering spirit back,
   When I forsake his ways;
And leads me, for his mercy's sake,
   In paths of truth and grace.

3 When I walk through the shades of death,
   Thy presence is my stay:
A word of thy supporting breath
   Drives all my fears away.

4 Thy hand, in sight of all my foes,
   Doth still my table spread;
My cup with blessings overflows,
   Thine oil anoints my head.

5 The sure provisions of my God
   Attend me all my days:
O may thy house be my abode,
   And all my work be praise!

23.3   F.M.

THE Lord my Shepherd is
   And He my soul will keep;
He knoweth who are his,
   And watches o'er his sheep:
Away with every anxious fear!
I cannot want, while He is near.

2   His wisdom doth provide
   The pasture where I feed;
Where the still waters glide
   Along the quiet mead,
He leads my feet, and when I roam,
O'ertakes, and brings the wanderer home.

3   Let me but feel Him near,
   Death's gloomy pass in view,
I'll walk without a fear
   The shadowy valley through.

With rod and staff my Shepherd's care
Will guide my steps, and guard me there.

4   My table richly spread,
      My foes stand silent by:
    I feed on living bread,
      My cruse is never dry;
    And surely love and mercy still
    Shall guard my steps to Zion's hill.

5   Still hope and grateful praise
      Shall form my constant song;
    Shall cheer my gloomiest days,
      And tune my dying tongue;
    Until my ransomed soul shall rise
    To serve him better in the skies.

23.4   L.M.

THE Lord my Shepherd is, no want I know;
   I feed in pastures green, safe-folded rest:
He leadeth me where quiet waters flow,
Restores when wandering, saves me when oppressed.

What though in lonesome shades of death I stray?
My guardian Thou, no evil can I fear:
Thy rod, thy staff shall be my constant stay;
In life, in death, my Comforter is near.

Before my foes my table still is spread;
My cup with countless blessings runneth o'er:
With holy oil thou dost anoint my head;
What shall I ask, what wilt thou give me, more?

O let thy goodness, wise and gracious God!
And mercy, lead me to thy seats above:
In the bright pathway all the fathers trod,
I seek my home, the kingdom of thy love.

23.5   C.M.

MY Shepherd is the Lord, I know
  No care or craving need,
I rest where his green pastures grow
  Along the quiet mead.

He leads me where the waters glide,
  The waters soft and still;
And homeward he will gently guide
  My wandering heart and will.

When through death's gloomy, lonesome vale
  I take my dreary way,
His rod of comfort will not fail,
  His staff shall be my stay.

My board for me is richly spread
  In spite of all my foes;
Fresh oil with joy embalms my head,
  My cup with grace o'erflows.

O nought but love and mercy wait,
  Through all my life, on me;
And I within my Father's gate
  For long, bright years shall be!

23.6   L.M.

SHEPHERD of the ransom'd flock,
  Lead us to the shadowing rock,
Where the cooling waters flow,
Where the fresh'ning pastures grow.

2 Grant, O Lord, that we may be
Ever glad to follow thee!
And with thankful heart rejoice,
When we hear thy gracious voice.

3 Saviour, when thy loved ones stray
From the new and living way,
Gently call thine own by name,
And our wandering steps reclaim.

4 Through the hours of darksome night
Keep us in thy watchful sight:
O'er each deadly foe prevail,
Let no harm thy fold assail.

5 Jesus, who thy life didst give,
Dying, that thy sheep might live;
May we in thy presence rest,
With eternal comfort blest.

6 Sing we then, to God above,
Praise eternal, as his love:
Praise him, all ye heavenly host,
Father, Son, and Holy Ghost.

23.7   S.M.

GREEN pastures and clear streams,
    Freedom and quiet rest,
Christ's flock enjoy, beneath his beams,
    Or in his shadow blest.

2   Secure amidst alarms
    From violence and snares,
The lambs he gathers in his arms,
    And in his bosom bears.

3 The wounded and the weak
    He comforts, heals, and binds;
  The lost he came from heaven to seek,
    And saves them when he finds.

4 Let earth and hell oppose,
    Let Satan take the field;
  Quenched are the darts of all their foes,
    Their Shepherd is their shield.

5 Conflicts and trials done,
    His glory they behold,
  Where Jesus and his flock are one,
    One Shepherd and one fold.

24 Day 5. Psalms 24—29. C.M.

THE earth is thine, O Lord most high!
    With all its ample store:
  The world, and all that dwell therein,
    Are thine for evermore.

2 Thou, Lord, hast built it on the seas,
    And with almighty hand
  On the deep waterflood hast made
    Its fabric firmly stand.

3 A nobler home the King of heaven
    For his own seat designed:
  O who shall to that sacred hill
    Desired admittance find?

4 The men, whose hands from lawless wrong,
    Whose lips from pride are free;
  Who still from slander keep their tongue,
    And yield their hearts to Thee.

5 On these the King of heaven will shower
   His plenteous blessings down :
New gifts of righteousness each hour
   Their righteous deeds shall crown.

6 So blest are all who seek thy face,
   And on thy help rely ;
Who soon shall tread, redeemed by grace,
   Thy sacred courts on high.

24.2   A.M.

OUR Lord is risen from the dead,
   Our Leader is gone up on high :
The powers of hell are captive led,
   Dragged to the portals of the sky.

2 There his triumphant chariot waits,
   And angels chant the solemn lay :
Lift up your heads, ye heavenly gates !
   Ye everlasting doors, give way !

3 Loose all your bars of massy light,
   And wide unfold th' ethereal scene ;
He claims these mansions as his right,
   Receive the King of glory in.

4 Who is the King of glory, who ?
   The Lord, that all his foes e'ercame ;
The world, sin, death, and hell o'erthrew ;
   And Jesus is the conqueror's name.

5 Lo ! his triumphal chariot waits,
   And angels chant the solemn lay :
Lift up your heads, ye heavenly gates !
   Ye everlasting doors, give way !

6 Who is the King of glory, who ?
   The Lord, of glorious power possessed ;
The King of saints and angels too,
   God over all, for ever blest !

25 S.M.

I LIFT my soul to Thee;
  My trust is in thy name:
O save me, Lord, and set me free
  From terror, guilt, and shame!

2 From dawn of opening day
   Till the dark evening rise,
 For Thee I wait, to Thee I pray
   With ever longing eyes.

3 O lead me in thy truth,
   My doubts and fears assuage;
 Forgive the follies of my youth,
   And sins of riper age.

4 The Lord is just and kind,
   The meek shall learn His ways;
 And every humble sinner find
   How plenteous is his grace.

5 On Thee I still would wait;
   O keep my soul from shame,
 And pardon, though my guilt be great,
   Through my Redeemer's name!

25.2 C.M.

HOW good and upright is the Lord
  To those who seek his face!
He cheers them, from his holy word,
  With rich supplies of grace.

2 With tender love He guides the meek,
   And leads them in his way:
 His mercy, while his face we seek,
   Will be our constant stay.

3 Our souls, amidst a world of care,
    Shall rest upon his word:
Full streams of comfort, pastures fair,
    His bounty will afford.

4 Thy lovingkindness, Lord, fulfil;
    Thy mercies call to mind;
And graciously continue still,
    As thou wert ever, kind.

5 From all the sins of early days
    In mercy set us free;
And lead us in thy holy ways,
    And bind our hearts to Thee.

6 O sweet delight and peace is theirs,
    Who on their God rely!
He guides them here, his love prepares
    Their mansion in the sky.

5.3   S.M.

MINE eyes and my desire
    Are ever to the Lord;
I love to plead his promises,
    And rest upon His word.

2   When shall the sovereign grace
    Of my forgiving God
Restore me from the dangerous ways
    My wandering feet have trod?

3   With every morning light
    My grief anew begins:
Look on my anguish and my pain,
    And pardon all my sins.

4 O keep my soul from death,
   Nor put my hope to shame!
 For I have placed my only trust
   In my Redeemer's name.

5 With humble faith I wait
   To see thy face again:
 Of Israel it shall ne'er be said,
   "He sought the Lord in vain."

26   C.M.

JUDGE me, O Lord! in Thee I trust;
   My footsteps shall not slide:
 O prove my heart, thou wise and just!
   Try me, as gold is tried.

2 Thy love I keep before my face
   In vision bright and clear,
 And in thy paths of truth and grace
   Will daily persevere.

3 Cleansed in his blood, who pleading stands
   Before thy mercy seat,
 With upright heart and blameless hands
   I'll worship at thy feet.

4 I love the place, where Thou dost dwell,
   My God, my heavenly King!
 My lips shall all thy wonders tell,
   And loud thy praises sing.

5 Far from the troubled haunts of strife
   My soul would ever flee;
 And live a calm and peaceful life,
   Devoted, Lord, to Thee!

6 O may Thy love with gentle rays
   Around my pathway shine!
Then in th' assemblies I will praise
   Thy majesty divine.

27   C.M.

THE Lord of glory is my Light,
   My strong defence is He:
What terror can my soul affright?
   What foes shall make me flee?

2 Though mighty hosts encamp around,
   My heart shall never fear:
Though armies rage, and trumpets sound,
   My help is always near.

3 One thing, O Lord, with deep desire
   I seek from day to day;
Within thy temple to inquire,
   And there devoutly pray.

4 There would I see thy heavenly face,
   Thy beauty most divine;
There learn thy messages of grace,
   And prove that Thou art mine.

5 Safe sheltered by thy gracious hand,
   My soul shall there abide:
High on a rock my feet shall stand,
   Above the surging tide.

6 Thy face I seek, thy praise I sing,
   Thy goodness I adore;
And near thy side, O God our King,
   Would dwell for evermore.

27.2 C.M.

ONE thing, with all my heart's desire,
   I seek and will pursue;
What thine own Spirit doth inspire,
   Lord, for thy servant do.

2 Grant me within thy courts a place,
   Among thy saints a seat,
For ever to behold thy face,
   And worship at thy feet.

3 "Seek ye my face!" without delay,
   When thus I hear Thee speak,
My heart would leap for joy, and say,
   "Thy face, Lord, will I seek."

4 O leave me not, when griefs assail,
   And earthly comforts flee!
When father, mother, kindred fail,
   My God! remember me.

5 Wait on the Lord! with courage wait;
   My soul, disdain to fear:
The righteous Judge is at the gate,
   Thy soul's redemption near.

27.3 B.M.

WAIT, O my soul, thy Maker's will;
   Tumultuous passions all be still:
Nor let a murmuring thought arise;
His ways are just, His counsels wise.

2 He in the thickest darkness dwells,
Performs his work, the cause conceals;
And though his footsteps are unknown,
Judgment and truth support his throne.

3 In heaven, in earth, in air and seas,
  He executes his firm decrees;
  And by his saints it stands confessed
  That what He does is ever best.

4 Wait, then, my soul, submissive wait;
  With reverence bow before his seat;
  And, midst the terrors of his rod,
  Trust in a wise and gracious God.

27.4   D.M

GOD is my strong salvation;
  What foe have I to fear?
In darkness and temptation
  My Light, my Help is near:
Though hosts encamp around me,
  Firm to the fight I stand;
What terror can confound me,
  With God at my right hand?

2 Place on the Lord reliance,
  My soul, with courage wait;
His truth be thine affiance,
  When faint and desolate:
His might thy heart shall strengthen,
  His love thy joy increase;
Mercy thy days shall lengthen,
  The Lord will give thee peace.

27.5   C.M.

THE Lord my strong salvation is,
  My helper, ever near:
While He is mine and I am His,
  What has my soul to fear?

One wish, one ardent wish is mine;
  Lord, grant my humble plea!
To dwell for ever near thy shrine,
  And find my all in Thee.

O give me at thy side a place!
  Secure from every harm;
Where I may daily see thy face,
  And feel thy helping arm.

From light to light, from strength to strength,
  My soul enlarge and raise;
Till from all bonds I burst at length
  To endless joy and praise.

28   C.M.

O LORD my Rock, I cry to thee,
  And spend in sighs my breath:
O keep not silence, lest I be
  Like those who sleep in death!

2 Draw not my soul, O Lord, away
  With men who frame deceit;
Who slight thy wondrous works, nor pray
  With reverence at thy feet.

3 The Lord hath heard my suppliant voice,
  My Strength, my Shield and King!
My thankful heart shall loud rejoice,
  My lips his mercy sing.

4 O save thy people! feed them still
  From thy exhaustless store;
With holy joy their spirit fill,
  And bless them evermore.

28.2   A.M.

BLEST be the Lord, who heard my prayer;
  The Lord, my shield, my help, my song!
He saved my soul from sin and fear,
And filled with praise my thankful tongue.

In the dark hour of deep distress,
By foes beset, of death afraid,
My spirit trusted in his grace,
And sought and found his heavenly aid.

O blest Redeemer of mankind!
Thy shield, thy saving strength shall be
The shield, the strength of every mind
That loves thy name, and trusts in thee.

Remember, Lord, thy chosen seed,
Israel defend from guilt and woe;
Thy flock in richest pastures feed,
And guard their steps from every foe.

Zion exalt, her cause maintain,
With peace and joy her courts surround;
In showers let endless blessings rain,
And all the earth thy praise resound.

29   C.M.

GIVE to the Lord, ye sons of might,
  All glory, strength, and praise!
Adore him in those realms of light,
  Where He his power displays.

2 With reverence bow before his feet,
  Who all your hosts hath made:
In holy beauty round his seat
  Be your high offerings paid.

3 Wide o'er the seas his voice sublime
  Is heard, when thunders roar;
And far above the waves of time
  He reigns for evermore!

4 He speaks, and like a startled child
  All nature shrinks with fear;
Hills, forests quake, and deserts wild:
  Jehovah's voice they hear.

5 High o'er the floods supreme He reigns
  On heaven's eternal hill;
Where angel choirs with rapturous strains
  His glorious temple fill.

6 The Lord on all his chosen race
  Will strength and peace bestow:
The souls, that humbly seek his face,
  Shall all his glory know.

29.2   I.M.

SING, ye sons of might, O sing
  Praise to heaven's eternal King!
Raise to him some new-taught song,
To his praise the notes prolong.

2 Hark! his voice in thunder breaks:
Hushed to silence, while He speaks,
Ocean's waves from pole to pole
Hear the awful accents roll.

3 Now the bursting clouds give way,
See! the vivid lightnings play;
Deserts wild, by man untrod,
Hear, dismayed, the voice of God.

4 He the swelling surge commands,
Fixed his throne for ever stands;
He his people shall increase,
Arm with strength, and bless with peace.

29.3   S.M.

GIVE glory to the Lord,
   His holy name revere:
The wonders of his voice record,
   That all who live may hear.

2 The voice of God is strong,
   The voice of God is grand:
It rolls, the sounding deep along,
   It breaks upon the land.

3 The voice of God can shake
   The solid earth around:
The voice of God the rock can break,
   That in the heart is found.

4 About his heavenly throne
   Ten thousand thousand sing:
O'er the vast flood he sits alone,
   The world's eternal King.

5 Almighty is his arm,
   Unchangeable his love:
He keeps his people here from harm,
   And bears them safe above.

29.4   C.M.

THE Lord our God is full of might,
   The winds obey his will:
He speaks, and in the heavenly height
   The rolling sun stands still.

2 Rebel, ye waves! and o'er the land
   With threat'ning aspect roar:
The Lord uplifts his awful hand,
   And chains you to the shore.

3 Howl, winds of night! your force combine;
   Without his high behest,
Ye shall not, in the mountain pine,
   Disturb the sparrow's nest.

4 His voice sublime is heard on high,
   When dreadful thunders roll:
Through heaven and earth the lightnings fly,
   Restrained by his control.

5 Ye nations, bend, in reverence bend!
   Ye kings, obey his word!
And bid the grateful song ascend,
   To praise th' eternal Lord.

30 Day 6. Psalms 30—34. K.M.B.

HEAVENLY Father, I will praise thee!
   Bless, my soul, his glorious name!
Powerful was his love, to raise thee
   From the depths of sin and shame.

2 Lord, I cried, and thou hast healed me,
   Snatched me from the opening grave:
Thou wast near, with might to shield me,
   Wise to guide, and strong to save.

3 Praise the Lord, ye saints! unsleeping
   Is the love that guards your way;
Short will be your night of weeping,
   Soon shall dawn the promised day:

4 Day of mercy, day of gladness!
   When the mourners dry their tears;
Dawning on the night of sadness,
   End of sorrows, doubts, and fears.

5 Day of days, all hopes transcending,
   Rich with peace, and light, and love!
Countless hearts and voices blending
   In eternal joys above.

6 I will give Thee thanks for ever,
   Till that promised morn arise:
Loudest anthems, ceasing never,
   Then shall fill the lofty skies.

30.2   C.M.

I WILL extol thee, O Most High!
   Who dost thy power employ,
To hear the mourners' plaintive cry,
   And turn their grief to joy.

2 In my distress to Thee I cried,
   Who kindly didst relieve,
And from the dark grave, yawning wide,
   My hopeless life retrieve.

3 Now to thy courts with songs of praise
   Shall humble souls repair,
And loud proclaim, in thankful lays,
   How vast thy mercies are.

4 Thy wrath has but a moment's reign,
   Thy favour no decay:
Thou soon wilt end our night of pain
   In joy's eternal day.

30. 3   A.M.

I PRAISE thee, Lord! my heart was faint,
  My feet were sinking to the grave;
But thou wast nigh to hear my plaint,
  To hear, to heal me, and to save.

2 Thine anger, O how soon it dies!
  Thy grace is life for evermore:
The sun may set on weeping eyes,
  But joy returns when night is o'er.

3 In song before the Lord rejoice,
  His praise let all his saints proclaim;
And still with thankful heart and voice
  Give glory to his holy name.

4 In prosperous times I dared to say,
  My mountain stands for ever sure:
But thou didst turn thy face away,
  And who that burden can endure?

5 To thee I raised my voice in prayer—
  "Lord, to my humble suit attend:
In pitying love thy servant spare,
  And be my Helper and my Friend!"

6 Now joy for mourning thou hast given,
  That I may bless thee all my days:
Let every saint in earth and heaven
  Swell the loud anthem of thy praise.

31   S.M.

O KEEP me, Lord, from shame!
  For still I trust in Thee:
Holy and righteous is thy name,
  From evil set me free.

2 Bow down thy gracious ear,
  And swift deliverance send;
 My Rock, my Fortress, always near
  Thy servants to defend.

3 The brightness of thy face
  In mercy, Lord, disclose;
 And shield me by thy heavenly grace
  From all my secret foes.

4 How great beyond compare
  To all who fear thy name,
 The treasures of thy goodness are,
  Through every age the same!

5 O love the Lord, his saints!
  And in his promise rest;
 Who cheers the mourner, when he faints,
  And comforts the distressed.

6 With courage still proceed,
  And on his love rely:
 His sovereign grace, in time of need,
  Will all your wants supply.

31.2   C.M.

MY times of sorrow and of joy,
  Great God, are in thy hand!
My choicest comforts are from Thee,
  And go at thy command.

2 If Thou should'st take them all away,
  Yet would I not repine:
 Before they were possessed by me
  They were entirely Thine.

3 Nor would I drop a murmuring word,
  Though the whole world were gone;
 But seek my happiness, O Lord!
  In Thee, in Thee alone.

4 'Midst changing scenes and dying friends,
  When life's deep shadows fall;
 On Thee my steadfast hope depends,
  Be Thou my all in all!

31.3   I.M.

SOVEREIGN Ruler of the skies,
  Ever gracious, ever wise;
All my times are in thy hand,
All events at thy command:

2 Times of sickness and of health,
 Times of penury and wealth;
 Times of trial and of grief;
 Times of triumph and relief:

3 Times the tempter's power to prove,
 Times to taste the Saviour's love;
 All must come, and last, and end,
 As shall please my heavenly Friend.

4 O thou gracious, wise, and just!
 Unto Thee my life I trust:
 May I always own thy hand,
 Still to the surrender stand!

5 Thee at all times I will bless;
 Having Thee, I all possess:
 How can I bereaved be,
 Since I cannot part with Thee?

31.4   S.M.

MY spirit on thy care,
    Blest Saviour, I recline:
Thou wilt not leave me to despair,
    For thou art Love divine.

2   In Thee I place my trust,
    On thee I calmly rest:
I know thee good, I know thee just,
    And count thy choice the best.

3   Whate'er events betide,
    Thy will they all perform:
Safe in thy breast my head I hide,
    Nor fear the coming storm.

4   Let good or ill befall,
    It must be good for me;
Secure of having Thee in all,
    Of having all in Thee.

31.5   CC.M.

THOU, gracious Lord, hast saved our souls
    From death and endless woe;
Thy wisdom all events controls,
    From thee all mercies flow:
Thou hast decreed that, even here,
    Thy faithful sons shall prove,
In weal and woe, midst toil and fear,
    The riches of thy love.

2 But O when life's brief term is o'er
    And saints in glory rise,
For them what blessings are in store,
    What joys beyond the skies!

A blest inheritance above,
    Prepared by grace divine,
To spend eternal days in love,
    Where all thy glories shine!

32 B.M.

HOW blest the man, with mercy crowned,
    Whose sins have all forgiveness found;
Whose deep transgressions, cover'd o'er
With pardoning blood, are seen no more!

2 How blest the man, to whom the Lord
Doth his own righteousness afford;
Whom mercy clears from every sin,
Whose heart conceals no guile within!

3 I made my guilt and sorrows known,
With deep contrition, at thy throne:
I said, I'll all my sins confess,
And seek Thy grace and righteousness.

4 Scarce had my breast the thought conceived,
Thy grace my anxious fears relieved;
Cleansed my whole soul with blood divine,
And sealed thy pardoning mercy mine.

5 O boundless love! the rich display
Shall teach the trembling lips to pray:
The penitent, with godly fear,
Shall plead, while mercy waits to hear.

32.2 S.M.

O BLESSED souls are they,
    Whose sins are covered o'er!
Divinely blest, to whom the Lord
    Imputes their guilt no more!

2 They mourn their follies past,
   And keep their hearts with care;
Their lips and lives, without deceit,
   Shall prove their faith sincere.

3 While I concealed my guilt,
   I felt the festering wound;
Till I confessed my sins to thee
   And ready pardon found.

4 Let sinners learn to pray,
   Let saints keep near the throne:
Our help, in times of deep distress,
   Is found in God alone.

32.3   A.M.

BLEST is the man, for ever blest
   Whose guilt is pardoned by his God;
Whose sins with sorrow are confessed,
And covered with his Saviour's blood.

2 Blest is the man, from whom the Lord
Doth all his load of shame remove;
Who claims no merit or reward,
But rests upon his Saviour's love.

3 From guile his heart and lips are free:
His humble joy, his holy fear,
With deep repentance well agree,
And join to prove his faith sincere.

4 How glorious is that righteousness
That hides and cancels all his sins!
His ransomed soul, renewed by grace,
With beams of heavenly lustre shines.

32. 4   C.M.

O BLESS the Lord, the Only Wise!
   Who gives the blind their sight,
And scatters round their wondering eyes
   A flood of sacred light.

2 He leads us still, in paths unknown,
   To his divine abode:
New gifts of grace are richly strewn
   Through all the heavenly road.

3 He guides his people with his eye,
   His arm preserves them still:
In every change his grace is nigh,
   Their souls with peace to fill.

4 O may we still his love adore,
   Till we the mount ascend,
Where toil and storms are known no more,
   And praise shall never end.

33   C.M.

REJOICE, ye righteous, in the Lord!
   To you the work belongs:
With harp and voice your praise record
   In full melodious songs.

2 His word is true, his works are right,
   Holy, and just, and wise:
His goodness floods the earth with light,
   His glory fills the skies.

3 The heavens and all their host arose
   At his supreme command;
And oceans fill, in calm repose,
   The storehouse he has planned.

4 He spake the word, and it was done;
    All worlds his voice obey:
  Let every tribe beneath the sun
    To Him their homage pay.

5 Ten thousand thoughts and counsels vain
    The sons of earth devise:
  Thy thoughts, O God, unchanged remain,
    Thy wisdom never dies.

6 O then, with psaltery, harp, and voice,
    Thy praises we'll proclaim;
  With heart and soul in Thee rejoice,
    And bless thy holy name.

33.2   E3.M.

YE holy souls, in God rejoice;
    Your Maker's praise becomes your voice;
  Great is your theme, your songs be new!
Sing of his name, his word, his ways,
His works of nature and of grace,
    How wise and holy, just and true!

Justice and truth he ever loves;
All the wide world his goodness proves,
    He filled the storehouse of the deep:
He spake, and gave all nature birth;
And fires, and seas, and heaven and earth
    His everlasting orders keep.

The eye of thy compassion, Lord,
Doth most secure defence afford,
    When wars and famine waste the land:
Thy watchful eye preserves the just,
Who make thy name their fear and trust,
    Safe in the shelter of thy hand.

In sickness, age, on tented field,
O great Physician, heavenly Shield,
   Send us salvation from thy throne!
We wait to see thy goodness shine,
Let us rejoice in help divine,
   For still we hope in Thee alone.

34   A.M.

LORD, I will bless thee all my days,
   Thy praise shall dwell upon my tongue:
My soul shall glory in thy grace,
While saints rejoice to hear the song.

O magnify the Lord with me;
Come, let us all exalt his name:
I sought the eternal God, and he
Has not exposed my hope to shame.

I told him all my secret grief,
My secret groaning reached his ears:
He gave my inward pain relief,
And calmed the tumult of my fears.

To Him the poor lift up their eyes,
And feel his heavenly goodness shine:
A beam of mercy from the skies
Fills them with light and joy divine.

His holy angels pitch their tents
Around the men that serve the Lord:
O fear and love him, all his saints!
Taste of his grace, and trust his word.

34.2   C.M.

O BLESS the Lord from day to day!
   How good are all his ways!
Ye humble souls, that love to pray,
   Assist my lips to praise.

2 When threat'ning sorrows round me stood,
    And endless fears arose,
He calmed the raging of the flood,
    And sent me sweet repose.

3 O sinners! come and taste his love,
    Come, learn his pleasant ways;
And let your own experience prove
    The sweetness of his grace.

4 He bids his angels pitch their tents
    Round where his children dwell:
What ills their heavenly care prevents
    No earthly tongue can tell.

5 His eyes awake to guard the just,
    His ears attend their cry:
When broken spirits dwell in dust,
    The God of grace is nigh.

34.3   A.M. B.

O TASTE and see that He is good,
    The King of heaven, who reigns on high!
His truth through ages firm hath stood,
His mercy reaches to the sky.

Good in the sunshine and the shower,
When summer skies are bright and warm:
Good, when the wintry tempests lower,
Amidst the whirlwind and the storm.

O taste and see that He is good,
The Lord of providence and grace!
He calms the surges of the flood,
And guards us from his holy place.

Good, when he smites, and when he heals,
And when he gives, or takes away:
Good, when his goodness he conceals,
In sorrow's dark and cloudy day.

O taste and see that He is wise!
Who chastens sore with grief and pain;
Then bids the light in darkness rise,
To cheer the mourner's heart again.

O teach us, Lord, to trust thy love,
To taste thy goodness, and adore!
In clearer light thy saints above
Shall see and praise thee evermore.

35   Day 7.   Psalms 35–37.   C.M. B.

O PLEAD my cause, thou God of grace!
   When men of strife assail:
Defend me from thy holy place,
   Nor let my foes prevail.

2 I trust in him who bore the cross,
   My soul from guilt to free;
And suffered such amazing loss,
   To bring the lost to Thee.

3 Through him preserve me from the foe,
   Still threatening to devour;
And saving health and peace bestow
   In trouble's darkest hour.

4 So shall my tongue through endless years
   Thy works of love proclaim:
I bless the Lord, who dries my tears,
   And praise his glorious name.

36   A.M.

HIGH in the heavens, eternal God!
   Thy goodness in full glory shines:
Thy truth shall break through every cloud
That veils and darkens thy designs.

2 For ever firm thy justice stands,
As mountains their foundations keep:
Wise are the wonders of thy hands;
Thy judgments are a mighty deep.

3 Thy providence is kind and large,
Both man and beast thy bounties share:
The whole creation is thy charge,
But saints are thy peculiar care.

4 My God! how excellent thy grace,
Whence all our hope and comfort springs:
The sons of Adam in distress
Fly to the shadow of thy wings.

5 From the provisions of thy house
We shall be fed with sweet repast:
There mercy like a river flows,
To bring salvation to our taste.

6 Life, like a fountain rich and free,
Springs from the presence of the Lord;
And in thy light our souls shall see
The glories promised in thy word.

36.2   C.M.

ABOVE these heavens' created rounds
   Thy mercy, Lord, extends:
Thy truth outlives the narrow bounds,
   Where time and nature ends.

2 Safety to all thy goodness brings,
   By thee sustained and blessed:
Beneath the shadow of thy wings
   Thy children love to rest.

3 From Thee, when earthly streams run low,
   And mortal comforts die,
Perpetual springs of life shall flow,
   And raise our pleasures high.

4 Though all created light decay,
   And death close up our eyes,
Thy presence makes eternal day,
   Where clouds can never rise.

36.3   C.M.

HOW great a being, Lord, is thine,
   Which doth all beings keep!
Thy knowledge is the only line
   To sound so vast a deep.

2 How good thou art, whose goodness is
   Our parent, nurse, and guide;
Whose streams do water Paradise,
   And all the earth beside!

3 Most pure and holy are thine eyes,
   Most holy is thy name:
Thy truth, thy mercy never dies;
   Thou ever art the same!

4 Thy veilèd brightness, God of grace!
   We humbly here adore:
Show us thy glory and thy face,
   That we may praise thee more.

36.4
B. M.

O THOU great Fountain, full and free!
  Communicate thy grace to me:
To me that sacred treasure give,
Which makes the dying sinner live.

2 To my poor, thirsty, barren heart,
  Thy sanctifying grace impart:
Diffuse the plenteous streams around,
And water all the parched ground.

3 To Thee O let my soul aspire,
  As on the wings of pure desire:
Let love within my bosom glow,
And faith and hope with vigour grow.

4 O let my graces ne'er decay,
  But flourish to eternal day!
Till heavenly love complete the plan,
And glory crown what grace began.

36.5
E. M.

O THOU, whom thoughtless men despise,
  Thou Only Good, thou Only Wise!
    My soul would thee adore:
Thy love the heaven of heaven transcends,
Thy faithfulness, thy truth extends
    Beyond where thought can soar.

2 Thy justice like the mountains stands,
  Vast are the wonders of thy hands,
    Thy judgments deep and broad;
And all thy creatures, man and beast,
Down from the loftiest to the least
    Thy bounty share, O God!

3 Blest more than all, the sons of grace,
　The favoured souls, that find a place
　　Beneath thy sheltering wing:
　How from thy table they are fed!
　How drink they, from the fountain-head,
　　The mercies of their King!

4 The springs of life are all with Thee:
　Light in thy light alone we see,
　　Creator, Father, Friend!
　Still on our souls thy graces shed;
　Still feed us with the living bread,
　　And keep us to the end.

37　　　　　　　　　　　　C.M.

O FRET not in the evil day,
　　When scorn and pride increase!
　Trust in the Lord, and hope and pray,
　　And He will give thee peace.

2 Rest in the Lord, in him abide,
　　To him commit thy way:
　Thy soul shall then be satisfied,
　　And nourished day by day.

3 He will perform thy heart's desire,
　　Protect and bless thee still:
　He loves the men, whose hearts aspire
　　To do his holy will.

4 How soon the years of prosperous sin,
　　Of pride and wrong shall cease!
　How soon a brighter age begin
　　Of heavenly love and peace!

5 Then suffering saints no longer grieve,
　　The meek in beauty shine;
And, crowned with endless joy, receive
　　A portion all divine.

37.2   C.M.

O GOD of love, how blest are they
　　Who in thy ways delight!
Thy presence guides them all the day,
　　And cheers them all the night.

2 Whene'er they faint, a mighty arm
　　Is nigh them, to uphold;
And sin and Satan cannot harm
　　The feeblest of thy fold.

3 The Lord is wise, the Lord is just,
　　The Lord is good and true;
And they, who in his promise trust,
　　Will find it bear them through.

4 His word will stay their sinking hearts,
　　Their feet shall never slide:
The heavens dissolve, the earth departs,
　　They safe in God abide.

37.3   B.M.

WHILE passing through the wilderness,
　　Full of temptations and distress,
What comfort does the thought afford,
Our steps are ordered by the Lord!

2 Though disappointments oft abound,
　　And sorrows may our souls surround,
We gain relief from this sweet word,
Our steps are ordered by the Lord.

3 When lost in life's bewildering maze,
And darkness overspreads our ways,
O 'tis a soul-reviving word,
Our steps are ordered by the Lord!

4 Soon shall we reach that land of joy,
Where pleasures are without alloy;
And there with gratitude record,
Our steps were ordered by the Lord.

37.4   C.M.

THE steps of all the just, O God,
   Are ordered by thy will:
Though thou afflict them with thy rod,
   Thy hand upholds them still.

2 Theirs is the sure, the better part;
   Their wants are all supplied:
Thy holy law is in their heart,
   Their steps shall never slide.

3 They shall possess a land of light,
   Of hope and peace and love;
There dwell rejoicing in thy sight,
   And never thence remove.

4 Thou, Lord, in each distressful hour,
   Wilt their salvation be;
And save them by thy mighty power,
   Because they trust in thee.

38   Day 8.   Psalms 38—43.   C.M.

IN anger, Lord, rebuke no more,
   Thy chastening stroke remove:
My wounded soul by grace restore,
   In wrath remember love.

2 Thine arrows pierce my inmost heart,
   Thy hand hath brought me low:
I mourn and groan with hidden smart,
   No rest or peace I know.

3 Lord, my desires to thee are known;
   And every secret tear,
The mourner's sigh, the prisoner's moan,
   Still reach thy gracious ear.

4 When friends and earthly helpers fail,
   Be near me, still, O Lord!
When powers of hell thy Church assail,
   Thy mighty help afford.

5 O soon return, and cheer my soul
   With beams of grace divine!
O make my wounded spirit whole,
   And seal me ever thine!

39   A.M.

HEAR me, O Lord! attend my cry,
   And gently mark each falling tear:
A lonely sojourner am I,
A pilgrim and a stranger here.

2 A desert land around me lies,
A land of shadows, cares, and woe:
How vain the wealth that sinners prize!
How few their fleeting days below!

3 Why should I fear from earth to part,
Or fix my hopes on earthly things?
Thou, O my God, my portion art;
From thee alone my comfort springs.

4 Remove the chastening of thy rod :
O spare me, and my strength restore !
Until my soul from earth to God
Returns, and I am seen no more.

39.2   C.M.

GOD of my life, look gently down,
   Behold the pains I feel :
But I am dumb before thy throne,
   Nor dare dispute thy will.

2 Diseases are thy servants, Lord !
   They come at thy command :
I'll not attempt a murmuring word
   Against thy chastening hand.

3 Yet I will plead with humble cries,
   Remove thy stroke, O God !
My strength consumes, my spirit dies
   Beneath thy chastening rod.

4 I'm but a sojourner below,
   As all my fathers were :
May I be well prepared to go,
   When I the summons hear.

5 But if my life be spared awhile
   Before my last remove,
O let me dwell beneath thy smile,
   Rejoicing in thy love !

39.3   S.M.

LORD, let me know mine end,
   How few my fleeting years ;
How swift and short the days I spend
   In this poor vale of tears !

2 Our life is but a span,
  Our age is nought with thee:
Man in his highest honour, man
  Is dust and vanity.

3 Dumb at thy feet I lie,
  For thou hast brought me low:
Remove thy judgments, lest I die;
  I faint beneath thy blow.

4 At thy rebuke the bloom
  Of man's vain beauty flies;
And grief shall, like the moth, consume
  All that delights our eyes.

5 Have pity on my fears,
  Hearken to my request;
Turn not in silence from my tears,
  But give the mourner rest.

6 O spare me, Lord, I pray!
  Awhile my strength restore;
Ere I am summoned hence away,
  And seen on earth no more.

39.4   H.M.

WHAT is our life? 'tis but a span:
 So frail the best estate of man;
  Disquieted in vain,
We walk but in an idle show,
And heap up riches as we go,
  Our harvest, toil and pain.

2 Yet is my hope, O Lord, in thee!
From guilt and anguish set me free;
  Beneath thy chastening breath,

    The pride of youth, and beauty's bloom,
  Like moth-worn raiment, doth consume
      Into the dust of death.

3 Lord, hear my prayer! attend my cry!
  Slight not my tears; for what am I,
    Who here before thee stand?
  A stranger and a sojourner
  With thee, as all my fathers were,
    A pilgrim in the land.

4 O spare me then a little space!
  Still let me dwell before thy face;
    Till, life's brief warfare o'er,
  In thy kind arms I sweetly rest,
  And, there of heavenly life possess'd,
    Am found on earth no more.

40   A.M.

I WAITED meekly for the Lord;
  He bowed his ear, and heard my cry;
My soul from depths of woe restored,
And brought his saving mercy nigh.

2 Firm on a rock my feet he placed,
  Deep sunk so late in miry clay:
  Now, O my soul, with joyful haste
  In thankful songs thy tribute pay.

3 Blest are the men, who put their trust
  In thee, O God, in thee alone!
  Thy word is true, thy ways are just,
  Thy wonders infinite, unknown.

4 See where the gates of heaven unfold,
  The Son descending from above;
  And saints and angels view, unrolled,
  The counsel of eternal love.

5 Behold, the heavenly Preacher stands,
   His Father's goodness to proclaim;
   And wears, engraven on his hands,
   Each humble, contrite sinner's name.

6 The load of all our guilt He bears,
   Burdened with curses, not his own;
   Yet still his Father's love declares,
   And makes his grace to mortals known.

7 Incarnate Saviour! Prince divine!
   Thy boundless mercy we adore:
   O may our souls be wholly Thine,
   In life, in death, and evermore!

41   C.M.

O TEACH us, Lord, with tender care
    To feel for the distressed!
With pitying heart their griefs to share,
    And cheer the troubled breast.

2 On men of grace thy mercy still
    Will gifts of grace bestow;
  With peace and light their bosom fill,
    And save from every foe.

3 In hours of sickness Thou wilt prove
    Their never-failing friend,
  Wilt guard them hourly with thy love,
    And keep them to the end.

4 Save me, O Lord, and heal my soul!
    Thy suffering child restore:
  O raise me up, and make me whole,
    And let me sin no more.

5 O fill my heart with tender love,
   Pure, gentle, like thine own!
Till, raised from earth to seats above,
   I stand before thy throne.

41.2   C.M.

O GRACIOUS God, when troubles lower,
   And sins and fears combine,
Around me in the darkest hour
   With beams of mercy shine!

2 From scenes of sorrow and distress
   My soul triumphant raise;
Till wondering foes thy power confess,
   And learn to sing thy praise.

3 In thee, O Lord, my help is found,
   Thy mercies ne'er shall fail:
With light and love my steps surround
   Through all this gloomy vale.

4 O still uphold me, King of grace!
   With power and love divine;
And bring me to behold thy face,
   Where thy bright glories shine.

42   A.M.

AS pants the hart for cooling springs,
   That sinks exhausted in the chase,
So thirsts my soul, O King of kings!
To reach thy sacred dwelling-place.

2 On bitter tears my soul hath fed,
   While foes deride my deep despair;
Say, where is thy Deliverer fled?
   Thy God, abandoned wanderer, where?

3 Oft dwell my thoughts on happier days,
　When mid thy courts, a willing throng,
　Our pleasure still was prayer and praise,
　And days were bright with festal song.

4 Yet still thy mercies, in my sight,
　Shall cheer me through the tedious day;
　Amidst the gloomy shades of night
　To thee I'll tune my grateful lay.

5 Why faint, my soul! or doubt his aid?
　Thy God will still his mercy prove:
　Within his courts thy thanks be paid
　For all his faithfulness and love.

42.2 K M.

GOD of grace! in hours of sadness
　　Thee will I remember still,
From thy Canaan's outmost border,
　Jordan's stream, and Hermon's hill.

2 Floods of dark and hopeless sorrow
　　O'er my fainting spirit sweep:
　Wave on wave, with solemn echoes,
　　Deep is calling unto deep.

3 Yet thy loving kindness daily
　　Thou wilt cause on me to rest;
　Nightly songs thou wilt awaken
　　In the darkness of my breast.

4 Still I pray and hope for mercy,
　　Still I rest upon thy word:
　Thou, my Rock, wilt not forsake me;
　　Thou art mine, O blessed Lord!

5 Why, my soul, cast down with sorrow?
    Why oppressed with doubt and fear?
Hope in God! I yet shall praise him;
    Heavenly comfort still is near.

6 I will praise thee daily, nightly,
    Through the desert while I roam;
And with nobler songs adore thee,
    Safe in my eternal home,

42.3   A.M.

I THIRST, but not as once I did,
    The vain delights of earth to share:
Thy wounds, Emmanuel, all forbid
That I should seek my pleasure there.

2 It was the sight of thy dear cross
    First weaned my soul from earthly things,
And taught me to esteem as dross
    The mirth of fools, and pomp of kings.

3 I want the grace that comes from Thee,
    And quickens all things where it flows;
And makes a worthless thorn, like me,
    Bloom as the myrtle and the rose.

4 Dear Fountain of delights unknown!
    No longer sink beneath the brim;
But overflow, and pour me down
    A living and life-giving stream.

5 For sure, of all the plants that share
    The notice of thy Father's eye,
None proves less worthy of his care,
    Or yields him meaner fruit than I.

43   C.M.

JUDGE me, O Lord! my cause maintain
   Against the sons of pride;
Nor let me seek the help in vain,
   To all thy saints supplied.

2 God of my strength! be ever near,
   And cast me not away:
Why should my soul, oppressed with fear,
   Go mourning all the day?

3 Send out thy light and heavenly truth,
   Sweet heralds of thy love:
Renew me with unfading youth,
   And guide to seats above.

4 High praise shall then thy temple fill,
   High praise my lips employ;
And thou wilt be my Father still,
   And mine exceeding joy.

5 Why, O my soul, oppressed with fear,
   Go mourning all the day?
Hope still in God, whose help is near,
   Thy light, thy health and stay!

43.2   B.M.

JUDGE me, O Lord! to thee I fly;
   New foes and fears my spirit try:
Plead thou my cause, my soul sustain,
And let the wicked rage in vain.

2 Send forth thy light and truth once more,
To thy blest house my steps restore:
Again thy presence let me see,
And find my joy in praising Thee.

3 Arise my soul, and praise him now;
The Lord is good, be faithful thou:
His nature changes not like thine;
Believe, and soon his face shall shine.

43.3   A.M.

O THOU who art my only stay,
  Why leav'st thou me in deep distress?
Why go I mourning all the day,
Whilst me insulting foes oppress?

2 Let me with light and truth be blessed;
Be these my guides to lead the way,
Till on thy holy hill I rest,
And in thy sacred temple pray.

3 Then will I there fresh altars raise
To God, who is my only joy;
And well-tuned harps with songs of praise
Shall all my grateful hours employ.

4 Why then cast down, my soul! and why
So much oppressed with anxious care?
On God, thy God, for aid rely,
Who will thy ruined state repair.

43.4   13.M.

JUDGE me, Lord, in righteousness;
  Plead for me in my distress:
Good and merciful Thou art,
Bind the bleeding, broken heart;
Cast me not despairing hence,
Be Thy love my confidence.

2 Send thy light and truth to guide
Me, far wandered, to thy side;

On thy holy hill to rest,
In thy tabernacle blest:
There to God, my chiefest joy,
Praise shall all my powers employ.

3 Why, my soul! art thou dismayed?
Why of earth or hell afraid?
Trust in God, disdain to yield;
While o'er thee He casts his shield;
He will make his face to shine,
Cheer thy path with love divine.

43.5   C.M.

O LORD our God, thy light and truth
   To all thy children send;
That we may serve thee in our youth,
   And love thee to the end.

2 O let thy all-victorious grace
   Our heedless steps restrain;
And teach us, Lord, to seek thy face,
   Which none shall seek in vain.

3 Now to the hills we lift our eyes,
   Whence our salvation springs:
O Sun of righteousness, arise
   With healing in thy wings!

4 Arise, and o'er this vale of tears
   Shine into perfect day:
Still heavenward, through succeeding years,
   Point out the pilgrim's way.

43.6   A.M.

O LORD, thy mercy from above
   Send down, our darkened souls transform;
The messenger of peace and love,
The bow of promise midst the storm.

2 Then guilty passions take their flight,
Sorrow, remorse, and anguish cease:
Religion's ways are ways of light,
And all her paths are paths of peace.

3 Ambition, pride, revenge depart,
And folly flies her chastening rod:
She makes the humble, contrite heart
A temple of the living God.

4 At her approach the grave appears
The gate of paradise restored:
Her voice the watching cherub hears,
And drops his double-flaming sword.

5 Baptized in her renewing fire,
May we the crown of glory gain,
Rise, when the host of heaven expire,
And reign with God, for ever reign!

43.7   A.M.

SEND out thy light and truth, O God!
With sound of trumpet from above:
Break not the nations with thy rod,
But draw them with the cords of love.

2 Before thee bid the idols fall,
Rend with thy truth each veil of lies;
The fulness of the Gentiles call,
Let Israel from the dust arise.

3 Now, for the travail of his soul,
Messiah's peaceful reign advance:
From sea to sea, from pole to pole,
He claims his vast inheritance.

4 O mighty King of glory, gird
  Thy sword for conquest on thy thigh:
  Be countless souls with sorrow stirred,
  And born anew beneath thine eye.

5 O may thy kingdom dawn at length,
  All earth's dark idols overthrown!
  Thy Church renew with saving strength,
  To bow with rapture at thy throne.

44. Day 9. Psalms 44—49. C.M.

O GOD! our fathers oft have told
    In our attentive ears,
How wonderful, in days of old,
    Thy mighty work appears.

2 Fierce, haughty nations thou didst drive
    From Canaan's promised land:
  In vain the proudest warriors strive
    With thine avenging hand.

3 Not Israel's courage, strength, or sword,
    To them possession gave;
  But thy right hand, thine arm, O Lord!
    Omnipotent to save.

4 We too, O Lord, thy name confess,
    And own thee sovereign King:
  O still to us, in our distress,
    The like deliverance bring!

5 What though the powers of earth and hell
    Were banded to destroy!
  Thou, Lord, the sons of pride wilt quell,
    And fill our hearts with joy.

6 In Thee we trust, to Thee we pray,
   Thy greatness we proclaim:
In God we triumph all the day,
   And bless thy glorious name.

44.2   13.M.

LORD, to us our sires have told
   All thy wondrous deeds of old;
How thy strong and powerful hand
Drove the heathen from the land;
How, with peace thy people blest,
Entered on their promised rest.

2 Not by mortal's feeble sword,
Not by arm of flesh, O Lord!
But by Thine, and thine alone,
Were their mighty foes o'erthrown:
Thine the voice the world obeys,
Lord! to Thee be all the praise.

3 Helpless we in danger's hour,
Weak our arms, and vain our power;
Yet by Thy almighty aid
We are more than conquerors made:
Thine the voice the world obeys,
Lord! to Thee be all the praise.

4 Wake from slumber, mighty Lord!
Now fulfil thy promised word:
Come, and hide thy face no more,
Gladness, peace, and light restore:
From the dust thy people raise;
Fill their lips with endless praise.

45   D.M.

MY heart, with zeal o'erflowing,
  Prepares a joyful song;
My lips, with fervour glowing,
  The welcome theme prolong;
The Saviour, meek and lowly,
  The Lord of boundless love;
The King, whose name is Holy,
  Who reigns in light above.

2 O fairer than the fairest
  Of all that dwell below,
What blessings Thou preparest
  On mortals to bestow!
In richest, largest measure,
  Grace in thy lips is poured;
Thou art the Father's pleasure,
  The everlasting Lord!

3 Gird on thy sword, O glorious,
  Most blessed Prince of peace!
Ride on, in might victorious;
  Make all oppression cease.
Sharp arrows from thy quiver
  Shall pierce through every foe;
The meek Thou wilt deliver,
  And bring the scorner low.

4 Thy throne, O God, abideth
  For ever firm and sure!
All worlds thy sceptre guideth,
  A sceptre just and pure;
For guilty rebels bleeding,
  Thy patience how divine!
And joy, all joys exceeding,
  Shall evermore be Thine.

5 Like cassia, myrrh, and aloes,
    With fragrance richly sweet,
Round Thee in heaven's high palace,
    What prayers and praises meet!
Those garments of salvation
    Adorn thee night and day;
While souls, thy new creation,
    Their constant homage pay.

6 In robes of purest whiteness,
    And raiment wrought in gold,
The church thy dazzling brightness
    Shall evermore behold:
All worlds shall bow before thee,
    All ages speak thy fame:
All heaven with joy adore thee,
    And triumph in thy name.

45.2   S.M.

MY Saviour and my King,
    Thy beauties are divine;
Thy lips with blessings overflow,
    And every grace is thine.

2   Now make thy glory known,
    Gird on thy dreadful sword;
And ride in majesty, to spread
    The conquests of thy word.

3   Strike through thy stubborn foes,
    Or melt their hearts t'obey;
While justice, meekness, grace and truth
    Attend thy glorious way.

4   Thy laws, O God, are right!
    Thy throne shall ever stand,
And thy victorious gospel prove
    A sceptre in thy hand.

45.3   B.M.

O KING of saints, supremely fair,
  With grace adorned beyond compare!
Descend with blessings from above,
And win the nations to thy love.

2 At Thy right hand our eyes behold
The Bride, arrayed in purest gold:
How glorious is her heavenly dress,
Her robe of joy and righteousness!

3 He forms her beauties like his own,
He calls and seats her near his throne:
Fair stranger, set thine eyes no more
On idols, known and loved before.

4 So shall the King the more rejoice
In thee, the favoured of his choice:
Let him be loved, and yet adored,
Thy Maker, and thy sovereign Lord!

5 O, happy hour! when thou shalt rise
To his fair palace in the skies;
And all thy sons, a numerous train,
Each like a prince in glory reign.

6 Let endless honours crown his head,
Let every age his praises spread:
With cheerful songs his saints approve
His vast and condescending love.

45.4   D.M.

WITH hearts in love abounding,
  Prepare we now to sing
A lofty theme, resounding
  Thy praise, almighty King!

Whose love, rich gifts bestowing,
  Redeemed the human race;
Whose lips, with zeal o'erflowing,
  Breathe words of truth and grace.

2 In majesty transcendent
  Gird on thy conquering sword;
In righteousness resplendent,
  Ride on, incarnate Word!
Ride on, triumphant speeding
  To glory and renown:
Thy power, all power exceeding,
  Shall smite the rebels down.

3 So reign, O God, in heaven
  Eternally the same!
And endless praise be given
  To Thy almighty name:
Clothed in thy dazzling brightness,
  Thy Church on earth behold,
In robe of purest whiteness,
  And raiment wrought in gold.

4 O let each Gentile nation
  Come gladly in thy train,
To share her great salvation,
  And join her grateful strain!
Then ne'er shall note of sadness
  Awake the trembling string;
One song of joy and gladness
  The ransomed world shall sing.

45.5   12.M.

O HOW blest, with holy song
  All thy praises to prolong!
Mighty King, by seers foretold,
Hope of saints in days of old!

Fairer Thou than sons of earth,
Born, a new and wondrous birth:
Lips of speechless grace are Thine,
Filled and stored with love divine.

2 Gird thy sword upon thy thigh,
Ride in prosperous majesty;
Truth and righteousness maintain,
Save the meek, the proud restrain:
Pierce and smite each stubborn foe,
Lay the haughty scorner low;
Bid the contrite mourners prove
All thy rich and tender love.

3 Thou, O Christ, art King alone!
Thine, an everlasting throne:
Righteous thy commands, and sure;
Thine a sceptre just and pure:
Grace and glory in thee meet,
Heavenly beauties, odours sweet;
Bliss untold to Thee is given,
Lord of earth and King of heaven!

4 O that we may hear thy voice,
In thy holy name rejoice,
Turn from meaner joys away,
Gladly thy commands obey!
Then, redeemed from earth, arise,
Meet our Captain in the skies;
Where thy bridal glories shine,
Filled and blessed with love divine!

45.6   A.M.

O MAY the Spirit from on high
   Kindle the fire of Christian love!
And may the saints' united cry
Speed swiftly to the throne above.

2 Expectant wait thy people, Lord!
Messiah's triumphs now to see:
Speak but thy light-imparting word,
And error's darkest night shall flee.

3 Gird on thy sword, most mighty Prince,
And ride in prosperous majesty:
Thy piercing truths shall soon convince,
And bend the people's hearts to Thee.

4 Ascend, O King of saints, thy throne!
And let thy banners be unfurled:
Demand the nations for thine own,
Arise, and bless a waiting world.

45. 7

GIRD on thy conquering sword,
　　Ascend thy shining car;
And march, Almighty Lord!
　　To wage thy holy war:
Before thy wheels in glad surprise
Let mountains sink, let valleys rise.

2 Beneath thine arrowy shower
　　Thy startled foes shall fall;
Made captive to thy power,
　　The power which conquers all:
Great King of kings! the world shall know
What wondrous things thine arm can do.

3 Lord, to the waiting soul
　　Bend thy triumphant way;
There every foe control,
　　There all thy might display:
In every breast erect thy throne;
O may we rest in Thee alone!

45.8   G2.M.

MY heart is full, and I must sing;
   My heart with praise is swelling;
And I must raise unto the King
   A song, his honour telling:
O fairer Thou than mortal race!
Thy lips o'erflow with heavenly grace,
   And so thou art confessèd
   Of God for ever blessèd!

2 Gird on thy sword, Most Mighty, take
   Thy majesty and glory:
Ride on for truth and meekness' sake;
   Ride on, while saints adore thee!
Great marvels shall thy right hand show,
Sharp arrows pierce each rebel foe,
   O God, who ever reignest,
   And holy rule maintainest!

3 O Church, the King's beloved Bride,
   Incline thine heart to hear him:
Thy former fancies cast aside;
   He is thy Lord, revere him:
So shall thy beauty be his choice,
So in thy love shall He rejoice;
   Tyre's daughters shall implore thee,
   And come with gifts before thee.

4 In broidered gold the Bride is seen,
   Her virgin train attend her;
To heaven's high palace comes the queen
   In pomp of royal splendour:
Instead of sires, through all the land
Thy sons shall rule, a princely band;
   Thy glory ceaseth never,
   Thy praise shall live for ever.

46   A.M.

GOD is our help, when ills abound,
   Our strength and refuge, always near:
When thickening dangers gloom around,
In Him we trust, we will not fear.

2 Not though the earth's foundations shake,
And mountains in the deep be hurled;
Though seas may roar, and lands may quake,
And dreadful tumult awe the world.

3 There is a river, pure and bright,
That cheers the city of our God:
Full streams of heavenly grace delight
The saints' secure and blest abode.

4 The heathen rage, the kingdoms rave;
God speaks, and earth dissolves with fear:
The Lord of hosts is strong to save,
And Israel's God our refuge near.

5 Come, see the works of God, for lo!
Wide desolations He doth send:
He snaps the spear, and breaks the bow;
He burns the chariot, war shall end.

6 Be still, and know that God alone
Is o'er the earth exalted high:
Safe are his saints beneath his throne;
The Lord of hosts is ever nigh.

46.2   A.M.

GOD is the refuge of his saints,
   When storms of sharp distress invade:
Ere we can offer our complaints,
Behold him present with his aid.

2 Let mountains from their seats be hurled
  Down to the deep, and buried there,
  Convulsion shake the solid world,
  Our faith shall never yield to fear.

3 Loud may the troubled ocean roar,
  In sacred peace our souls abide;
  While every nation, every shore
  Trembles, and dreads the swelling tide.

4 There is a stream, whose gentle flow
  Supplies the city of our God;
  Life, love, and joy still gliding through,
  And watering our divine abode.

5 That sacred stream, Thy holy word,
  That all our raging fear controls:
  Sweet peace thy promises afford,
  And give new strength to fainting souls.

6 Zion enjoys her Monarch's love,
  Secure against each threat'ning hour;
  Nor can her firm foundations move,
  Built on His truth, and armed with power.

46.3   G.M.

GOD is our sure defence, our aid
   In time of tribulation:
Our heart shall never be dismayed,
   Though fail the earth's foundation;
Though o'er the hill the floods ascend,
Though billows roar, and ocean rend
   The mountain peaks asunder.

2 A stream beside God's holy shrine,
   A pure and gliding river,
  Makes glad the seat of power divine,
   She stands unmoved for ever:

God in the midst of Zion dwells,
Her comfort, when wild tumult swells,
He comes at break of morning.

3 He bids the sounds of war to cease,
The bow, the spear he breaketh;
Her Saviour comes, the Prince of peace,
To judgment soon he waketh:
O'er all the earth his name is high;
The Lord of hosts, our Help, is nigh,
Our refuge never-failing.

47   C.M.

EXTOL the Lord, the Lord most high,
King over all the earth;
Exalt his triumphs to the sky
In songs of sacred mirth.

2 God is gone up with loud acclaim,
And trumpet's tuneful voice:
Sing praise, sing praises to his name!
Sing praises, and rejoice.

3 Sing praises to our God, sing praise
To every creature's King:
His wondrous works and glorious ways
All tongues and kindreds sing.

4 God sits upon his holy throne,
And o'er the heathen reigns:
His power through all the world is known,
And truth his throne sustains.

5 Princes! around his footstool throng;
Kings! in the dust adore:
Earth and her shields to God belong;
Sing praises evermore!

47.2   C.M.

O FOR a shout of sacred joy
   To God, the sovereign King!
Let every land their tongues employ,
   And hymns of triumph sing.

2 Jesus our Lord ascends on high:
   His heavenly guards around
Attend him, rising through the sky,
   With trumpet's joyful sound.

3 While angels shout, and praise their King,
   Let mortals learn their strains:
Let all the earth his honours sing;
   O'er all the earth he reigns.

4 Rehearse his praise with awe profound,
   Let knowledge lead the song;
Nor mock him with a solemn sound
   Upon a thoughtless tongue.

5 The western islands are the Lord's,
   There Abraham's God is known;
While powers and princes, shields and swords,
   Submit before his throne.

47.3   S.M.

THOU art gone up on high,
   O Christ, our glorious King!
And all the armies of the sky
   Thy praise perpetual sing.

2   Thou art gone up on high,
     And on the Father's throne
  Art crowned with endless majesty,
     In power and love unknown.

3 The Lord the Saviour reigns,
  Victorious o'er the grave:
 His arm a sinking world sustains,
  Omnipotent to save.

4 Princes, the shields of earth,
  To Him your offerings bring:
 Let all the lands with sacred mirth
  Adore the eternal King.

47. 4   E2.M.

THE Lord ascendeth up on high;
  The Lord hath triumphed gloriously,
 In power and might excelling:
Hell and the grave are captive led;
Lo! he returns, our glorious Head
  To his eternal dwelling.

2 The heavens with joy receive our Lord,
 By saints, by angel hosts adored;
  O day of exultation!
 O earth, confess thy glorious King!
 His rising, his ascension sing
  With grateful adoration.

3 Our great High Priest hath gone before,
 Thence on his Church his grace to pour
  And bring to us salvation:
 O may our hearts to him ascend!
 May all within us upward tend,
  Where lies our expectation.

4 Draw all our hearts, O Lord, to thee!
 Our minds from every burden free
  Of earthly care and pleasure;
 And when our mortal days shall end,
 O may our souls to thee ascend,
  Our everlasting Treasure!

48   S.M.

GREAT is the Lord our God,
   And let his praise be great:
He makes the churches his abode,
   His most delightful seat.

2   The temples of his grace,
   How beautiful they stand!
The honours of our native place,
   And bulwarks of our land.

3   In Zion God is known,
   A refuge in distress:
How bright has his salvation shone
   In all her palaces!

4   Oft have our fathers told,
   Our eyes have often seen,
How well our God secures the fold,
   Where his own sheep have been.

5   In every new distress
   We'll to his house repair;
We'll think upon his wondrous grace,
   And seek deliverance there.

48.2   S.M.

FAR as thy name is known,
   The world declares thy praise:
Thy saints, O Lord, before thy throne
   Their songs of honour raise.

2   Let strangers walk around
   The city where we dwell;
Compass and view the holy ground,
   And mark the building well.

3 How decent and how wise !
 How glorious to behold !
Beyond the pomp that charms the eyes,
 Or rites adorned with gold.

4 The God we worship now
 Will guide us till we die ;
Will be our God while here below,
 And ours above the sky.

48.3   C.M.

HOW honoured is the holy place,
 Where we adoring stand !
Zion, the glory of the earth,
 And beauty of the land.

2 Bulwarks of mighty grace defend
 The city where we dwell :
The walls, of strong salvation made,
 Defy the assaults of hell.

3 Lift up the everlasting gates,
 The doors wide open fling :
Enter, ye nations, that obey
 The statutes of our King.

4 Here ye shall taste unmingled joys,
 And live in perfect peace ;
Ye that have known Jehovah's name,
 And ventured on his grace.

5 Trust in the Lord, for ever trust,
 And banish all your fears :
Strength in the Lord Jehovah dwells,
 Eternal as his years.

6 He will abase the sons of pride,
   His arm shall bring them low;
And raise the needy near his side
   Where joys eternal flow.

48.4   E2.M.

GREAT is the Lord: O let us raise
   To Him within his city praise,
     Upon his holy mountain!
How beautiful is Zion's hill!
The city where He dwelleth still,
   Of power the only Fountain.

2 God in her palaces is known,
   Her refuge his eternal throne;
     Her kingly foes shall wonder:
In trouble they shall haste away;
The winds their ships, in wild dismay,
     Shall break with storms of thunder.

3 As we have heard, so have we seen,
How God his Zion's strength has been,
     To stablish her foundations:
Lord! of thy loving kindness we
Have thought within thy house, to Thee
     Be praise from farthest nations.

4 Thy hand is full of righteousness;
Thee Judah's joyful daughters bless,
     Thy righteous acts adoring:
O mark her bulwarks, tell her towers!
For Zion's God and Guide is ours,
     Our life in death restoring.

49   C.M.

WHY should I fear in days of ill,
    When foes beset me round?
Or why forget my God, who still
    My life with love hath crowned?

2 The proud their riches boast in vain;
    Their wealth can never save:
The great, the noble, speed amain
    To darkness and the grave.

3 How foolish they, whose heart's desires
    And hopes are fixed below!
Sons following still their heedless sires
    In paths that lead to woe.

4 O Thou, whose mighty grace hath power
    To ransom souls from death!
Be with me in my dying hour,
    Receive my parting breath.

5 So shall I wait, beneath thine eyes,
    Embraced by love divine,
The day, when all thy saints shall rise,
    In heavenly bliss to shine.

50   Day 10. Psalms 50—55. A4.M.

THE mighty God, the Lord hath spoken,
    And bids the trembling earth draw nigh:
The silence of long ages broken,
    He speaks in thunder from the sky.

2 Forth from the heavenly Zion shining,
    In perfect beauty He appears:
Love, wisdom, majesty combining,
    Bright are the diadems he wears,

3 A fiery stream devours before him,
  And cloud and tempest veil his form:
The countless hosts of heaven adore him,
  Amidst the darkness and the storm.

4 He speaks, and all the nations tremble;
  Heaven, earth, and hell his voice obey:
In solemn awe his saints assemble,
  The world's dim shadows flee away.

5 O who can stand, when Thou appearest
  In robes of majesty divine!
Though now each contrite sigh Thou hearest,
  What terrors then will round thee shine!

6 O mighty God! O Lord most holy!
  Prepare us for that solemn day:
O shield and guard us! save us wholly!
  Thy pardoning grace to us display.

51   S.M.

HAVE mercy, gracious Lord!
  Thy wondrous love reveal:
O let my soul, by grace restored,
  Thy lovingkindness feel!

2 My sins I dare not hide;
  But grievous though they be,
Thy mercies, like a flowing tide,
  Are yet more full and free.

3 Now, for my Saviour's sake,
  Thy pardoning bounty show;
And by the blood of sprinkling make
  My spirit white as snow.

4   O let me hear again
      Thy kind, forgiving voice!
  The bones, which thou hast broken, then
      Shall with new strength rejoice.

5   O cast me not away!
      Thy holy joys restore:
  With grace uphold me day by day,
      That I may fall no more.

51.2   B.M.

GREAT God! create my heart anew,
    And form my spirit pure and true:
O make me wise, betimes to spy
My danger and my remedy.

2 Behold, I fall before thy face;
    My only refuge is Thy grace:
No outward forms can make me clean;
The leprosy lies deep within.

3 Jesus, my Lord! thy blood alone
    Hath power sufficient to atone:
Thy blood can make me white as snow,
Not aught beside could cleanse me so.

4 While guilt disturbs and breaks my peace,
    Nor flesh nor soul hath rest or ease:
Lord, let me hear thy pardoning voice,
And make my broken bones rejoice.

51.3   B M.

O THOU that hear'st, when sinners cry!
    Though all my crimes before thee lie,
Behold them not with angry look,
But blot their memory from Thy book.

2 Create my nature pure within,
And form my soul averse from sin:
Let thy good Spirit ne'er depart,
Nor hide thy presence from my heart.

3 I cannot live without thy light,
Cast out and banished from thy sight:
Thy holy joys, O God, restore,
And guard me, that I fall no more.

4 Though I have grieved thy Spirit, Lord,
His help and comfort still afford;
And let my soul come near thy throne,
To plead the merits of thy Son.

5 O may thy love inspire my tongue!
Salvation shall be all my song;
And all my powers shall join to bless
The Lord, my Strength and Righteousness.

51.4   C.M.

LORD, I have sinned; but O forgive!
   Nor cast me quite away:
Restore my soul, and bid me live,
   And be my future stay.

2 O let me from my fall arise,
   More watchful and more strong!
Light up my dim and tearful eyes,
   And fill my mouth with song.

3 On Christ's prevailing sacrifice
   I all my hopes recline:
A broken spirit thou wilt prize,
   And such, O Lord, be mine!

4 Give me a meek, dependent heart
   For all my days to come;
Nor let thy Spirit e'er depart,
   Till I am safe at home.

51.5   C.M.

O GOD of mercy, hear my call!
   My load of guilt remove:
Break down this separating wall,
   That bars me from thy love.

2 Give me the presence of thy grace;
   Then my rejoicing tongue
Shall speak aloud thy righteousness,
   And make thy praise my song.

3 No blood of goats, or heifer slain,
   For sin could e'er atone:
The death of Christ shall still remain
   Sufficient and alone.

4 A broken heart, with sin opprest,
   Our God will ne'er despise;
Nor crush the souls, that humbly rest
   On Christ's own sacrifice.

52   C.M.

O WHO can tell the countless ills,
   From lips of pride that flow!
When passions rage, and tumult fills
   God's heritage below.

2 All peace and love thy words devour
   O thou deceitful tongue!
Devising mischief hour by hour,
   Thy pleasure, fraud and wrong.

3 But God shall take thee soon away,
   The sounds of strife shall cease;
 While holy lips their tribute pay
   In hymns of joy and peace.

4 Then, like some green, fair olive tree,
   Within thy courts I'll stand;
 And, filled with heavenly wonder, see
   The judgments of Thy hand.

5 When pride is hushed, and evil tongues
   Are mute in endless shame,
 Our souls, O Lord, in thankful songs
   Will praise thy holy name.

53   E.M.

THE Lord, from heaven his lofty throne,
   The God of majesty unknown,
 Looked down on earth below;
 To mark the little, faithful band,
 To see if sinners understand,
   And seek their God to know.

2 Alas! they all are gone aside;
 Men of deceit, the sons of pride
   In every place abound:
 Like olive berries, few and lone,
 Or gleaning grapes, the vintage done,
   The righteous scarce are found.

3 But see! th' ungodly shrink with fear;
 The mighty Lord will soon appear,
   And put his foes to shame:
 Our God the scorners will despise,
 And help his servants from the skies,
   Who fear his holy name.

4 Soon, Lord, let thy salvation come!
 O bring the captive wanderers home!
  Bid Zion weep no more:
 Then Israel's sons shall loud rejoice,
 And all the Gentiles, heart and voice,
  Thy holy name adore.

54   C.M.

SAVE me, O God! and by thy name
  Preserve from every ill:
 O let me ne'er be put to shame!
  Give ear, and bless me still.

2 See! hell's dark powers against me rise;
  And strangers fierce and strong,
 Blind to thy presence, still devise
  Their works of fraud and wrong.

3 Thou wilt uphold me, O my God!
  With help from day to day:
 Each haughty foe, beneath thy rod,
  Shall waste and pass away.

4 Then will I freely sacrifice
  To thee, my God, my King!
 Like incense shall my praise arise,
  My lips thy goodness sing.

5 Thou, gracious Lord, from every snare
  Hast set my spirit free:
 My soul, released from toil and care,
  Hath found its rest in Thee.

55   C.M.

O GOD of mercy, hear my cry!
  Behold me in the dust:
 What should I be, or whither fly,
  If Thou wert not my trust?

2 O that my weary soul had wings!
   How swiftly would I flee
From earthly men and earthly things,
   To dwell, my God, with Thee!

3 How sweet it is to turn from all,
   Thy converse, Lord, to claim;
At morn, and noon, and eve, to call,
   And find Thee still the same!

4 Ye saints! to God your burdens bring,
   And He your strength will be:
To earthly props let others cling,
   I trust, O Lord, in Thee!

55.2   C.M.

FAR from the world, O Lord, I flee,
   From strife and tumult far!
From scenes, where Satan wages still
   His most successful war.

2 The calm retreat, the silent shade
   With prayer and praise agree;
And seem by thy sweet bounty made
   For those who worship Thee.

3 There, if thy Spirit touch the soul,
   And grace her mean abode,
O with what peace, and joy, and love
   She communes with her God!

4 There, like the nightingale, she pours
   Her solitary lays;
Nor asks a witness of her song,
   Nor sighs for human praise.

5 Author and Guardian of my life,
　　Sweet source of life divine,
　And, all harmonious names in one,
　　My Saviour, thou art mine!

6 What thanks I owe thee, and what love,
　　A boundless, endless store,
　Shall echo through the realms above,
　　When time shall be no more!

55.3   C.M.

O HAD I pinions like a dove,
　　Swift rising through the air,
How would I flee, and far remove
　From scenes of strife and care!

2 To some wild desert would I go,
　　And seek a peaceful home,
　Where storms of malice never blow,
　　Temptations never come.

3 Vain hope! from all the rage of hell,
　　By change of scene to fly:
　He, who alone the storm can quell,
　　In every place is nigh.

4 God shall preserve my soul from fear,
　　Or shield me when afraid:
　Ten thousand angels must appear,
　　If He command their aid.

5 By morning light I seek his face,
　　At noon repeat my cry;
　The night shall hear me ask his grace,
　　Nor will he long deny.

6 I cast my burdens on the Lord,
    The Lord sustains them all:
My courage rests upon his word,
    His saints shall never fall.

55.4   A.M.

O CAST thy burdens on the Lord,
    My soul, in hours of deep distress!
And lean upon his faithful word,
When thickening dangers round thee press.

2 Sustained by his almighty power,
Firm as a rock thou shalt abide:
His tender love from hour to hour
Shall all thy feeble footsteps guide.

3 At morn, and noon, and evening, pray,
And gracious answers shall be given,
To cheer and bless thee day by day,
And lead thee safe from earth to heaven.

55.5   N2.M.

O HAD I the wings of a dove,
    I'd make my escape, and be gone!
I'd mix with the spirits above,
Who encompass yon heavenly throne;
I'd fly from all labour and toil
To the place where the weary have rest;
I would haste from contention and broil
To the peaceful abode of the blest.

2 How happy are they, who no more
Have to fear the assaults of the foe!
Arrived on the heavenly shore,
Who have left all their conflicts below;

Afar from all danger and fear,
Where remembrance enhances their joys;
As the storm, when escaped, will endear
The retreat which the haven supplies.

3 Around the magnificent throne,
Where the Lamb all his glory displays,
United for ever in one,
And singing for ever his praise,—
O when shall the veil be removed,
And round me this brightness be poured;
To meet Him, whom absent I loved,
And to see, whom unseen I adored!

4 O then, never more shall the fears,
The trials, temptations, and woes,
Which darken the valley of tears,
Intrude on my blissful repose!
Or if yet remembered above,
Remembrance no sadness will raise;
They will only be signs of thy love,
And themes for my wonder and praise.

56   Day 11. Psalms 56—61.   C.M.

O THOU most holy, just, and true!
   In Thee I place my trust;
Nor will I fear what man can do,
   The offspring of the dust.

2 My wanderings all to Thee are known,
   With every secret tear:
The contrite sigh, the sufferer's groan
   Still reach thy gracious ear.

3 When to thy throne I raise my cry,
   The powers of darkness flee;
So swift is prayer to reach the sky,
   So near is God to me!

4 Thy solemn vows are on me, Lord!
    Thou shalt receive my praise:
I'll sing how faithful is thy word,
    How righteous all thy ways.

5 Thou hast redeemed my soul from death;
    O set thy prisoner free!
That heart and soul, and life, and breath
    May be employed for Thee.

56.2   12.M.

HELP me, Lord! I trust in thee;
    To thy sheltering side I flee:
Powers of hell in dark array
Mark my footsteps day by day:
Doubts and fears my heart assail,
But thy promise cannot fail:
Still I hope in thee, my Lord!
All my trust is in thy word.

2 Thou dost on my wanderings look,
    All my tears are in thy book;
When my spirit cries to Thee,
All my foes shall turn and flee.
Thou wilt cast the haughty down,
Save the meek, the lowly crown,
Fill my lips with joy and praise,
Guide and bless me all my days.

3 Thou hast saved my soul from death,
    Lord, to Thee I yield my breath:
Humbly for thy help I call,
Suffer not thy child to fall:

May I walk before thee here,
Live devoted to thy fear;
May I dwell with thee above,
In the land of light and love!

57   A.M.

MY God! in whom are all the springs
Of boundless love, and grace unknown,
Hide me beneath thy spreading wings,
Till the dark cloud be overblown.

Up to the heavens I send my cry,
The Lord will my desires perform;
He sends his angels from the sky,
And saves us from the threatening storm.

Be thou exalted, O my God!
Above the heavens, where angels dwell:
Thy power on earth be known abroad,
And land to land thy wonders tell!

My heart is fixed, my song shall raise
Immortal honours to Thy name:
Awake, my tongue! to sound his praise,
My tongue, the glory of my frame.

High o'er the earth his mercy reigns,
And reaches to the utmost sky:
His truth to endless years remains,
When lower worlds dissolve and die.

Be thou exalted, O my God!
Above the heavens where angels dwell;
Thy power on earth be known abroad,
And land to land thy wonders tell.

58   C.M.

O SOLEMN joy of righteous souls,
    To see thy judgments, Lord!
And, when thy thunder loudest rolls,
    To rest upon thy word!

2 O solemn hour! when wrath shall light
    On all the sons of pride,
And sinners call, with vain affright,
    On rocks, their shame to hide!

3 And can thy people, Lord, rejoice
    Thy lifted arm to see?
Or hear in peace that awful voice,
    Which makes the wicked flee?

4 Though clouds and darkness veil thy throne,
    They turn to Calvary still:
Its depths of grace and love unknown
    With peace their bosom fill.

5 O Lamb of God, thou Judge divine!
    When rocks and hills remove,
In wrath we see thy mercy shine,
    And know that God is love.

59   12.M.

SAVE me, Lord, from every foe;
    Life, and health, and peace bestow;
Free me from the power of sin,
Snares without, and lusts within:
Disappoint the lying tongue,
Stay the course of crime and wrong;
Make the powers of darkness flee,
Let thy Church thy glory see.

2 So, my God! at morning hour
I will sing thy mighty power,
And, when evening shadows fall
On the God of mercy call;
Unto Thee will gladly raise
Songs of never-ceasing praise;
And, when future storms arise,
Trust Thy care, which never dies.

60   C.M.

O GOD, the Lord of heavenly grace!
   We faint beneath thy hand:
Unveil the brightness of thy face,
   And heal the troubled land.

2 A glorious banner give to those,
   Who on thy truth depend;
And still before their numerous foes
   Their righteous cause defend.

3 So heathen lands shall own Thy might,
   And distant tribes obey;
While Israel's sons with joy unite
   Their grateful thanks to pay.

4 Through Thee triumphant we shall stand,
   Secure from every foe;
Till conflicts cease, and every land
   Thy power and glory know.

60.2   B.M.

REPULSED, dispersed, chastised by Thee,
   O grant us, Lord, thy face to see!
And let thy people, once thy care,
Again thy favouring presence share.

2 How trembles the divided land
　Beneath the terrors of thy hand!
　O Thou, the God whom we adore,
　Its breaches heal, its peace restore!

3 Our hopes, in man reposed in vain,
　O let thy strength, great God, sustain!
　And may we, on thy aid reclined,
　In Thee a firm protection find.

4 O help us, Lord! our foes subdue,
　Our sins forgive, our strength renew:
　O may we more than conquerors prove,
　Sustained and cheered by heavenly love!

60.3   C.M.

THROUGH foes and dangers, sin and death,
　　A pilgrim band, we move
To Canaan's promised land, beneath
　　The flag of heavenly love.

Almighty, omnipresent grace
　　Goes with us all the way;
And nothing can impede our race,
　　With Christ our guide and stay.

The empire of the world is His,
　　By Him from Satan won:
He speaks the word, and, lo! it is;
　　He wills, and all is done.

Though we are weak, the Lord is strong,
　　On Him our hopes depend:
We cannot dwell in darkness long,
　　While blest with such a Friend!

61 S.M.

WHEN, overwhelmed with grief,
　My heart within me dies,
Helpless, and far from all relief,
　To heaven I lift mine eyes.

2　O lead me to the Rock
　That's high above my head!
And make the covert of Thy wings
　My shelter and my shade.

3　Within thy presence, Lord!
　For ever I'll abide:
Thou art the tower of my defence,
　The refuge where I hide.

4　Thou giv'st me, Lord, the lot
　Of those that fear thy name:
If endless life be their reward,
　I shall possess the same.

62　Day 12.　Psalms 62—67.　12.M.

TRULY, Lord, my soul doth wait
　Humbly at thy temple gate;
Foes may rage, but rage in vain,
Men of blood shall all be slain;
Like a tottering, broken wall,
Envious men of malice fall;
But the souls who trust in Thee
Shall thy saving mercy see.

2 Wait, my soul, upon the Lord,
Ever trust his faithful word;
Earthly joys may fleet away,
God shall be thy constant stay:

He will make the light arise,
Dawning bright in wintry skies;
He will guide thee to the end,
God, thy everlasting Friend.

3 Surely mortal men are dust,
Place in God alone thy trust:
Right and good are all his ways,
Righteous are his gifts of grace:
Power belongs to God alone,
Plead thy wants before his throne:
Mercy, Lord, belongs to thee;
Let thy saints thy glory see!

62.2 C.M.

WHEN dangers press, and fears invade,
    O may we ne'er rely
On man, who, in the balance weighed,
    Is light as vanity!

2 Riches, how soon they fly away!
    Health's blooming cheek grows pale;
Vigour and strength must soon decay,
    And worldly wisdom fail.

3 But God, our God, is still the same
    As at that solemn hour,
When thunders spake his awful name,
    His majesty and power.

4 And still sweet mercy's voice is heard,
    Proclaiming from above,
That good and gracious is the Lord,
    That all his works are love.

5 In Thee we trust, in Thee alone,
   On Thee for help rely;
And lay our wants before thy throne,
   Whose love shall never die.

63   A.M.

GREAT God, indulge my humble claim!
   Thou art my hope, my joy, my rest:
The glories that compose thy name
Stand all engaged to make me blest.

2 Thou Great and Good, thou Just and Wise!
Thou art my Father and my God;
And I am thine by sacred ties,
Thy son, thy servant, bought with blood.

3 With heart and eyes, and lifted hands
For Thee I long, to Thee I look;
As travellers in thirsty lands
Pant for the cooling waterbrook.

4 With early feet I love to appear
Among thy saints, and seek thy face:
Oft have I seen thy glory there,
And felt the power of sovereign grace.

5 My life itself, without thy love,
No taste of pleasure could afford:
'Twould but a tiresome burden prove,
If I were banished from the Lord.

6 I'll lift my hands, I'll raise my voice,
While I have strength to pray or praise;
This work shall make my heart rejoice,
And spend the remnant of my days.

63.2   C.M.

EARLY, my God, without delay
   I haste to seek thy face;
My thirsty spirit faints away,
   Without thy quickening grace.

2 So pilgrims on the scorching sand,
   Beneath a burning sky,
Long for some cooling stream at hand,
   And they must drink or die.

3 I've seen thy glory and thy power
   Through all thy temple shine:
My God! repeat that heavenly hour,
   That vision, so divine!

4 Not life itself, with all its joys,
   Can my best passions move,
Or raise so high my cheerful voice,
   As thy forgiving love.

5 Thus, till my last expiring day,
   I'll bless my God and King:
Thus will I lift my hands to pray,
   And tune my lips to sing.

63.3   A.M.

O LORD, within thy sacred gates,
   Where I so oft have sought for Thee,
Again my longing spirit waits
   The fulness of delight to see.

2 More dear than life itself, thy love
My heart and tongue shall still employ;
Thy praise to sing, thy grace to prove,
My peace, my glory, and my joy.

3 In blessing thee with grateful songs
   My happy life shall glide away;
   The praise, that to thy name belongs,
   Hourly with lifted hands I'll pay.

4 Abundant sweetness, while I sing
   Thy love, my ravished heart o'erflows;
   Secure in thee, my God and King,
   Of glory that no period knows.

5 Thou art my soul's delightful choice,
   Thou, mercy's unexhausted spring;
   O God, who bidd'st my heart rejoice
   Beneath the shadow of thy wing!

63.4   C.M.

O GOD of love, my God thou art!
   To Thee I early cry:
Refresh with grace my thirsty heart,
   For earthly springs are dry.

2 Thy power, thy glory, let me see,
   As seen by saints above:
'Tis sweeter, Lord, than life to me,
   To share and sing thy love.

3 I freely yield thee all my powers,
   Yet ne'er my debt can pay:
The thought of Thee, at midnight hours,
   Turns darkness into day.

4 Lord, thou hast been my help, and Thou
   My refuge still shalt be:
I follow hard thy footsteps now,
   Thy face when shall I see?

63.5 A.M.

O GOD, thou art my God alone!
  Early to Thee my soul shall cry;
A pilgrim in a land unknown,
A thirsty land, whose springs are dry.

2 Yet, through this rough and thorny maze,
  I follow hard on thee, my God:
Thy hand, unseen, upholds my ways;
I safely tread where Thou hast trod.

3 Thee, in the watches of the night,
When I remember on my bed,
Thy presence makes the darkness light,
Thy guardian wings are round my head.

4 Better than life itself thy love,
More dear than all besides to me;
For whom have I in heaven above,
Or what on earth, compared to Thee?

5 Praise with my heart, my mind, my voice,
For all thy mercies I will give;
My soul shall still in God rejoice,
My tongue shall bless thee while I live.

64 12.M.

HEAR my prayer, O God of love!
  Let my soul thy mercy prove;
Save me from the snares of hell,
Shield and guard thy servant well:
When temptations fierce assail
Never let thy promise fail;
Keep thy child, I humbly pray,
Steadfast in the evil day.

2 So the people of thy choice
  Shall aloud in Thee rejoice;
  Feeble children of the dust
  In thy gracious words shall trust;
  Upright hearts to thee shall sing,
  Praise their good and gracious King,
  Daily learn thy grace to prove,
  Glory in thy perfect love.

65   A.M.

O THOU, who to our humble prayer
  Dost always bend thy listening ear;
To Thee shall all mankind repair,
And at thy gracious throne appear.

2 Our sins, though numberless, in vain
  To stop thy flowing mercy try:
  Thou dost o'erlook the guilty stain,
  And streams of cleansing grace supply.

3 By wondrous acts, O God most just!
  Have we thy gracious answer found:
  In Thee remotest nations trust,
  And those whom stormy waves surround.

4 God by his strength sets fast the hills;
  With matchless power from age to age,
  The sea's loud roaring waves He stills,
  And angry crowds' tumultuous rage.

5 Thy goodness does the circling year
  With fresh returns of plenty crown;
  And where thy glorious paths appear,
  The fruitful clouds drop fatness down.

6 They drop on barren deserts, changed
  Full soon to pastures fresh and green:
The hills around, in order ranged,
  In beauteous robes of joy are seen.

7 So, mighty Lord! with showers of grace,
  Make glad thy heritage below;
And lead us to that happier place,
  Where life's full streams for ever flow.

65.2   C.M.

'TIS by thy strength the mountains stand,
  God of eternal power!
The sea grows calm at thy command,
  And tempests cease to roar.

2 Thy morning light and evening shade
  Successive comforts bring:
Thy plenteous fruits make harvest glad,
  Thy flowers adorn the spring.

3 The clouds, like rivers raised on high,
  Pour out, at thy command,
Abundant blessings from the sky,
  To cheer the thirsty land.

4 The softened ridges of the field
  Permit the corn to spring;
The valleys rich provision yield,
  And the poor labourers sing.

5 The various months thy goodness crowns,
  How bounteous are thy ways!
The bleating herds spread o'er the downs,
  And shepherds shout thy praise.

65.3   B.M.

PRAISE, Lord, for thee in Zion waits,
  Prayer shall besiege thy temple gates:
All flesh shall to thy courts repair,
And find, through Christ, salvation there.

2 Our spirits faint, our sins prevail;
Leave not our trembling heart to fail:
O thou that hearest prayer, descend,
And still be found the sinner's Friend!

3 How blest thy saints! how safely led!
How sweetly kept! how richly fed!
Saviour of all in earth and sea,
How happy they who rest in Thee!

4 Thy hand sets fast the mighty hills,
Thy voice the troubled ocean stills;
Evening and morning hymn thy praise,
And earth thy bounty wide displays.

5 The year is with thy goodness crowned,
Thy clouds drop wealth the world around:
Through Thee the deserts laugh and sing,
And nature smiles, and owns her King.

6 Lord, on our souls thy Spirit pour,
Light, beauty, peace, and joy restore:
O let thy love our springtide be,
And make us all bear fruit to Thee.

65.4

O THOU God who hearest prayer,
  All shall come to Thee, that live;
Sins too great for us to bear
Thou wilt pity and forgive;

Grant, O Lord, thy saving grace !
Wonderful thy truth is found ;
Hope of earth's remotest race,
Hope of ocean's utmost bound.

2 Heavenly Father! from thy store
Earth receives the wealthy rain ;
And thy fountains, gushing o'er,
Raise for man the needful grain :
Earth, by thy soft dews prepared,
Fills her furrows, smooths her soil,
And her crops with rich reward
Bless the labourers' happy toil.

3 With thy gifts the year is crowned ;
Clouds, thy chariots, from on high
Scatter o'er the desert ground
Showers of blessing as they fly :
Gladness girds the mountain height,
Fleecy downs with gladness sing :
Vales, with gleaming harvest white,
Shout for gladness, shout and sing.

65.5   G3.M.

TO thee, O Lord, our hearts we raise
  In hymns of adoration ;
To thee bring sacrifice of praise
  With shouts of exultation :
Bright robes of gold the fields adorn,
  The hills with joy are ringing ;
The valleys stand so thick with corn,
  That even they are singing.

2 We come before thee, day by day,
    Thy bounteous hand confessing;
Before thy presence, Lord, we lay
    The firstfruits of thy blessing:
By Thee the souls of men are fed
    With gifts of grace supernal:
Thou, who dost give us daily bread,
    O give us bread eternal!

3 We bear the burden of the day,
    And often toil seems dreary;
But labour ends with sunset ray,
    And rest is for the weary:
May we, the angel reaping o'er,
    Be ne'er at last rejected,
Christ's golden sheaves for evermore,
    To garners bright elected.

4 O blessed is that land of God,
    Where saints abide for ever!
Where golden streams speed fast and broad,
    Where flows the crystal river:
The strains of all the holy throng
    Are there for ever blending;
Thrice blessed is that harvest song,
    Which never knows an ending.

66   C.M.

HOW terrible in power art thou,
    O God, our heavenly King!
To Thee shall every creature bow,
    And hills and valleys sing.

2 Come, see the wonders God hath wrought,
    When Israel's tribes of yore,
Through mighty floods in safety brought,
    Stood on the desert shore.

3 How did the ransomed host rejoice,
    And praise Jehovah's name!
Harp answering harp, voice answering voice,
    His greatness to proclaim.

4 Age after age has passed away,
    But God is sovereign still:
His eyes the sons of men survey
    From heaven's eternal hill.

5 In vain would haughty rebels strive
    Against their Maker's hand:
His power, who kills and makes alive,
    No creature can withstand.

6 O bless our God, whose love sustains
    Our life from day to day!
Let heaven and earth in loudest strains
    Their grateful homage pay.

66.2   I.M.

SING the great Jehovah's praise,
    Trophies to his glory raise:
Say,—How wonderful thy deeds!
Lord, thy power all power exceeds.

2 Let the many-peopled earth,
All of high and humble birth,
Worship our eternal King,
Hymns unto his honour sing.

3 We through fire, with flames embraced,
We through raging floods have passed;
Safe, by thy conducting hand,
Brought into a wealthy land.

4 We will to thy house repair
 Worship, and thy power declare;
 Offerings on thine altar lay
 All our vows devoutly pay.

66.3   C.M.

O ALL ye lands, rejoice in God!
 Sing praises to his name :
Let the whole earth with one accord
 His wondrous acts proclaim.

2 O let his faithful servants tell
 How, by redeeming love,
Their souls are saved from death and hell,
 To share the joys above!

3 Tell how the Holy Spirit's grace
 Forbids their feet to slide;
And, while they run the Christian race,
 Vouchsafes to be their guide.

4 Sing, sing, ye saints! and shout for joy,
 Ye ransomed of the Lord!
Be grateful praise your sweet employ,
 His presence your reward.

66.4   K2.M.

EARTH, with all thy thousand voices,
 Praise in songs th'eternal King!
Praise His name, whose praise rejoices
 Ears that hear, and tongues that sing.
Lord! from each far-peopled dwelling
 Earth shall raise the glad acclaim :
All shall kneel, thy greatness telling,
 Sing thy praise, and bless thy name.

2 Come and hear the wondrous story,
    How our mighty God of old
In the terrors of his glory
    Back the flowing surges rolled:
Walled within the threatening waters,
    Free we passed the fettered wave;
Then was joy to Israel's daughters,
    Loud they sang his power to save.

3 Bless the Lord, who ever liveth,
    Sound his praise through every land;
He our dying souls reviveth,
    By his arm upheld we stand:
When we made our supplication,
    When our voice in prayer was strong,
Straight we found his glad salvation,
    Now his mercy fills our tongue.

67   C.M.

SHINE, mighty God! on Britain shine
    With beams of heavenly grace:
Reveal thy power through all our coasts,
    And show thy smiling face.

2 Amidst our isle, exalted high,
    Do Thou our glory stand;
And, like a wall of guardian fire,
    Surround the favoured land.

3 Earth shall obey her Maker's will,
    And yield a full increase;
Our God will crown his chosen isle
    With fruitfulness and peace.

4 May our Redeemer scatter round
    His choicest blessings here;
And let creation's utmost bound
    Behold, adore, and fear.

5 So shall Thy name from shore to shore
    Sound, all the earth abroad;
And distant nations know and love
    Their Saviour and their God.

67.2   F.M.

RISE, gracious God, and shine
    In all thy saving might,
And prosper each design
    To spread thy glorious light:
Let healing streams of mercy flow,
That all the earth thy truth may know.

2   O bring the nations near,
    That they may sing thy praise!
  Let all the people hear,
    And learn thy holy ways:
Reign, mighty God! assert thy cause,
And govern by thy righteous laws.

3   Put forth thy glorious power!
    The nations then will see,
  And earth present her store
    In converts, born of Thee:
God, our own God, his Church will bless,
And earth shall yield her full increase.

4   Let every land, renewed
    In righteousness divine,
  With all the saints of God
    In songs of praise combine:
Join, all on earth, rejoice and sing,—
All glory to th' eternal King.

67.3   C.M.

SHINE on our souls, O King of grace!
   With rays of beauty shine:
O let thy favour crown our days,
   And all their course be Thine!

2 Renew, with each returning hour,
   The visits of thy love:
Still on our souls thy blessings shower,
   And raise our hearts above.

3 With Thee let every week begin,
   Each day be spent for Thee;
And grace each hour new triumphs win,
   Until thy face we see.

4 So cheer us through the desert road,
   Till all our labours cease,
And bring us to the sweet abode
   Of everlasting peace.

68   Day 13.   Psalms 68–70.   A.M.

LET God arise, and all his foes
   Flee from his presence in dismay;
As wax, in fire that melting flows,
Or smoke the tempest drives away.

2 But let the righteous loud rejoice
In God, the Lord who rules on high;
And praise Jehovah, heart and voice,
Whose chariot is the lofty sky.

3 The Father of the fatherless
In heaven's high dwelling-place is He:
To Him, in times of deep distress,
The widow and the orphan flee.

4 He frees the prisoner from his chains,
Restores the wanderers, when they roam:
The lonely pilgrim He sustains,
Cheers with sweet love, and guides him home.

5 So, when through deserts lone and waste
The chosen warriors took their way,
Earth trembling shook, the skies in haste
To Israel's God their homage pay.

6 Like dew, the sacred camp around,
The manna from the skies was poured;
And gracious rains the parched ground
To sudden life and joy restored.

7 The ransomed tribes, through Jordan's flood,
Passed onward to their promised rest;
A land enriched with every good,
With God's abundant favour blest.

8 O still to wandering pilgrims, Lord!
Be showers of grace in mercy given;
And may the manna of thy word
Refresh us in our way to heaven.

68.2   A.M.

To God your voice in anthems raise,
  Jehovah's awful name he bears:
In Him rejoice, extol his praise,
Who rides upon high rolling spheres.

2 His chariots numberless! his powers
Are heavenly hosts that wait his will:
His presence now fills Zion's towers,
As once it honoured Sinai's hill.

3 Lo! freed from bonds, and service mean,
Thy ransomed warriors shine as bright
As doves, in golden lustre seen,
Or silvered o'er with paler light.

4 Ascending high in triumph, Thou
Captivity hast captive led:
Through Thee thy people vanquish now
The powers of darkness, once their dread.

5 Even rebels shall partake thy grace,
And humble proselytes repair
To worship at thy dwelling-place,
And all the world pay homage there.

6 For benefits each day bestowed
Daily be thy great name adored,
O thou, our Saviour and our God!
Of life and death the sovereign Lord.

68.3   C2.M.

O GOD, when thou didst lead the way
   Before thy people's face,
In fire by night, and cloud by day,
   To guide thy chosen race;
Earth trembling shook, the veilèd skies
   Grew dark with sudden fear:
Old Sinai, startled with surprise,
   Beheld its God so near.

2 Thou, Lord, on thine inheritance
   Didst send a gracious rain;
And, cheered beneath thy quick'ning glance,
   Its pastures smiled again:
There for thy poor thou didst provide
   A portion richly blest;
And safe thy weary wanderers guide,
   To reach their promised rest.

3 Praised be the Lord, who doth fulfil
   His covenant day by day;
And with new loving mercies still
   Delights to bless our way :
He is our God, from whom alone
   Health and salvation spring :
O worship humbly at his throne,
   The great, eternal King!

68.4   A M.

O SON of God, ascended high,
   And seated on thy Father's throne !
Thine is the power, the victory,
And might and majesty unknown.

2 Thou on thy people wilt bestow
The gifts and gladness of thy love;
That God may dwell with men below,
And rebels rise to seats above.

3 Thy Spirit's grace in plenteous showers,
A gracious rain, shall soon be given;
Till deserts bloom with spring-tide flowers,
And earth grow bright with joys of heaven.

68.5   B.M.

WE bless the Lord, the just, the good,
   Who fills our hearts with joy and food;
Who pours his blessings from the skies,
And loads our days with rich supplies.

2 He sends the sun his circuit round,
To cheer the fruits, and warm the ground :
He bids the clouds, with plenteous rain,
Refresh the thirsty earth again.

3 'Tis to his care we owe our breath,
  And all our near escapes from death:
  Safety and health to God belong;
  He heals the weak, and guards the strong.

4 The Lord, that bruised the serpent's head,
  On all the serpent's seed shall tread;
  The stubborn sinner's hope confound,
  And smite him with a lasting wound.

5 His own right hand his saints shall raise
  From the deep earth, or deeper seas,
  And bring them to his courts above,
  To taste his everlasting love.

68.6   C.M.

O SING to God, ye heathen lands,
    To life and hope restored!
Let Ethiopia stretch her hands
    In prayer before the Lord.

2 Ascribe ye strength to Israel's God,
    Who reigns enthroned on high:
  In paths no mortal foot hath trod,
    He rides upon the sky.

3 How wonderful in power art Thou,
    Supreme, eternal King!
  All the wide earth to Thee shall bow,
    And ceaseless praises sing.

69   C.M.

FATHER, I sing thy wondrous grace,
    I bless my Saviour's name;
He brought salvation for the poor,
    And bore the sinner's shame.

2 His deep distress has raised us high;
  His duty and his zeal
Fulfilled the law which mortals broke,
  And finished all thy will.

3 This shall his humble followers see,
  And set their hearts at rest;
They by his death draw near to Thee,
  And live for ever blest.

4 Let heaven, and all that dwell on high,
  To God their voices raise;
While lands and seas assist the sky,
  And join t'advance the praise.

69.2   C.M.

LORD, I would stand with thoughtful eye
  Beneath thy fatal tree,
And see thee bleed, and see thee die,
  And think, what love to me!

2 Dwell on the sight, my stony heart,
  Till every pulse within
Shall into contrite sorrow start,
  And hate the thoughts of sin.

3 Didst thou for me, my Saviour, brave
  The scoff, the scourge, the gall,
The nails, the thorns, the spear, the grave,
  While I deserved them all?

4 O help me some return to make;
  To yield my heart to Thee,
And do and suffer for thy sake,
  As Thou didst then for me!

70   K4.M.

HASTE, O Lord! my soul deliver
   From the threat'ning powers of hell;
Let sharp arrows from thy quiver,
   All their might and malice quell:
Backward let thy foes be driven,
Speed thy victory, King of heaven.

2 Lowly hearts, in hours of sadness,
   Rest upon thy tender love;
Fill them, Lord, with heavenly gladness,
   All thy mercy let them prove;
May the souls, who seek thy face,
Triumph in thy heavenly grace!

3 Heavenly Father, still be near me;
   See! my spirit waits for Thee:
With thy tender favour cheer me,
   Set thy prisoned captive free;
Shield me daily with thy love,
Guide me safe to joys above.

71   Day 14. Psalms 71—74.   C.M.

MY God, my everlasting hope,
   I live upon thy truth:
Thy hands have held my childhood up,
   And strengthened all my youth.

2 Still has my life new wonders seen,
   Repeated every year:
Behold, the days that yet remain,
   I trust them to thy care.

3 Cast me not off when strength declines,
   When hoary hairs arise;
And round me let thy glory shine,
   Whene'er thy servant dies.

4 Then, in the history of my age,
   When men review my days,
They'll read thy love in every page,
   In every line thy praise.

71.2   C.M.

MY Saviour, my almighty Friend!
   When I begin thy praise,
Where will the growing numbers end,
   The numbers of thy grace?

2 Thou art my everlasting trust,
   Thy goodness I adore;
And since I knew thy grace at first,
   I speak thy glories more.

3 My feet shall travel all the length
   Of the celestial road;
And march with courage, in thy strength,
   To see my Father, God.

4 When I am filled with sore distress
   Beneath the load of sin,
I'll plead thy perfect righteousness,
   And mention none but Thine.

5 How will my lips rejoice to tell
   The victories of my King!
My soul, redeemed from sin and hell,
   Shall thy salvation sing.

6 Awake, awake, my tuneful powers!
   With this delightful song
I'll entertain the darkest hours,
   Nor think the season long.

D.M.

HAIL to the Lord's Anointed,
   Great David's greater son!
Hail, in the time appointed,
   His reign on earth begun!
He comes to break oppression,
   To set the captive free,
To take away transgression,
   And rule in equity.

2 He shall come down, like showers
   Upon the fruitful earth,
And love, joy, hope, like flowers,
   Spring in his path to birth:
Before Him on the mountains
   Shall Peace, the herald, go;
And righteousness, in fountains,
   From hill to valley flow.

3 Arabia's desert ranger
   To Him shall bow the knee,
The Ethiopian stranger
   His glory come to see:
With offerings of devotion
   Ships from the isles shall meet,
To pour the wealth of ocean
   In tribute at his feet.

4 Kings shall fall down before him,
   And gold and incense bring;
All nations shall adore him,
   His praise all people sing:
For He shall have dominion
   O'er river, sea, and shore;
Far as the eagle's pinion,
   Or dove's light wing can soar.

5 For Him shall prayer unceasing
    And daily vows ascend,
  His kingdom still increasing,
    A kingdom without end:
  The mountain dews shall nourish
    A seed in weakness sown,
  Whose fruit shall spread and flourish,
    And shake like Lebanon.

6 O'er every foe victorious,
    He on his throne shall rest,
  From age to age more glorious,
    All blessing, and all blest:
  The tide of time shall never
    His covenant remove;
  His name shall stand for ever,
    The King of peace and love!

72.2   H 2. M.

HASTEN, Lord, the glorious time,
  When, beneath Messiah's sway,
Every nation, every clime,
Shall the gospel's call obey:
Then shall wars and tumults cease,
Then be banished grief and pain;
Righteousness, and joy, and peace,
Undisturbed shall ever reign.

2 As, when soft and gentle showers
Fall upon the thirsty plain,
Springing grass and blooming flowers
Clothe the wilderness again;
So thy Spirit shall descend,
Softening every stony heart,
And his sweetest influence lend,
Holy beauties to impart.

3 Time shall sun and moon obscure,
Seas be dried, and rocks be riven;
But His reign shall still endure,
Endless as the days of heaven:
Bless we, then, our gracious Lord,
Ever praise his glorious name;
All his mighty acts record,
All his wondrous love proclaim.

72.3   F.M.

FAR as the isles extend,
   To the vast ocean's bound,
Let kings to Jesus bend,
   And pour their offerings round;
Arabia, raise the song divine,
And Afric, join t' exalt his praise.

2 All princes shall adore,
   And gifts and honours bring,
To hail the Saviour's power,
   To crown Immanuel king:
Remotest lands shall homage pay,
And earth obey his high commands.

3 His eye with pity spares
   Th' afflicted and oppressed;
Their names the Saviour wears
   Engraven on his breast:
He from on high salvation sends,
Their life defends, and hears their cry.

4 From each deceitful foe
   He will redeem their soul,

His quickening grace bestow,
And make the wounded whole:
Through endless days his name shall live,
And still receive perpetual praise.

72. 4'   A.M.

FALL down, ye nations, and adore
   Jehovah on the mercy seat;
Like prostrate seas on every shore,
That cast their billows at your feet.

2 Come from the East with gifts, ye kings!
With gold, and frankincense, and myrrh:
Where'er the morning spreads her wings,
Let man to God his vows prefer.

3 Come from the West! the bond, the free,
His easy service make your choice:
Ye isles of the Pacific sea,
Like halcyon nests, in God rejoice.

4 Come from the South! through desert sands,
A highway for the Lord prepare:
Let Ethiopia stretch her hands,
And Lybia pour her soul in prayer.

5 Come from the North! let Europe raise
In all her languages one song:
Give God the glory, power, and praise,
That to his holy name belong.

6 With smiles, O earth, thy Maker meet;
Nations! before your Saviour fall:
Redemption is in him complete,
The gospel now is preached to all.

73. B3.M.

O LORD, to thy deep wisdom blind,
How dull was once my thoughtless mind!
But still thy goodness kept me Thine;
My hand is in the hand divine:
Thy love shall guide me, till I see
Thy glorious face, and rest with Thee.

2 Whom else could heaven itself provide?
What firmer friend, what surer guide?
And if for love on earth I pine,
What earthly love can equal Thine?
In peace I rest, my terrors o'er,
Strong in thy strength for evermore.

3 O foolish hearts, whose senseless pride,
From thee, my Father, turns aside!
Nearest to thee, my God, is best;
In Thee my hope I firmly rest:
O let me to the world proclaim,
The wonders of thy glorious name!

73.2 A.M.

WHOM have I, Lord, in heaven but thee?
Or whom desire on earth beside?
My weary spirit still would flee
For refuge to thy sheltering side.

2 When doubts and fears my peace assail,
And vexing thoughts my bosom fill,
My heart may faint, my courage fail,
But thou, my Rock, art with me still.

3 How sad and mournful is their doom,
Who wander from thy paths astray!
When lightnings flash, and tempests gloom,
What terrors will their souls dismay!

4 But Thou, my helper, always nigh,
　With gentle love my soul wilt cheer,
　And guide me wisely with Thine eye,
　Till safe in glory I appear.

5 Then, raised from death to endless joy,
　Within thy courts my soul shall dwell,
　Where praise shall every tongue employ,
　And saint to saint thy glories tell.

73.3   C.M.

WHOM have we, Lord, in heaven but Thee?
　　And whom on earth beside?
Where else for succour shall we flee,
　Or in whose strength confide?

2 Thou art our portion here below,
　　Our promised bliss above;
In heaven and earth we nought can know
　　So precious as thy love.

3 When heart and flesh, O Lord, shall fail,
　　Thou wilt our spirits cheer,
Support us through life's thorny vale,
　　And calm each anxious fear.

4 Yes, Thou, our only guide through life,
　　Wilt health and strength supply,
Support us in death's fearful strife,
　　And welcome us on high.

73.4   16.M.

LORD of earth! thy forming hand
　Well this glorious frame hath planned,
Woods that wave, and hills that tower,
Ocean rolling in its power;

All that strikes the gaze unsought,
All that charms the lonely thought;
Friendship, gem transcending price,
Love, a flower from Paradise;
Yet, amid this scene so fair,
Should I cease thy love to share,
What were all its joys to me?
Whom have I on earth but Thee?

2 Lord of heaven! beyond our sight
Rolls a world of purer light;
There, in love's unbounded reign,
Parted hands shall meet again:
Martyrs there and prophets high
Shine, a glorious company;
While immortal music rings
From ten thousand seraph strings.
Oh, the scene is passing fair!
Yet shouldst Thou be absent there,
What were all its joys to me?
Whom have I in heaven but Thee?

3 Lord of heaven and earth! my breast
Seeks in Thee its only rest:
I was lost; thy accents mild
Homeward lured thy wandering child:
I was blind; thy healing ray
Drove the long eclipse away:
Source of every joy I know,
Solace of my every woe,
O should once thy light divine
Cease upon my soul to shine,
What were earth or heaven to me?
Whom have I in each but Thee?

74 C.M.

O LORD, defend us! as of old,
    Thy hand salvation wrought;
When safely to their promised fold,
    Thy chosen flock were brought.

2 Even in the wilderness, thy hand
    With plenty strewed their road;
And from the rock, at thy command,
    Refreshing waters flowed.

3 The sun, obedient to thy will,
    Renews his daily light;
Seasons and times thy word fulfil,
    And all proclaim thy might.

4 Arise, O Lord, and plead my cause,
    Against the oppressor's power:
O keep the saints, that love thy laws,
    Safe in each trying hour.

5 Thy covenant of heavenly grace,
    Bear daily, Lord, in mind;
And may the poor, who seek thy face,
    Thy constant succour find.

75 Day 15. Psalms 75—78. E.M.

THAT thou, O Lord, art ever nigh,
    Though veiled in awful majesty,
  Thy mighty works declare:
Thy hand this earthly frame upholds,
Thine eye the universe beholds
  With providential care.

2 Thou settest up and castest down,
　The ruler's power, the monarch's crown
　　Thy hands alone bestow:
　In Thee all creatures live and move,
　Thou reign'st supreme in heaven above,
　　And in the earth below.

3 Great King of kings, and Lord of lords,
　Whose hand chastises and rewards,
　　Thee only we adore:
　To Thee the voice of praise shall rise
　In hallelujahs to the skies,
　　Till time shall be no more.

76   A.M.

IN Judah, Lord, thy name was known
　By wondrous works in time of old;
In Zion stood thine ancient throne,
And Salem was thy chosen fold.

2 There sank beneath thy vengeful blow
　The Assyrian, in his hour of pride;
　Shield, sword, and buckler, spear and bow,
　Prince, warrior, chief, who Thee defied.

3 Zion, how excellent thy fame!
　More glorious than the hills of prey;
　While, mute in silence, death, and shame,
　Thy vanquished foes around thee lay.

4 Thou, Lord, for judgment didst appear,
　The nations trembled, and were still;
　While distant lands, with holy fear,
　Brought offerings to thy sacred hill.

5 So, mighty God, in every age,
   The wrath of man shall work thy praise:
   When floods arise, and tempests rage,
   Thy love its mightiest power displays.

6 Ye nations! worship at his throne,
   Your solemn vows with reverence bring;
   For Zion's God is God alone,
   The true, the everlasting King.

77. D.M.

IN time of tribulation,
   Hear, Lord, my feeble cries!
With humble supplication,
   To Thee my spirit flies:
My heart with grief is breaking,
   Scarce can my voice complain;
Mine eyes, with tears kept waking,
   Still watch and weep in vain.

2 The days of old in vision
   Bring vanished bliss to view;
The years of past fruition
   Their joys in pangs renew:
Remembered songs of gladness,
   Through night's lone silence brought,
Strike notes of deeper sadness,
   And stir desponding thought.

3 Hath God cast off for ever?
   Can time his truth impair?
His tender mercies never
   Shall I presume to share?
Hath He his loving kindness
   Shut up in endless wrath?
No! this is mine own blindness,
   That cannot see his path.

4 I call to recollection
    The years of his right hand;
And, strong in his protection,
    Again through faith I stand:
Thy deeds, O Lord, are wonder;
    Holy are all thy ways:
The secret place of thunder
    Shall utter forth thy praise.

5 Thee, with the tribes assembled,
    O God, the waters saw;
They saw thee, and they trembled,
    Turned, and stood still with awe:
The clouds shot hail, they lightened;
    The earth reeled to and fro:
The fiery pillar brightened
    The gulf of gloom below.

6 Thy way is in great waters,
    Thy footsteps are not known;
Let Adam's sons and daughters
    Confide in Thee alone:
Through the wild sea Thou leddest
    Thy chosen flock of yore:
Still on the waves Thou treadest,
    And thy redeemed pass o'er.

77.2   C.M.

THY way, O God, is in the sea,
    Thy paths we cannot trace;
Nor comprehend the mystery
    Of thine unbounded grace.

2 As through a glass, we dimly see
    The wonders of thy love:
How little do we know of Thee,
    Or of the joys above!

3 'Tis but in part we know thy will,
  We bless Thee for the sight:
When will thy love the rest reveal
  In glory's clearer light?

4 Our souls shall then with joy survey
  Thy mercy's brightest rays,
And spend an everlasting day
  In wonder, love, and praise.

78   B.M.

GREAT God! how oft did Israel prove,
  By turns thine anger and thy love:
There in a glass our hearts may see
How fickle and how false they be.

2 Oft, when they saw their brethren slain,
They mourned, and sought the Lord again;
Called him the Rock of their abode,
Their high Redeemer, and their God.

3 Their prayers and vows before him rise,
As flattering words or solemn lies;
While their rebellious tempers prove
False to his covenant and his love.

4 Yet did his sovereign grace forgive
The faithless tribes, and bade them live;
His anger oft away He turned,
Or else with gentler flame it burned.

5 He saw their flesh was weak and frail,
He saw temptations sore prevail;
The God of Abraham loved them still,
And led them to his holy hill.

78.2   C2.M.

O PRAISE our great and gracious Lord,
   And call upon his name!
To strains of joy tune every chord,
   His mighty acts proclaim:
Tell how He led his chosen race
   To Canaan's promised land;
Tell how his covenant of grace
   Unchanged shall ever stand.

2 He gave the shadowing cloud by day,
   The moving fire by night;
To guide his Israel on their way,
   He made their darkness light:
And have not we a sure retreat,
   A Saviour, ever nigh?
The same clear light, to guide our feet,
   The Dayspring from on high?

3 We too have manna from above,
   The bread that came from heaven;
To us the same kind hand of love
   Hath living waters given:
A Rock we have, from whence the spring
   In rich abundance flows;
That Rock is Christ, our Priest, our King,
   Who life and health bestows.

4 O let us prize this heavenly food,
   And trust our heavenly Guide!
So shall we find death's fearful flood
   Serene as Jordan's tide;
And safely reach that happy shore,
   The land of peace and rest,
Where angels worship and adore,
   In God's own presence blest.

78.3   C.M.

HOW good, how faithful, Lord, art Thou!
   How false and stubborn we!
O teach us at thy feet to bow,
   And yield our all to Thee!

2 Our fathers, in their darkest hours,
   From Thee obtained relief:
O let their mercies, Lord, be ours,
   But not their unbelief!

3 The rocks were cleft to slake their thirst,
   Thy manna was their food;
And still thy bonds they daily burst,
   Thy will each hour withstood.

4 The same kind Father, Lord, thou art,
   The same dark rebels we:
O touch with grace each erring heart,
   And win us all to Thee!

79   Day 16. Psalms 79—85.   D.M.

O GOD, the King of nations!
   Incline thy gracious ear:
What grievous desolations
   Within thy Church appear!
See! scattered into corners,
   The faithful scarce are found;
While troops of haughty scorners
   Profane thy holy ground.

2 Pour out thy wrath, we pray thee,
   On all the sons of pride;
That nations may obey thee,
   Who once thy power defied:

Remember not transgressions,
   Our sins of former days,
But hear our intercessions,
   And tune our lips to praise.

3 O may the prisoners' sighing
   Still reach thy throne on high!
And keep the souls from dying,
   Appointed now to die:
So we, thy sheep, for ever
   Thy goodness will proclaim,
And strive, with meek endeavour,
   To tell thy wondrous fame.

79.2   S.M.

THOU gracious God, and kind,
   O cast our sins away!
Nor call our former guilt to mind,
   Thy justice to display.

2   Thy tenderest mercies show,
     Thy richest grace prepare;
Ere yet, with guilty fears laid low,
   We perish in despair.

3   Save us from guilt and shame,
     Thy quickening grace reveal;
And, for the glory of Thy name,
   Our sins and sickness heal.

4   So we, thy flock, thy choice,
     The people of thy love,
Shall in thy care through life rejoice,
   But praise Thee best above.

80.   A.M.

O ISRAEL'S Shepherd, Joseph's Guide!
  Our prayers to Thee vouchsafe to hear:
Thou that dost on the cherubs ride,
Again in solemn state appear.

2 O Thou, whom heavenly hosts obey,
  How long shall thy fierce anger burn?
  How long thy suffering people pray,
  And to their prayers have no return?

3 Do Thou convert us, Lord, do thou
  The lustre of thy face display;
  And all the ills we suffer now,
  Like scattered clouds, shall pass away.

4 Behold the vineyard made by Thee,
  Which thy right hand did guard so long;
  And keep the Branch from danger free,
  Which for thyself Thou madest strong.

5 So shall we still continue free
  From all the load of guilt and shame;
  And, quickened and revived by Thee,
  Will always praise thy holy name.

6 Do Thou convert us, Lord, do thou
  The lustre of thy face display;
  And all the ills we suffer now,
  Like scattered clouds, will pass away.

80.2   C.M.

SHEPHERD of Israel, God of grace!
  Thy saving health display;
Shine from thy holy dwelling-place,
  And turn our night to day.

2 Shine on our inward darkness, shine!
    Convert our hearts to Thee:
  We rest upon thy arm divine;
    Arise, and set us free.

3 We faint beneath thy chastening power,
    And seek relief in vain:
  O send thy Spirit's quickening shower,
    And all will smile again.

4 From light to light, from grace to grace,
    O bid us onward move!
  Till we behold thy glorious face
    Without a cloud above.

80.3   B.M.

RETURN, O Lord of hosts, return!
    Nor let thy drooping vineyard mourn:
Turn us to Thee, thy love restore;
We shall be saved, and sigh no more.

2 Lord, when thy vine in Egypt grew,
  Thou wast its hope and glory too;
  Attacked in vain by all its foes,
  Till the fair Branch of promise rose!

3 Fair Branch! of old ordained to shoot
  From Judah's stem, of David's root;
  Thy first-born Son, adorned and blessed
  With gifts of grace above the rest.

4 O for His sake attend our cry!
  Shine on thy churches, lest they die:
  Turn us to Thee, thy love restore;
  We shall be saved, and sigh no more.

80.4
K4.M.

SEE the vineyard early planted
  In this barren world below :
Let thy people's prayer be granted,
  Keep it, Lord! from every foe :
Fears and dangers far remove,
Tend it with thy ceaseless love.

2 Thine almighty hand has made it;
  Hide it from the wintry blast :
Let no foot of beast invade it,
  No rude hand its beauty waste :
Hear thy people when they pray;
Keep thy vineyard night and day.

3 Drooping plants revive and nourish,
  Let them thrive beneath thy hand ;
Let the weak grow strong and flourish,
  Blooming fair at thy command :
Let the fruitful yield thee more,
Laden with a richer store.

4 Further, Lord, be thou entreated;
  Plant the barren waste around :
Let thy work be thus completed,
  And no sterile spot be found :
Let the earth a vineyard be,
Consecrated, Lord, to thee !

80.5
C.M.

O VINEYARD of the Lord, how blest
  How safe a lot is thine !
No foes shall now thy peace molest,
  Preserved by grace divine.

2 The choicest wine thy plants shall yield,
    Still watered day by day;
The Lord himself thy sun, thy shield,
    And thy perpetual stay.

3 O sweet and lovely paradise!
    Where fruits of grace abound,
And plants are training for the skies
    Throughout the holy ground.

4 In vain shall banded foes conspire
    To mar thy holy peace :
Like thorns and briers, burned with fire,
    Their fury soon shall cease.

5 Thine ancient vineyard, Lord, restore;
    Let Zion's mercy come;
And Israel's ransomed sons adore
    The grace that leads them home.

80.6   M2.M.

O KING of mercy, from thy throne on high
    Look down in love, and hear our humble cry!

Thou tender Shepherd of the blood-bought sheep,
Thy feeble, wandering flock in safety keep.

O gentle Saviour! by thy death we live;
To contrite sinners life eternal give.

Thou art the Bread of heaven, on Thee we feed;
Be near to help our souls in time of need.

Thou art the mourner's stay, the sinner's Friend
Sweet Fount of joy and blessings without end.

O come and cheer us with thy heavenly grace,
Reveal the brightness of thy glorious face!

In cooling cloud by day, in fire by night,
Be near our steps, and make our darkness light.

Go where we go, abide where we abide,
In life, in death, our Comfort, Strength, and Guide.

O lead us daily with thine eye of love,
And bring us safely to our home above!

81   S.M.

SING to the Lord aloud,
  Our mighty, glorious King!
In joyful bands his temple crowd,
  The harp and psaltery bring.

2   Such festal songs of praise
     The King of heaven decreed,
When Israel's tribes in ancient days
     From bondage sore He freed.

3   Through every later age,
     For nobler mercies still,
High festal songs thy Church engage
     Around thy sacred hill.

4   We bless the Father's name,
     Enthroned in light on high:
We bless the eternal Son, who came
     In lowly love to die.

5   We praise, with songs divine,
     The Spirit, Lord of love,
Who makes our darkened souls to shine
     With sunlight from above.

6   O blessed are the songs,
     When ransomed sinners meet,
  And each the notes of joy prolongs
     Before the Saviour's feet!

7   Our mouth we open wide,
     For Israel's God to fill;
  And He, who once their wants supplied,
     Will bless his people still.

81.2   C.M.

O GOD our strength! to thee the song
    With grateful hearts we raise:
To Thee, and Thee alone, belong
    All worship, love, and praise.

2 In trouble's dark and gloomy hour
    Thine ear hath heard our prayer;
  And graciously thine arm of power
    Hath saved us from despair.

3 Led by the light thy word imparts,
    Ne'er may we bow the knee
  To idols, which our wayward hearts
    Set up instead of Thee.

4 So shall thy choicest gifts, O Lord!
    Be to thine Israel given:
  Its plenteous stores shall earth afford,
    And train their souls for heaven.

81.3   S.M.

SING to the Lord our might,
   With holy fervour sing:
Let hearts and instruments unite
   To praise our heavenly King.

2 The Sabbath to our sires
  In mercy first was given:
The Church her Sabbaths still requires,
  To speed her on to heaven.

3 We still, like them of old,
  Are in the wilderness;
And God is near his chosen fold,
  To pity and to bless.

4 Then let us open wide
  Our mouths for Him to fill;
And He, that Israel then supplied;
  Will help his Israel still.

82   A.M.

MID stately halls of royal power,
 Where earthly lords their pomp display,
Unseen He stands from hour to hour,
The Lord, whom angel hosts obey.

2 How long, ye gods! will ye despise
 The God supreme, whose name ye bear?
How long with violence and lies
 The friendless and the weak ensnare?

3 Defend the poor, their cause maintain,
 And rid them from the oppressor's hand:
Let none for justice plead in vain,
 The works of violence withstand.

4 They know not, Lord, and will not know;
 Onward they walk in darkness still:
Thy laws they strive to overthrow,
 The voice of thine eternal will,

5 Once glorious names to you were given,
Gods, lords, and sons of God most high:
Now, wasted by the frown of heaven,
Like men ye fall, like princes die!

6 Arise, O God, and judge the earth;
To weary hearts deliverance bring:
Our world renew with second birth,
And reign, the true, eternal King!

83 D.M.

KEEP silence, Lord, no longer,
  But hear thy people's cry;
Thy foes are waxing stronger,
  And lift their heads on high:
Against thy Church, conspiring,
  With one consent they rage;
And, filled with zeal untiring,
  A deadly warfare wage.

2 Their rival hosts are blended,
  Their numbers still increase;
By mightier hate suspended,
  Their ancient discords cease:
Around the Church, thy dwelling,
  Immanuel's sacred land,
In warlike strength excelling,
  On every side they stand.

3 O make them like the Tyrians
  And Edomites of old;
Or fierce and proud Assyrians,
  Those wolves around thy fold:
Let all their hosts be scattered,
  Like Midian's vast array;
As Jabin's army, shattered,
  In helpless ruin lay.

4. As fire consumes the stubble,
   Like chaff before the flame,
So fill them, Lord, with trouble,
   Their faces clothe with shame:
Then heathen lands, awaking,
   Thy mighty power shall own,
And, idol-gods forsaking,
   Shall worship Thee alone.

84   A.M.

HOW lovely, how divinely sweet,
   O Lord, thy sacred courts appear!
Fain would my longing spirit meet
The glories of thy presence there.

2 O blest the men! blest their employ,
Whom thine abundant favours raise
To dwell in these abodes of joy,
And sing Thy never-ceasing praise!

3 One day within thy sacred gate
Affords more real joy to me
Than thousands in the tents of state;
The meanest place is bliss with Thee.

4 God is our Sun! our brightest day
From his reviving presence flows:
God is our Shield! through all our way
To guard us from surrounding foes.

5 He pours his choicest blessings down,
Profusely down, on hearts sincere;
And grace shall guide, and glory crown,
The happy favourites of his care.

6 O Lord of hosts! thou God of grace!
How blest, how highly blest, is he
Who trusts Thy love, and seeks Thy face,
And fixes all his hopes on Thee!

84.2   L.M.

LORD of hosts, how lovely fair,
  Even on earth, thy temples are!
Here thy waiting people see
Much of heaven, and much of Thee.

2 From Thy gracious presence flows
Bliss that softens all our woes;
While thy Spirit's holy fire
Warms our hearts with pure desire.

3 Here we supplicate thy throne,
Here we make thy glories known;
Here we learn Thy righteous ways,
Taste thy love, and sing thy praise.

4 Thus with festive songs of joy
We our happy lives employ;
Love, and long to love Thee more,
Till from heaven to earth we soar.

84.3   B.M.

HOW pleasant, how divinely fair,
  O Lord of hosts, thy dwellings are!
With strong desire my spirit faints
To meet the assemblies of thy saints.

2 My flesh would rest in thine abode,
My longing heart cries out for God:
My God, my King! why should I be
So far from all my joys, and Thee?

3 Blest are the saints, who dwell on high
Around Thy throne of majesty!
Thy brightest glories shine above,
And all their work is praise and love.

4 Blest are the souls that find a place
Within the temples of Thy grace!
There they behold thy gentler rays,
And seek thy face, and learn thy praise.

5 Blest are the men, whose hearts are set
To find the way to Zion's gate:
God is their strength, and through the road
They lean upon their helper, God.

6 Cheerful they walk with growing strength,
Till all shall meet in heaven at length;
Till all before Thy face appear,
And join in nobler worship there.

84.4   D.M.

VOICE unto voice is telling,
  Through heaven's wide azure coasts,
How amiable Thy dwelling,
  Lord of the starry hosts!
My spirit, to thee turning,
  Sore struggles to be free:
My inmost soul is yearning,
  O living God! for Thee.

2 In Thee, O thou most holy!
  My heart and flesh rejoice:
Thou wilt not spurn the lowly,
  Nor hide thee at my voice:
Thrice happy they, who, weary,
  Their strength from Thee renew:
Although their path be dreary,
  Thy arm will bear them through.

3 On through the vale of sorrow,
 Oft treading sad and slow,
From Baca's wells they borrow
 Fresh vigour, as they go:
From strength to strength, ascending,
 They journey onward still,
Their toils and dangers ending
 In praise on Zion's hill.

84.5   C.M.

THY earthly dwellings, Lord, are fair;
 More fair Thy courts above:
When shall I rise, and banquet there
 On thy eternal love?

2 Happy the birds, that round Thy shrine
 Can daily sing and roam:
I with their songs would mingle mine,
 And choose with them my home.

3 Tis sweet within Thy house to come,
 And all thy mercies trace;
Within thy arms to find a home,
 And see thee face to face.

4 O happy seasons, spent with Thee,
 Within thy house of prayer!
I'd rather there a servant be,
 Than reign a king elsewhere.

5 The Lord will grace and glory give,
 A sun and shield is He:
How happy, Lord! how safe they live,
 Who trust their all to Thee.

84.6   C4.M.

O LORD of hosts, my soul cries out,
   How lovely thine abode!
My pining heart and flesh aspire,
   To Thee, the living God:
The wild bird there has found its rest,
And there the swallow builds her nest:
O happy, in thy courts who dwell,
And evermore thy praises tell.

2 Yea, happy they, whose strength Thou art,
   Who seek thy holy hill;
They, passing through this vale of tears,
   Find springs of comfort still:
From strength to strength they shall proceed,
Their feet to Zion thou wilt lead,
There to behold, O God, thy face,
There to enjoy thy endless grace.

3 O better than a thousand days,
   One day of joy with Thee!
Better to watch thy doors, than dwell
   Where mirth and feasting be:
Lord God of armies, hear our prayer!
O God of Jacob, hear and spare;
On thine Anointed look, and send
Thy grace, to help us and defend.

4 God is a shield to save, a sun
   To lighten and to bless;
No good will He withhold from those
   Who walk in holiness:
O God of hosts, almighty Lord!
Blest are the souls who trust thy word;
By Thee redeemed, renewed, forgiven,
The sons of God, the heirs of heaven!

84.7

HOW pleasant, Lord of hosts, how dear
    The tents of thine abode!
My longing soul faints to be near
    Thy dwelling-place, O God!
How blest, who dwell around thy shrine
    With ever-growing praise!
Blest are the men, whose strength is Thine,
    Who keep in heart thy ways.

2 They, passing through the vale of pain,
    With streams the valley fill;
New blessings, with thy heavenly rain,
    Come mantling soft and still:
They shall proceed from strength to strength
    Along their weary road;
In Zion they appear at length
    Before the mighty God.

3 O gracious, everlasting Lord!
    Our prayers with mercy crown:
O King of heaven, thine ear afford!
    O God our Shield, look down!
In Thee we trust, by Thee we live,
    Our Hope, our heavenly Friend!
Thou, Lord, wilt grace and glory give,
    And blessings without end.

84.8   L.M.

HOW lovely, how beloved is Thine abode,
    Lord of the hosts of heaven, thou King of saints!

My heart cries out for Thee, the living God,
And for thy courts my spirit longs and faints.

Beneath Thine altars, on the far hill-side,
The sparrow and the swallow build their nest:
My Father, bid me come to Thee, and hide
A child's deep yearnings in a Parent's breast.

Blessèd are they, who in Thy temple dwell,
And utter forth thy praises day and night;
There drinking, from thy love's exhaustless well,
Pure crystal draughts of comfort and delight.

Enough: let earth its richest feast prepare,
Thy presence and thy smile are more than all;
One day within Thy house, one whispered prayer,
Than years of mirth in pleasure's festive hall.

In dark and danger, sun and shield art Thou,
And grace and glory spring from Thee alone,
The refuge of thy pilgrim people now,
Their home for ever, gathered round thy throne.

85   C.M.

O LORD, the night of woe is past,
  The dawn begins to rise:
Rich showers of mercy rain at last,
  Like manna, from the skies.

2 Thou hast forgiven Thy people's sin,
  And turned thy wrath away:
New life and love and peace begin,
  With mercy's opening day.

3 Turn us, O God our Saviour, turn!
  And let thine anger cease:
No longer let thy people mourn,
  While foes and fears increase.

4 Wilt thou for ever hide Thy face?
 For ever turn away?
O Lord, revive us by thy grace!
 Thy pardoning love display.

5 So, meekly listening to thy voice,
 Thy words of peace divine;
Our souls shall in thy name rejoice,
 Sealed evermore for Thine!

85.2   H2.M.

LORD, thine heart in love hath yearned
 On thy lost and fallen land;
Israel's face is homeward turned,
Thou hast freed thy captive land:
Thou hast borne thy people's sin,
Covered all their deeds of ill;
All thy wrath is gathered in,
All thy burning anger still.

2 Art thou not a God to turn,
 And revive our souls again?
That thy people's heart may burn
With the gladness of thy reign:
Show us now thy tender love,
Thy salvation, Lord, impart:
I the voice divine would prove,
Listening in my silent heart.

3 Mercy now and justice meet,
 Peace and truth for aye embrace;
Truth from earth is springing sweet,
Justice looks from her high place:

Marking out her Maker's way,
Righteousness shall go before;
God his goodness will display,
Earth shall yield her plenteous store.

85.3   S.M.

LORD, thou art love divine!
  I yield my heart to Thee:
Fetters and darkness long were mine,
  But grace hath set me free.

2   The Saviour's blood is spilt,
    The day of mercy come;
And to his cross from sin and guilt
    I flee, and find a home.

3   Thy work, O Lord, complete!
    Thy daily grace impart:
Direct aright my wandering feet,
    Upstay my sinking heart.

4   Still let me onward move,
    Rejoicing more and more;
Till I behold Thy face above,
    And at thy feet adore.

85.4   G3.M.

HOW faithful, Lord, thy loving word,
  Of old to Jacob spoken!
Thy land hath seen its sons restored,
  Their captive fetters broken:
Thy grace hath pardoned all their sin,
  And covered their transgression;
No more in wrath thy hand shall smite,
  Nor yield them to oppression.

2 For ever shall thine anger burn,
    And whelm our hearts with sadness?
Return, O God our help, return
    To bring us hope and gladness!
Show us thy pardoning mercy, Lord!
    And grant us thy salvation:
Speak peace to all who love thy word;
    O bless thy chosen nation!

3 Mine ear shall hearken to the voice
    Of God, the Lord most holy;
For He will bid his saints rejoice,
    When they depart from folly:
The Lord's salvation still is nigh
    To those who truly fear him;
That glory in our land may dwell,
    And all the world revere him.

4 Mercy and truth together meet,
    Peace, righteousness, in union;
Truth springs from earth, the skies to greet,
    Heaven holds with earth communion:
All good to us the Lord shall give,
    Our land rich fruits supplying;
And ransomed saints new life receive,
    Immortal and undying.

85.5   A.M.

HOW near is thy salvation, Lord!
    To souls that love thy holy name:
The glorious promise of thy word
Surrounds them, like a wall of flame.

2 Mercy and truth for ever meet
  In our Immanuel's work divine;
  And ransomed souls, in Him complete,
  With beams of heavenly lustre shine.

3 O blessed gift! O wondrous birth!
  God's only Son to us is given:
  Truth springs exulting from the earth,
  And holy love looks down from heaven.

4 The righteous Lord will now bestow
  Rivers of joy and heavenly peace:
  Where streams of gospel mercy flow,
  Our land shall yield her full increase.

5 Truth, heavenly truth, prepares his way,
  And lights the path our Saviour trod:
  Our wandering feet no more shall stray,
  But mark his steps, and keep the road.

86 Day 17. Psalms 86—89. C.M.

ALMIGHTY Father, wise and just!
  To my complaint attend:
Preserve me, for in Thee I trust,
  And on thy love depend.

2 Thou, Lord, art good; nor good alone,
    But rich in pardoning grace,
  To all who kneel before Thy throne,
    And humbly seek thy face.

3 O hearken to my earnest prayer!
    My suppliant cry receive:
  On Thee I cast my grief and care,
    A gracious answer give.

4 Among the gods is none like Thee,
　　No works are like to thine:
All nations thou hast made shall see
　　How bright thy wonders shine.

5 O teach me, then, thy holy ways,
　　With love my soul inflame;
Unite my heart to sing thy praise,
　　And fear thy holy name.

6 Some gracious tokens, Lord, bestow
　　Of pardon freely given:
Comfort thy servant here below,
　　And guide me safe to heaven.

87　　　　　　　　　　　C.M.

O ZION! glorious things to come
　　Of thee thy prophets sing;
Thou dwelling-place, and earthly seat
　　Of heaven's eternal King.

2 Dark Egypt's sons and Babylon
　　To thee shall soon be known;
The Tyrian and the Philistine
　　Be numbered with thine own.

3 Lo! from Arabia's shores afar,
　　The region of the morn,
New names to Zion's mount are come,
　　New souls to God are born.

4 Thy birthright, free and unconfined,
　　Glad strangers now shall share;
And, born anew to God, shall find
　　Their home of comfort there.

87.2 K4.M.

FOUNDED in the holy mountains,
　　Zion stands for ever sure;
Watered still with living fountains,
　　Clear as crystal, bright and pure:
Safe from all the rage of hell;
There Jehovah loves to dwell.

2 Names renowned in heathen story,
　　Egypt, Babel, Tyre, and Rome,
Yield the palm of higher glory,
　　Zion, to thy favoured home:
Souls are born for heaven in thee,
All the world thy fame shall see.

3 Soon from earth's remotest nations
　　Shall thy exiled sons return,
Come with tears and supplications,
　　Look on Him they pierced, and mourn:
New born souls their voices raise,
Fill thy courts with songs of praise.

4 Heavenly Zion! home immortal!
　　Life's pure river flows in thee;
Angels guard each shining portal,
　　Heaven and earth thy brightness see:
There, enthroned for evermore,
Ransomed hosts their Lord adore.

88　　　　　　　　　　　　D.M.

LORD God of my salvation,
　　To thee, to thee I cry!
O let my supplication
　　Arrest thine ear on high!

Distresses round me thicken,
   My life draws nigh the grave:
Descend, O Lord, to quicken!
   Descend, my soul to save!

2 Thy wrath lies hard upon me,
   Thy billows o'er me roll;
My friends all seem to shun me,
   And foes beset my soul:
Where'er on earth I turn me,
   No comforter is near;
Wilt thou, too, Father, spurn me?
   Wilt Thou refuse to hear?

3 No! banished and heart-broken,
   My soul still clings to Thee!
The promise thou hast spoken
   Shall still my refuge be:
So hours of gloom and sadness
   May future joys increase;
Soon lost in years of gladness,
   In hope and heavenly peace.

89   C.M.

MY never-ceasing songs shall show
   Thy mercies, gracious Lord!
And make succeeding ages know
   How faithful is thy word.

2 The sacred truths Thy lips reveal
   Shall firm as heaven endure:
Stamped with thy covenant's holy seal,
   The eternal grace is sure.

3 How long to David's race was given
   The promised earthly throne!
But nobler gifts are sealed in heaven
   To David's greater Son.

4 His seed for ever shall possess
   A throne above the skies:
The meanest subject of his grace
   Shall to that glory rise.

5 Lord God of hosts! thy wondrous ways
   Are sung by saints above;
And saints on earth their honours raise
   To thine unchanging love.

89.2   C.M.

ANCIENT of mercies as of days,
   To Thee I lift my song:
My joy shall be to speak thy praise,
   And still the theme prolong.

2 Set up above the starry sky,
   Thy promise shall endure;
Thy words of truth, that cannot die,
   From age to age more sure.

3 Thine is the earth, and Thine the skies,
   Created at thy will:
The waves at thy command arise,
   At thy command are still.

4 Oh! happy that true flock of Thine,
   On whom the loving light
Of thy sweet countenance shall shine,
   To cheer them day and night!

5 Thou, Lord, wilt go before their face
   From youth to latest age:
Thy tender love shall still embrace
   Thy chosen heritage.

89.3   C.M.

O GOD of hosts, our King and Lord,
   What power is like to Thine!
How true and faithful is thy word!
   Thy glories how divine!

2 Thou rulest, Lord, the stormy deep:
   When its proud waves arise,
A word of Thine can bid them sleep,
   Calm as the summer skies.

3 Beneath thy mighty arm of old
   Sank Rahab's haughty pride:
The seas o'er horse and chariot rolled,
   Who Israel's God defied.

4 The starry heavens, O Lord, are Thine,
   Who all their worlds hast made:
Thy power and wisdom, all divine,
   Earth's deep foundations laid.

5 Eternal righteousness and grace
   Thy throne support below:
Truth, mercy, peace, before Thy face,
   Like sacred heralds go.

6 By Thee sustained, Messiah's throne,
   For ever firm shall stand;
And distant realms, and tribes unknown,
   Shall own his high command.

7 O blest are they, who know the sound
   Of pardon freely given!
Light, love, and joy their steps surround,
   Along their path to heaven.

89.4   C.M.

BLEST are the souls that hear and know
    The gospel's joyful sound:
Peace shall attend the path they go,
    And light their steps surround.

2 Their joy shall bear their spirits up,
    Through their Redeemer's name:
His righteousness exalts their hope,
    Nor Satan dares condemn.

3 They glory in his cross alone,
    They conquer by his grace;
And near the King's eternal throne
    Shall soon possess a place.

4 The Lord, our glory and defence,
    Strength and salvation gives:
Israel, thy King for ever reigns,
    Thy God for ever lives.

89.5   C.M.

THY mercies, O my God and King!
    My soul shall still pursue:
How blest, who feel them while they sing,
    And find them ever new!

2 As bright and lasting as the sun,
    As lofty as the sky,
From age to age Thy truth shall run,
    And chance and change defy.

3 The covenant of the King of kings
    Shall stand for ever sure:
Beneath the shadow of thy wings
    Thy saints repose secure.

4 In earth below, in heaven above,
    Lord, who is like to Thee!
  O spread the gospel of thy love,
    Till all thy glory see!

89.6   E.M.

THE heavens declare thy wondrous fame,
  Thy truth the saintly choirs proclaim;
    Where dwells thy peer, O Lord?
Who sits above the cloudy height,
Who reigns among the sons of light,
    Like Thee to be adored?

2 Thine are the heavens, the earth is Thine,
  The starry spheres, on high that shine,
    By Thee to being came:
  The north and south thy powerful voice
  Created, Tabor's heights rejoice,
    And Hermon, in Thy name.

3 An arm is Thine of peerless might,
  Strong is thy hand, and in the height
    Thy right hand rules supreme:
  Justice and judgment base Thy throne,
  Before thee love and truth flow on,
    An everlasting stream!

4 O blest the people, Lord, who know
  The joyful sound, and as they go,
    Behold Thy guiding face:
  With endless joy thy name they bless,
  While round them shine thy righteousness,
    Thy goodness, and thy grace.

89. 7

O COMFORT to the weary!
   O balm to the distressed!
To lean, when life is dreary,
   Upon the Saviour's breast:
Amidst its cares and sorrows,
   To feel him always nigh;
While earth a radiance borrows,
   From hopes beyond the sky.

2 O sweetness beyond measure,
   To taste the Saviour's love!
And know our choicest treasure
   Is safe with him above:
To prove his care, how tender,
   His providence, how wise!
Our Guardian and Defender,
   Whose goodness never dies.

3 O Saviour meek and lowly,
   Our never-failing friend!
Teach us to trust thee wholly,
   And on thy grace depend:
In mercy watching o'er us,
   Whene'er our feet may stray,
With gentle love restore us,
   And lead us in thy way.

4 When sorrows, Lord, o'ertake us,
   Thy promises are sure;
Thou never wilt forsake us,
   Thy mercies still endure:
Soon may we stand before thee,
   And see thee face to face,
Where saints with joy adore thee,
   And ever sing thy praise.

90   Day 18.   Psalms 90—94.   D.M.

O GOD, the Rock of Ages!
  Who evermore hast been,
What time the tempest rages,
  Our dwelling-place serene;
Before thy first creations,
  O Lord, the same as now,
To endless generations,
  The everlasting, Thou!

2 Our days are like the shadows,
  On sunny hills that lie;
Or grasses in the meadows,
  That blossom but to die;
A sleep, a dream, a story
  By strangers quickly told;
An unremaining glory
  Of things that soon are old.

3 O Thou, who canst not slumber,
  Whose light grows never pale!
Teach us aright to number
  Our years, before they fail:
On us thy mercy lighten,
  On us thy goodness rest;
And let thy Spirit brighten
  The hearts Thyself hast blessed.

4 Lord, crown our faith's endeavour
  With beauty and with grace;
Till, clothed in light for ever,
  We see thee face to face;
A joy no language measures,
  A fountain brimming o'er;
An endless flow of pleasures,
  An ocean without shore.

90.2   C.M.

RETURN, O God of love, return!
  Earth is a weary place;
How long shall we, thy children, mourn
  Our absence from thy face?

2 Let heaven succeed our painful years,
  Let sin and sorrow cease;
And, in proportion to our fears,
  So make our joys increase.

3 Almighty God, reveal thy love,
  And not thy wrath alone!
O let our sweet experience prove
  The mercies of thy throne!

4 Thy wonders to thy servants show,
  Make thy own work complete;
Then shall our souls thy glory know,
  Adoring at thy feet.

5 Then shall we shine before Thy throne,
  In all thy beauty, Lord!
And, trusting in thy grace alone,
  Reap a divine reward.

90.3   G.M.

LORD, thou hast been thy people's rest,
  Through all their generations;
Their refuge, when by dangers pressed,
  Their hope in tribulations:
Thou, ere the mountains had their birth,
Or ever Thou hadst formed the earth,
  Art God from everlasting.

2 The sons of men return to clay,
	When Thou the word hast spoken;
   As with a torrent torn away,
	Or like a dream when broken:
   A thousand years are, in Thy sight,
   Like one brief watch amidst the night,
	Or yesterday departed.

3 At morn we flourish like the grass,
	With dews and sunshine lighted;
   But, ere the cool of evening pass,
	The rich array is blighted:
   Thus do Thy chastisements consume,
   Youth's tender leaf, and beauty's bloom,
	We fade at thy displeasure.

4 Lord, teach us so to mark our days,
	That we may prize them duly;
   O guide our feet in wisdom's ways,
	That we may love thee truly!
   Return, O Lord! our grief behold,
   And with thy goodness, as of old,
	O fill our souls for ever!

90.4   E.M.

O GOD of glory, God of grace,
	From age to age our dwelling-place!
   Before thy throne we bow:
Ere the vast mountains rose of yore,
When they and earth shall be no more,
   The same, O Lord, art Thou!

2 Man's generations rise and pass,
	Like morning flowers, or summer grass,
	   The creatures of thy breath:

Our life runs onward, like a stream,
We shine and vanish like a dream,
  The prey of sin and death.

3 Unnumbered ills beset our path,
Our days grow dark beneath thy wrath,
  And yet how heedless we!
O touch with grace each erring heart!
Thy wisdom to each soul impart,
  And win us all to Thee.

4 We faint, we sink beneath Thy frown,
O send thy healing mercy down,
  To light our coming years!
Then, though our days be short and few,
Thy grace will bear us safely through,
  Beyond the reach of tears.

90.5   S2.M.

OUR guilty deeds, O Lord,
  Our sins in darkness done,
To thee are all revealed in light,
  More clear than mid-day sun:
  If Thy fierce anger burn,
  Our days grow dim and old,
We die, and to our dust return,
  Life's weary tale is told.

2   Fixed is our mortal date
    At threescore years and ten;
Should death a little longer wait,
  Life is but sorrow then:
  O teach us, day and night
  How swift the season flies!
How brief the whole, to learn aright
  The wisdom of the wise!

3 How long, O gracious Lord!
　　Shall we for mercy pray?
O turn again, relenting, turn,
　　And wash our guilt away!
Thy beauty, glorious Lord,
　　O may it round us shine!
Thy prospering grace through life afford,
　　And make us wholly Thine!

91　　　　　　　　　　　　D.M.

O LORD, in might excelling,
　　Whose glory fills the sky,
A safe and secret dwelling,
　　Thy sheltering wings supply!
My Refuge, Fortress, Treasure!
　　My God, in whom I trust!
Kind, gracious beyond measure,
　　To children of the dust.

2 When hell's dark powers assail me,
　　And life is sad and drear,
Thy love shall never fail me,
　　Thy help is always near:
Like bird, that shelters nightly
　　The young ones in her nest,
Thy mercy, shining brightly,
　　Shall bring me peace and rest.

3 No terror shall appal me,
　　Though plagues around me fly;
No evil shall befall me,
　　Since thou, my God, art nigh:
Thy angels shall uphold me,
　　And keep me in thy ways;
Thy arms of love enfold me,
　　My lips be filled with praise.

4 Daily, O Lord, defend me,
   For still I trust in Thee;
And constant succour lend me,
   While to the cross I flee:
I plead my Saviour's merit;
   O lift my soul on high!
And raise me to inherit
   A home beyond the sky.

91.2   K2.M.

CALL Jehovah thy salvation,
   Rest beneath th'Almighty's shade:
In his secret habitation
   Dwell, nor ever be dismayed:
There no tumult can alarm thee,
   Thou shalt dread no hidden snare;
Guile nor violence can harm thee,
   In eternal safeguard there.

2 From the sword at noonday wasting,
   From the noisome pestilence,
In the depth of midnight blasting,
   God shall be thy sure defence:
Fear not then the deadly quiver,
   When a thousand feel the blow;
Mercy shall thy soul deliver,
   Though ten thousand be laid low.

3 Though the winds and waves be swelling,
   God shall bear thee safe through all;
Plague shall not come nigh thy dwelling,
   Thee no evil shall befall:
He shall charge his angel legions,
   Watch and ward o'er thee to keep;
Though thou walk through hostile regions,
   Though in desert wilds thou sleep.

4 Since, with pure and firm affection,
   Thou on God hast set thy love,
With the wings of his protection
   He will shield thee from above:
Thou shalt call on him in trouble,
   He will hearken, He will save;
Here for grief reward thee double,
   Crown with life beyond the grave.

91.3   B.M.

HE that hath made his refuge, God,
   Shall find a most secure abode;
Shall walk all day beneath His shade,
And there at night shall rest his head.

2 What though a thousand at thy side,
At thy right hand ten thousand died?
Thy God his chosen people saves,
Amidst the dead, amidst the graves.

3 But if the fire, or plague, or sword,
Receive commission from the Lord
To smite his saints among the rest,
Their very pains and death are blest.

4 The sword, the pestilence, or fire,
Shall but fulfil their best desire,
From sins and sorrows set them free,
And bring Thy children, Lord, to Thee.

91.4   C.M.

INCARNATE God! the soul, that knows
   Thy name's mysterious power,
Shall dwell in undisturbed repose,
   Nor fear the trying hour.

2 Thy wisdom, faithfulness, and love
   To feeble, helpless worms,
A buckler and a refuge prove
   From enemies and storms.

3 Angels, unseen, attend the saints,
   And bear them in their arms,
To cheer the spirit when it faints,
   And guard their life from harms.

4 The angels' Lord himself is nigh
   To them that love his name:
He still will save them, when they cry,
   And put their foes to shame.

5 Crosses and changes are their lot,
   Long as they sojourn here;
But since their Saviour changes not,
   What have the saints to fear?

91.5   12.M.

LORD of hosts, how blest is he,
   Who has sought repose in Thee!
Sheltered safe beneath thy wings,
Guarded by the King of kings!
Thou, O Lord, my refuge art;
Draw to thee this wayward heart:
Bid me dwell, in loving rest,
In the covert of thy breast.

2 How should he be overcome,
Who hath found in Thee his home?
Round him, in a fiery band,
Ministering angels stand:
Safe he speeds his conquering way,
Where the lion lurks to slay;
Treads the crested dragon down,
Hasting to his heavenly crown.

3 Hark! the voice of love divine,
"Fear not, trembler, thou art Mine."
God himself is near thy side,
Strong to succour, wise to guide:
Call on Him in want and woe,
He will guard thee here below;
And, when all thy strife is past,
Bear thee to himself at last.

91.6   C.M.

THERE is a safe and secret place,
  Beneath the wings divine,
Reserved for all the heirs of grace;
  O be that refuge mine!

2 The least, the feeblest there may hide,
  Uninjured and unawed:
While thousands fall on every side,
  He rests secure in God.

3 He feeds in pastures, large and fair,
  Of love and truth divine:
O child of God, O glory's heir,
  How rich a lot is thine!

4 A hand almighty to defend,
  An ear for every call;
An honoured life, a peaceful end,
  And heaven to crown it all!

92   12.M.

THOU, who art enthroned above,
  Thou, by whom we live and move,
O how sweet, with joyful tongue,
To resound Thy praise in song!

When the morning paints the skies,
When the sparkling stars arise,
All thy favours to rehearse,
And give thanks in grateful verse.

2 Sweet the day of sacred rest,
When devotion fills the breast;
When we dwell within thy house,
Hear thy word, and pay our vows;
Notes to heaven's high mansion raise,
Fill its courts with joyful praise,
With repeated hymns proclaim
Great Jehovah's awful name.

3 From Thy works our joys arise,
O thou only good and wise!
Who thy wonders can declare?
How profound thy counsels are!
Warm our hearts with holy fire,
Grateful fervours still inspire;
All our powers, with all their might,
Ever in thy praise unite.

92.2   B3.M.

HOW good to praise thee, glorious Lord!
   Thy name in grateful songs record;
To tell thy love at morning light,
Thy faithfulness to listening night;
While joyful strains to heaven aspire,
From lute and sweetly sounding lyre.

2 Thy mighty deeds with songs of joy,
O Lord, my grateful heart employ:
How vast the wonders Thou hast wrought,
Untold, unnumbered, passing thought!
To proud and worldly hearts unknown,
But treasures for the meek alone.

3 Like palm trees fair the just are seen,
Like stately cedars, strong and green,
And, firmly planted near thy side,
Still faithful in thy courts abide:
From day to day thy truth they prove,
Upheld and blest by heavenly love.

92.3 B.M.

HOW blest the souls, O Lord, who stand
In gardens planted by thy hand!
May we within thy courts be seen,
Like cedars clad in living green.

2 There grow thy saints in faith and love,
Blest with thine influence from above:
Not Lebanon, with all her trees,
Yields such a comely sight as these.

3 The plants of grace shall ever live;
Nature decays, but grace must thrive:
Time, that doth all things else impair,
Still makes them flourish bright and fair.

4 Laden with fruits of age, they show
The Lord is holy, just, and true:
None that attend his grace shall find
A God unfaithful or unkind.

93 A4.M.

THE Lord is King of kings, he reigneth,
Girdled with everlasting might:
His powerful arm the world sustaineth,
His robes are majesty and light.

2 The earth upon the seas He founded,
By laws for ever firm and sure:
His throne, by angel hosts surrounded,
Through endless ages must endure.

3 The streams of mighty waters, flowing,
    Send up their voices to the sky:
Wild ocean's floods, in fury growing,
    Toss their tumultuous waves on high.

4 Calm on his heavenly throne abiding,
    The Lord their fury will restrain:
Beneath his mighty hand subsiding,
    The stormy waters sleep again.

5 Thy word is sure, Thy name is holy,
    O King of glory, God of grace!
From age to age the meek and lowly
    Find in thy house a welcome place.

93.2   A.M.

WITH glory clad, with strength arrayed,
    The Lord, that o'er all nature reigns,
The world's foundations firmly laid,
And the vast fabric still sustains.

2 How surely stablished is thy throne,
Which shall no change or period see!
For thou, O Lord, and thou alone,
Art God from all eternity!

3 The floods, O Lord, lift up their voice,
And toss their troubled waves on high;
But God above can still their noise,
And make the angry sea comply.

4 Thy promise, Lord, is ever sure;
Unchanged and firm thy laws remain;
And in thy dwelling, bright and pure,
Eternal holiness shall reign.

93.3   I.M.

HIGH above created things
   Reigns the glorious King of kings,
Seated in approachless light,
Self-arrayed in awe and might.

2 Everlasting is His throne;
Heaven and earth are all his own;
Fashioned by his wondrous hand,
Subject to his high command.

3 Ocean lifts its voice on high,
Angry waves assault the sky;
Calmly o'er them sits the Lord,
And controls them by his word.

4 Midst the roaring of the sea,
Sweet it is to him to flee:
He is faithful, He is near,
Wherefore should his children fear?

93.4   F.M.

THE Lord Jehovah reigns,
   His throne is built on high;
The garments He assumes
   Are light and majesty:
His glory shines with beams so bright,
No mortal eye can bear the sight.

2 The thunders of his hand
   Keep the wide world in awe:
His wrath and justice stand
   To guard his holy law;
And where his love resolves to bless,
His truth confirms and seals the grace.

3   Through all his ancient works
      Surprising wisdom shines,
  Confounds the powers of hell,
      And breaks their dark designs:
Strong is his arm, and shall fulfil
His great decrees, his sovereign will.

4   And can this mighty King
      Of glory condescend,
  And will he write his name,
      My Father, and my Friend?
I love his name, I love his word;
Join, all my powers, and praise the Lord!

93.5   F.M.

GOD rules in realms of light,
    Enrobed with glory round;
With majesty of might,
    As with a garland, bound:
He shall restrain the world he made,
Nor change invade his steadfast reign.

2   Thy throne, more old than time,
      Stands changeless as of yore;
  Above earth's stormy clime
      Firm fixed for evermore;
Though men may rise in wrathful mood,
Like ocean's flood, that threats the skies.

3   Though round us fierce and loud
      The madd'ning tumult roar,
  Like boisterous surges proud,
      That scourge the sounding shore;
Though with wild cry the floods rejoice,
More dread thy voice, O Lord most high!

4 Thy voice, in chiding heard,
   Shall bid the discord cease;
 Thy true and glorious word
   Shall bring perpetual peace;
And saints shall see fair holiness
For ever bless their home with Thee.

93.6   O.M.

YE servants of God, your Master proclaim,
  And publish abroad his wonderful name;
The name all-victorious of Jesus extol,
His kingdom is glorious, and rules over all.

2 The waves of the sea have lift up their voice,
But mightier is He, who bids us rejoice:
Amidst their loud roaring our Saviour is here;
While we are adoring, He always is near.

3 God ruleth on high, almighty to save;
And still He is nigh, his presence we have:
The great congregation his triumph shall sing,
Ascribing salvation to Jesus our King.

4 Salvation to God, who sits on the throne,
Let all cry aloud, and honour the Son:
Our Saviour's high praises the angels proclaim,
Fall down on their faces, and worship the Lamb.

5 Then let us adore, and give Him his right,
All glory and power, all wisdom and might;
All honour and blessing, with angels above,
And thanks never ceasing, and infinite love.

94 C.M.

O WHEN will sinners understand?
   O when will fools be wise?
And own their mighty Maker's hand,
   The Sovereign of the skies?

2 With matchless skill He plants the ear,
   He moulds the seeing eye:
Shall he not see the proud, and hear
   The mourner's plaintive cry?

3 He forms the powers of every soul,
   Thought, memory, reason, will:
Shall not His eyes observe the whole,
   And judge the nations still?

4 O blest are they, who humbly trust
   In God, our gracious King!
He soon will rise to help the just,
   And full deliverance bring.

95   Day 19.   Psalms 95—101.   B.M.

O COME, loud anthems let us sing,
   Loud thanks to our almighty King!
For we our voices high should raise,
When our salvation's Rock we praise.

2 Into His presence let us haste,
To thank him for his favours past;
To him address, in joyful songs,
The praise that to his name belongs.

3 For God the Lord, enthroned in state,
Is with unrivalled glories great;
The depths of earth are in his hand,
Her secret wealth at his command,

4 The roaring ocean's vast abyss,
  Its floods, by sovereign right are His;
  The strength of hills, that reach the skies,
  Subjected to his empire lies.

5 O let us to his courts repair,
  And bow with adoration there!
  Down on our knees devoutly fall,
  And on the Lord our Maker call.

95.2   S.M.

COME, sound his praise abroad,
   And hymns of glory sing:
Jehovah is the sovereign God,
   The universal King.

2   He formed the deeps unknown,
     He gave the seas their bound;
The watery worlds are all his own,
     And all the solid ground.

3   Come, worship at his throne,
     Come, bow before the Lord,
We are his work, and not our own,
     He formed us by his word.

4   To-day attend his voice,
     Nor dare provoke his rod:
Come, like the people of his choice,
     And own your gracious God.

5   O may we ne'er refuse
     His words of heavenly grace;
Nor Egypt's bondage blindly choose,
     Like Israel's stubborn race!

6 Thy saints, O Lord, how blest!
Their Paradise, how fair!
But they, who scorn Thy promised rest,
Shall never enter there.

95.3 N2.M.

O COME, let us sing to the Lord,
In God our salvation rejoice!
In psalms of thanksgiving record
His praises, with heart and with voice:
For God is the King, and he reigns
In glory supreme on his throne;
His wisdom all nature sustains,
And the strength of the hills is his own.

2 The sea is the Lord's, he hath made
The wild waves their dwelling to know;
The earth is the Lord's, he hath laid
Its deeper foundations below:
He spoke, and the mountains upreared
Their snow-mantled peaks to the sky;
The forests and valleys appeared,
And sent up their voices on high.

3 O come, let us kneel at the feet
Of our Maker, and humbly adore!
O give him the praise that is meet,
His mercy's deep wonders explore!
For we are his flock, whom he feeds
Amidst the green pastures of love;
O blest are the people he leads
To dwell in his presence above!

95.   K.M.

TO the God of all creation
   Sing aloud with cheerful voice:
In the Rock of our salvation
   Now with heart and soul rejoice.

2 In His presence let us gather
   With glad hearts and thankful lays,
And before our heavenly Father
   Show our joy in psalms of praise.

3 He is King o'er all the nations,
   God above all gods is He;
In his hand are earth's foundations,
   The strong hills and rolling sea.

4 He created land and ocean,
   And the wilds by man untrod:
Kneeling low in deep devotion,
   Bless your Maker and your God.

96   C.M.

SING to the Lord a noble song,
   Ye tribes of every name:
Let all the earth with heart and tongue
   His glorious deeds proclaim.

2 He made the heavens, the worlds of light,
   The stars that gem the sky:
He reigns in everlasting might,
   Midst angel hosts on high.

3 Honour and majesty are Thine,
   O God, the King of heaven!
And strength and beauty most divine
   To all thy saints are given.

4 O then, in glad and joyful strains
   Your humble offerings bring !
Proclaim, the Lord our Saviour reigns,
   The universal King.

5 Praise Him, who stooped from heaven to
   To suffer, bleed, and die :   [save,
His love hath opened, through the grave,
   Our pathway to the sky.

6 He comes,—let earth and heaven rejoice,
   And floods of ocean roar,—
To bless the people of his choice,
   And reign for evermore.

96.2   C.M.

SING to the Lord, ye distant lands,
   Ye tribes of every tongue:
His new-discovered grace demands
   A new and nobler song.

2 Say to the nations, Jesus reigns,
   God's own almighty Son;
His power the sinking world sustains,
   And grace surrounds his throne.

3 Let an unusual joy surprise
   The islands of the sea :
Ye mountains, sink ! ye valleys rise !
   Prepare the Lord his way.

4 Behold, He comes, he comes to bless
   The nations as their God,
To show the world his righteousness,
   And send his truth abroad.

5 Lord, when thy voice shall raise the dead,
    And bid the world draw near,
May we with joy lift up our head,
    And see the Judge appear!

96.3   K2.M.

RAISE the psalm: let earth adoring,
    Through each kindred, tribe, and tongue,
To her God his praise restoring,
    Raise her new and holy song:
Bless his name, each farthest nation;
    Sing his praise, his truth display:
Tell anew his high salvation,
    With each new return of day.

2 Tell it out beneath the heaven,
    Through each kindred, tribe, and tongue:
Tell it out from morn till even,
    Still in unexhausted song:
Say that God for ever reigneth,
    He who set the world so fast;
He who still its state sustaineth,
    Till the day of doom to last.

3 Loud proclaim, the day is coming,
    When that righteous doom shall be;
Then new joys shall heaven illumine,
    Gladness shine o'er earth and sea:
Yea, the far resounding ocean
    Shall its thousand voices raise;
All its waves, in glad commotion,
    Chant the fulness of his praise.

4 Let earth's forests, fields and flowers,
    All put on their choice array;
Sparkle clear, in leafy bowers,
    Dew-drops bright on every spray:
Lo! the Judge, to earth descending,
    Righteous judgment shall ordain:
Fraud and wrong for ever ending,
    Truth, immortal truth, shall reign!

97   B.M.

HE reigns, the Lord the Saviour reigns;
    Praise him aloud in joyful strains:
Let the whole earth in songs rejoice,
And distant islands join their voice.

2 Deep are his counsels, and unknown,
But grace and truth support his throne:
Though gloomy clouds his way surround,
Justice is their eternal ground.

3 In robes of judgment, lo! He comes,
Shakes the wide earth, and rends the tombs:
Before him burns devouring fire,
The mountains melt, the seas retire.

4 His enemies, with sore dismay,
Fly from the sight, and shun the day:
Then lift your heads, ye saints, on high,
And sing, for your redemption's nigh.

97.2   B.M.

THE Lord is come! the heavens proclaim
    His birth, and Gentiles learn his name:
An unknown star directs the road
Of eastern sages to their God.

2 All ye bright armies of the skies,
 Go, worship where the Saviour lies:
 Angels and kings before him bow,
 Ye gods on high, and gods below!

3 Let worthless idols strew the ground,
 And their own worshippers confound;
 But Judah, shout! and Zion, sing!
 And earth, confess thy sovereign King.

97.3   B.M.

TH' Almighty reigns, exalted high
 O'er all the earth, o'er all the sky:
Though clouds and darkness veil his feet,
His dwelling is the mercy-seat.

2 O ye that love his holy name,
 Hate every work of sin and shame:
 He guards the souls of all his friends,
 And from the snares of hell defends.

3 Immortal light and joys unknown
 Are for the saints in darkness sown:
 Those glorious seeds shall spring and rise,
 And the bright harvest bless their eyes.

4 Rejoice, ye righteous, and record
 The sacred honours of the Lord:
 None but the soul, that feels his grace,
 Can triumph in his holiness.

97.4   C.M.

JEHOVAH reigns, let all the earth
 In God their King rejoice;
Let all the isles, with sacred mirth,
 In praise unite their voice.

2 For thou, O God, art seated high,
    O'er all the earth enthroned;
Unrivalled in thy majesty,
    Supreme Creator owned.

3 O ye that love Him, turn away
    From every thought of ill;
His mercy then, from day to day,
    Shall your best hopes fulfil.

4 Bright seeds are sown of glorious light,
    A harvest for the just;
And gladness stored for hearts upright,
    To recompense their trust.

5 Rejoice, ye nations, in the Lord!
    Remembering, while ye sing,
How holy is the name and word
    Of our eternal King.

98   C.M.

SING to the Lord a new-made song,
    Who wondrous things hath done:
With his right hand and holy arm
    The victory He hath won.

2 The Lord hath through the astonished world
    Displayed His saving might;
And made his righteous acts appear
    In all the heathen's sight.

3 Of Israel's house His love and truth
    Have ever mindful been:
Wide earth's remotest parts the power
    Of Israel's God have seen.

4 Let, therefore, earth's inhabitants
　　Their cheerful voices raise;
　And all, with universal joy,
　　Resound their Maker's praise.

98.2　　　　　　　　　　　　　　C.M.

JOY to the world, the Lord is come!
　　Let earth receive her King;
Let every heart prepare him room,
　　And heaven and nature sing.

2 Joy to the earth! the Saviour reigns;
　　Let men their songs employ;
While fields and floods, rocks, hills, and
Repeat the sounding joy.　　　　[plains,

3 No more let sins and sorrows grow,
　　Nor thorns infest the ground:
He comes to make his blessings flow
　　Far as the curse is found.

4 He rules the world with truth and grace,
　　And makes the nations prove
The glories of his righteousness,
　　And wonders of his love.

98.3　　　　　　　　　　　　　　F.M.

HILLS of the North, rejoice!
　　River and mountain spring:
Hark to the advent voice,
　　Valley and lowland, sing:
Though absent long, your Lord is nigh,
He judgment brings and victory.

2   Isles of the Southern seas!
        Deep in your coral caves
    Pent be each warring breeze,
        Lulled be your restless waves:
    He comes to reign with boundless sway,
    And make your wastes his great highway.

3   Lands of the East, awake!
        Soon shall your sons be free;
    The sleep of ages break,
        And rise to liberty:
    On your far hills, long cold and gray,
    Has dawned the everlasting day.

4   Shores of the utmost West!
        Ye that have waited long,
    Unvisited, unblest,
        Break forth to swelling song:
    High raise the note that Jesus died,
    Yet lives and reigns, the Crucified!

5   Shout, while ye journey home,
        Songs be in every mouth,
    "Lo, from the North we come,
        From East, and West, and South.
    City of God, the bond are free;
    We come to live and reign in thee."

99   D.M.

THOU, Lord, in heavenly glory
    Dost reign for evermore;
Let nations fear before thee,
    And all the earth adore:
How great the awful splendour
    Of thy eternal throne!
And heaven's bright armies render
    Their praise to Thee alone.

2 Thou, too, art wise and holy,
   O King of righteousness!
Messiah, meek and lowly,
   True, faithful, full of grace.
How did thy saints revere thee,
   O Lord, in elder days!
We, too, will love and fear thee,
   And celebrate thy praise.

3 Thou, in thy cloudy pillar,
   Didst lead them through the flood,
O kind and wise Fulfiller
   Of every promised good!
They sinned, and thou didst chasten;
   They wandered, thou didst guide;
They loitered, thou didst hasten;
   Their wants were all supplied.

4 Their sins with daily pardon
   Thy mercies did remove;
Their path, like Eden's garden,
   Bloomed fresh with heavenly love.
O then, with hearts and voices,
   Exalt our glorious King!
While Israel still rejoices
   His holy name to sing.

99.2   S.M.

THE great Jehovah reigns,
   Let all the nations fear;
Let sinners tremble at his throne,
   And saints be humble there.

2   Jesus the Saviour reigns,
   Let earth adore its Lord;
Bright cherubs his attendants stand,
   Swift to fulfil his word.

3 In Zion is his throne,
   His honours are divine:
 His Church shall make his wonders known,
   For there his glories shine.

4 How holy is his name!
   How terrible his praise!
 Let heaven and earth aloud proclaim
   The wonders of his grace.

100 A.M.

WITH one consent let all the earth
   To God their cheerful voices raise,
Glad homage pay with awful mirth,
And sing before him songs of praise:

2 Convinced that He is God alone,
   From whom both we and all proceed,
 We whom he chooses for his own,
   The flock that he vouchsafes to feed.

3 O enter then his temple gate,
   Thence to his courts devoutly press,
 And still your grateful hymns repeat,
   And still his name with praises bless.

4 For He's the Lord, supremely good,
   His mercy is for ever sure:
 His truth, which always firmly stood,
   To endless ages shall endure.

100.2 A.M.

SING to the Lord with joyful voice,
   Let every land his name adore:
Ye ocean floods, in Him rejoice;
Sound his high praise on every shore.

2 Ye nations, bow before His throne,
With solemn fear, with sacred joy!
Know that the Lord is God alone,
He can create, and He destroy.

3 His sovereign power, without our aid,
Made us of clay, and formed us men;
And when like wandering sheep we strayed,
He brought us to his fold again.

4 We are his people, we his care,
Our souls, and all our mortal frame:
What lasting honours shall we rear,
Almighty Maker, to thy name?

5 We'll crowd thy gates with thankful songs,
High as the heavens our voices raise;
And earth, with her ten thousand tongues,
Shall fill thy courts with sounding praise.

6 Wide as the world is Thy command,
Vast as eternity thy love:
Firm as a rock thy truth shall stand,
When rolling years shall cease to move.

100.3   D.M.

O SERVE the Lord with gladness,
  In holy, happy bands!
Away with grief and sadness,
  Be joyful, all ye lands!
Come, and bow down before him!
  Into his presence throng,
Ye nations! and adore him
  With lute and holy song.

2 Know, all the earth, for ever,
    Our Lord is God alone;
We are his offspring, never
    Will He forsake his own.
O people born to praise him,
    The sheep of his own fold,
Awake, awake! and raise him
    The pleasant hymns of old.

3 O come with loud thanksgiving,
    And fill his courts with praise:
New mercies still receiving,
    New songs of gladness raise.
His glory heaven declareth,
    His goodness earth has known;
And truth with mercy shareth
    His everlasting throne.

100.4   L2.M.

PRAISE ye the Lord, ye tribes of earth,
    adore him!
Ye distant isles, to Him your homage bring!
Serve him with gladness, come with joy before
O praise the true, the everlasting King! [him;

The Lord is God, from Him alone proceedeth
Our life, our reason, memory, thought, and will:
We are his people, whom he hourly feedeth,
The sheep he guides in pleasant pastures still.

O enter then his gates with loud thanksgiving!
Loud in his courts his noble deeds proclaim!
Sing of his might, the True, the Everliving;
Be thankful unto him, and bless his name.

For He is good, his mercy lasts for ever,
High as the heavens, like mountains firm and sure;
For He is wise, his counsel changeth never;
His truth to endless ages must endure.

101 C.M.

OF mercy and of judgment, Lord!
   My daily song shall be:
O let my soul, by grace restored,
   Thy pardoning mercy see!

2 In paths of truth and righteousness
   My footsteps hourly guide:
With peace and love thy servant bless,
   And keep me near thy side.

3 Let envy, malice, fraud, and wrong
   Be banished far away:
May only those to me belong,
   Who fear from Thee to stray.

4 On earth the faithful of the land
   My chosen friends shall be;
Until before Thy face I stand,
   Thy perfect love to see.

101.2 D.M.

MY song shall be of mercy;
   To Thee, O Lord, I sing,
Who all my life hast hid me
   Beneath thy sheltering wing;
Who still, in love so patient,
   This mortal journey through,
Hast followed me with goodness,
   And blessings ever new.

2 My song shall be of judgment:
   All-wise and holy God!
Thou makest all thy children
   To pass beneath thy rod:
Thou scourgest whom Thou lovest,
   And oh, my soul shall tell
That in thy fiercest anger
   Thou doest all things well.

3 My song shall be of mercy:
   Come, ye who love the Lord,
Who know that He is gracious,
   Who trust his faithful word;
Tell out his works with gladness,
   With me exalt his name,
Whose love endures for ever,
   To endless years the same.

4 My song shall be of judgment:
   Ye who his chastenings feel,
O faint not, nor be weary!
   He wounds, that He may heal:
Yea, bless the hand that smiteth,
   And in your grief confess
That all His ways are wisdom,
   And truth, and righteousness.

5 Of mercy and of judgment,
   O Lord, to thee we sing,
O Father, Son, and Spirit!
   O great, eternal King!
For only Thou art holy,
   For Thou art Lord alone;
And mercy still, and judgment,
   Are pillars of thy throne.

102 Day 20. Psalms 102–104. C.M.

WHEN I pour out my soul in prayer,
  Do thou, O Lord, attend!
To thine eternal throne of grace
  Let my sad cry ascend.

2 My days, just hastening to their close,
  Are like an evening shade;
My beauty does, like withered grass,
  With waning lustre fade.

3 But thine eternal years, O Lord!
  No length of time can waste;
The memory of thy wondrous works
  From age to age shall last.

4 Thou shalt arise, and Zion view
  With an unclouded face:
For now her time is come, thine own
  Appointed day of grace.

5 Her scattered ruins by thy saints
  With pity are surveyed;
They grieve to see her lofty towers
  In dust and darkness laid.

6 Thy name and glory soon, O Lord,
  All heathen kings shall fear;
When Thou shalt Zion build again,
  And in full state appear.

102.2 C.M.

LET Zion from the dust arise,
  The promised hour is come;
Our God will hearken from the skies,
  And bring her wanderers home.

2 How long her sacred walls have lain
   In ruin and decay!
Her children mourned, and mourned in
   Their hopes had died away.   [vain,

3 Arise, O Lord! and Zion's sons
   Once more from bondage free:
Thy saints take pleasure in her stones,
   Her dust with favour see.

4 Her walls of old to Thee were dear,
   Her peace thy constant care:
In glorious brightness, Lord, appear;
   Their ruined heaps repair.

5 O hear the prisoner's mournful sigh,
   The burdened captive free;
And let the outcast's plaintive cry
   Ascend, O Lord, to Thee.

6 So all the earth shall fear Thy name,
   Thy matchless glories own;
Kings, princes, lords, thy truth proclaim,
   And worship at thy throne.

102.3   A.M.

IT is the Lord our Saviour's hand
   Weakens our strength amidst the race:
Disease and death, at His command,
Arrest us, and cut short our days.

2 Spare us, O Lord! aloud we pray,
   Nor let our sun go down at noon:
Thy years are one eternal day,
   And must thy children die so soon?

3 Yet, in the midst of death and grief,
This thought our sorrow shall assuage,
Our Father and our Saviour live,
Christ is the same through every age.

4 The starry curtains of the sky
Like garments shall be laid aside;
But still thy throne is firm on high,
Thy Church for ever must abide.

5 Before thy face thy Church shall live,
And near thy throne thy children reign;
This dying world they shall survive,
And the dead saints be raised again.

102.4   C.M.

LORD, end not Thou my mortal life,
  When half is scarcely past:
Thy years, from worldly changes free,
  To endless ages last.

2 The strong foundations of the earth
  Of old by Thee were laid;
Thy hands the beauteous arch of heaven
  With wondrous skill have made.

3 Thou, Lord, for ever shalt endure;
  They soon shall pass away;
And, like a garment long outworn,
  Shall tarnish and decay.

4 Thou to the children of thy saints
  Wilt lasting quiet give:
Their happy race, by faith secure,
  Shall in thy presence live.

102.5   C2.M.

O LORD, from Salem's ruined walls
   Goes up the ceaseless cry,
Each watchman, God-ordainèd, calls,
   And, wistful, scans her sky;
For 'tis thy will that, day and night,
   We never hold our peace,
Till Thou on Zion break in light,
   And bid her mourning cease.

2 [We will not give thee rest, O Lord,
   We will besiege thy throne,
We will obey thy gracious word,
   And leave thee not alone;
In silence never canst thou be,
   Until our prayer thou hear,
And bid the trump of Jubilee
   Proclaim the joyful year.]

3 To favour Zion, lo! the hour,
   Thine own set hour, is come;
The time to manifest thy power,
   And fetch thy banished home:
For why? thy servants with desire,
   Her ancient landmarks learn,
They search her dust, her stones admire,
   And o'er her ruins yearn.

4 Arise, O Lord! thine Israel bless;
   O speed the promised day,
That joyful, mournful day of grace,
   And take the veil away:
Then shall they know the piercèd One,
   And gaze on him they slew,
And mourn, as for an only son,
   For Him—Messiah true!

5 O Christ! thy Church thy glory sings,
    For many crowns are thine,
O King of saints! O King of kings!
    O King of David's line!
Great King of righteousness and peace,
    Melchisedec divine!
Now let thine Israel's exile cease,
    Bid Salem rise and shine!

103   B.M.

BLESS, O my soul! the living God;
    Call home thy thoughts that rove abroad:
Let all the powers within me join
In work and worship so divine.

2 Bless, O my soul! the God of grace;
His favours claim thy highest praise:
Why should the wonders He has wrought
Be lost in silence, and forgot?

3 'Tis He, my soul, that sent his Son
To die for crimes which thou hast done:
He owns the ransom, and forgives
The hourly follies of our lives.

4 Not half so far hath nature placed
The rising morning from the west,
As his forgiving grace removes
The daily guilt of those He loves.

5 Then, O my soul, with joyful tongue
Proclaim his mercies in thy song:
From age to age his truth shall reign,
Nor children's children hope in vain.

103.2   S.M.

O BLESS the Lord, my soul!
  Let all within me join,
And aid my tongue to bless his name,
  Whose favours are divine.

2   O bless the Lord, my soul!
  Nor let his mercies lie
Forgotten in unthankfulness,
  And without praises die.

3   'Tis He forgives thy sins,
  'Tis He relieves thy pain:
'Tis He that heals thy sicknesses,
  And makes thee young again.

4   He crowns thy life with love,
  When ransomed from the grave:
He that redeemed thy soul from hell
  Hath sovereign power to save.

5   His wondrous works and ways
  He made by Moses known,
But sent the world his truth and grace
  By his beloved Son.

103.3   A.M.

MY soul, inspired with sacred love,
  God's holy name for ever bless;
Of all his favours mindful prove,
And still thy grateful thanks express.

2 'Tis He that all thy sins forgives,
  And after sickness makes thee sound;
From danger He thy life retrieves,
  By him with grace and mercy crowned.

3 The Lord abounds with tender love,
And plenteous stores of heavenly grace;
His wakened wrath doth slowly move,
His willing mercy flies apace.

4 As far as 'tis from east to west,
So far has He our sins removed;
Who, with a father's tender breast,
Has such as fear him always loved.

5 The Lord, the universal King,
In heaven has fixed his lofty throne;
To Him, ye angels, praises sing:
My soul, rejoice in Him alone.

03.4   C.M.

HOW shall I sing that Majesty
Which angels do admire!
Let dust in dust and ashes lie;
Sing, sing, ye heavenly choir!

2 Thousands of thousands stand around
Thy throne, O God most high!
Ten thousand times ten thousand sing
Thy praise, but who am I?

3 Thy brightness unto them appears,
Whilst I thy footsteps trace:
A sound of God comes to mine ears,
But they behold thy face.

4 They sing, because Thou art their Sun:
Lord send thy beams on me!
Where once thy heavenly light hath shone,
There hallelujahs be.

5 O bless the Lord, ye sons of light!
    His glories still proclaim;
Let saints and angels all unite
    To praise his holy name.

103.5   K4.M.

O MY soul! thy powers combining,
    Bless the Lord's most holy name;
O my soul! till life's declining,
    Bless the Lord, his praise proclaim:
Thine infirmities he healed,
He thy peace and pardon sealed.

2 He with tender love hath crowned thee,
    Satisfied thy mouth with good,
From the snares of death unbound thee,
    Eagle-like, thy youth renewed:
Rich in loving-kindness He,
Slow to wrath, to favour free.

3 Far as east and west are parted,
    He our sins hath borne away:
Like a father, loving-hearted,
    Still He spares us day by day:
Well he knows our feeble frame,
He remembers whence we came.

4 He, from age to age enduring,
    He, the true, the faithful Lord,
Still his people's bliss ensuring,
    Keeps the covenant of his word:
Children's children He will bless,
Fill his Church with endless peace.

104   O.M.

MY soul, praise the Lord! speak good of his name,
With majesty clothed, with honour and might:
O Lord! let our praises thy greatness proclaim,
Whose throne is in heaven, whose robe is the light.

As curtains the sky Thou stretchest out wide;
Within the great deep thy chambers retire:
The clouds are thy chariots, on winds thou dost ride;
Thine angels are spirits, thy ministers fire.

How manifold, Lord, the works thou hast wrought!
In earth and in heaven thy glory we see:
Thy wisdom and riches surpass all our thought,
Such wisdom as only belongeth to Thee!

By angels in heaven of every degree,
And saints upon earth, all praise be addressed,
As it has been, now is, and always shall be,
To God in three persons, one God ever blest!

104.2   12.M.

GOD of glory, God of might!
Seated in approachless light;
Dwelling where the skies surround,
Like a tent, the blue profound;
Walking on the tempest loud,
Riding on the rolling cloud;
Seated on creation's throne,
Thou art King, and Thou alone!

2 At the voice of Thy command
Rose of old the breathing land,
And the murmuring waters fled
Down to their appointed bed;
There to rage, and there to roar,
But to pass their bounds no more,
Save to feed the fruitful rills,
Leaping down a thousand hills.

3 This wide world is in Thy hand;
Thine the sea, and thine the land;
When Thou breathest on the earth,
Plant and flower awake to birth:
Lord of providence and grace,
Filling, ruling time and space,
Praise from all that live be Thine,
Praise immortal and divine!

104.3

PRAISE, O my soul! the Lord: how great,
How wonderfully bright
In majesty, thy robe of state,
And raiment of the light;
Wide spreading for thy glorious tent
The curtains of the firmament.

2 His chamber-beams the waters vast,
The clouds his chariot form;
He rides upon the wingèd blast,
And curbs the raging storm:
At his command bright angels fly,
And the swift lightnings fire the sky.

3 All creatures wait on Thee, and live
Beneath thy wise control;

'Tis thine in season due to give,
 They gather up Thy dole:
Thy opening hands dispense their food,
 And satisfy their mouths with good.

4 O Lord, thy glorious majesty,
 For evermore shall last:
Glad in his works the Lord shall be;
 His look on earth is cast,
And lo! it quakes with touch of fire,
Its mountains smoke, its seas retire.

5 As long as life endures, my tongue
 Unto the Lord shall sing;
While being lasts, my thankful song
 Shall praise my God and King:
Praise, O my soul, his name, record
His power and glory, praise the Lord!

104.4   C.M.

O LORD, the everlasting God!
 Worship and praise are thine:
With Thee hath empire its abode,
 And majesty divine.

2 With light Thou hast thyself arrayed,
 And spread heaven's tent on high;
And on the mighty waters laid
 Thy chambers in the sky.

3 Thou sendest forth the pleasant springs,
 That run among the hills:
By them the wild bird sits and sings,
 The air wild music fills.

4 Thy showers of blessing from on high
    Refresh the thirsty land :
Thou dost the whole earth satisfy,
    So bounteous is Thy hand.

5 The moon her wonted season knows,
    And hastes her course to run ;
Thou hast ordained, since time arose,
    The circuits of the sun.

6 Soon as he riseth on the earth,
    Man wakes from his repose,
And to his labours goeth forth,
    Until the evening close.

7 How manifold, O Lord, are these,
    The works of thy right hand !
Thy wealth replenishes the seas,
    Thy riches fill the land.

104.5   C.M.

ALL creatures wait upon thy will,
    And cry to Thee for food :
Thou, Lord, dost their desire fulfil,
    And think on them for good.

2 They gather what Thou dost supply,
    Thou hidest thy face, they mourn ;
Thou tak'st away their breath, they die,
    And to their dust return.

3 Soon Thou dost send thy Spirit forth :
    Then, through her wide domain,
Earth travails to a second birth,
    And all things live again.

4 The glory of the Lord shall stand,
   While day shall follow night :
He in the works of his right hand
   Shall ever take delight.

5 I'll sing to thee, O Lord, as long
   As I have life and breath :
My joy shall be in Thee, my song
   Shall praise thee unto death.

105   C.M.

O THANK and bless Jehovah's name,
   Sound through the world his praise :
Aloud his mighty deeds proclaim,
   And humbly seek his face.

2 His covenant He hath kept in mind
   For numerous ages past :
The same for thousand ages more
   Unchanged shall ever last.

3 To guide his people, day by day
   The shadowing cloud was spread;
Their course, through all their desert way,
   His fiery pillar led.

4 They thirsted, and the smitten rock
   Poured forth a plenteous tide ;
And manna from the skies above
   Their hunger still supplied.

5 O wondrous stream ! O food divine !
   The types of heavenly grace :
So Christ his people still supplies
   Through all the wilderness.

6 O may the same almighty Hand
   Still guide our pilgrim way,
Until we reach the promised land
   Of everlasting day!

106   B.M.

TO God the great, the ever blest,
   New songs of honour be addressed:
His mercy firm for ever stands;
Give him the thanks his love demands.

2 Who knows the wonders of Thy ways?
Who shall fulfil thy boundless praise?
Blest are the souls that fear thee still,
And joy to do thy holy will.

3 Remember how thy mercy freed
   From Egypt's bonds thy chosen seed;
And with the same salvation bless
The meanest suppliant of thy grace.

4 O may I see thy tribes rejoice,
   And aid their triumph with my voice!
This is my glory, Lord, to be
Joined to thy saints, and near to Thee.

107   Day 22. Psalms 107—109.   B.M.

GIVE thanks to God! he reigns above;
   Kind are his thoughts, his name is Love:
His mercy ages past have known,
And ages long to come shall own.

2 Let the redeemed of the Lord
   The wonders of his grace record;
Like Israel, whom of old he chose,
And rescued from their mighty foes.

3 He feeds and clothes us all the day,
  He guides our footsteps, lest we stray:
  He guards us with a powerful hand,
  And brings us to the promised land.

4 O let the saints with joy record
  The truth and goodness of the Lord!
  How great his works! how kind his ways!
  Let every tongue pronounce his praise.

107.2   B.M.

FROM age to age exalt his name,
  God and his grace are still the same:
He fills the hungry soul with food,
And feeds the poor with every good.

2 When to the Lord we raise our cries,
  He makes the dawning light arise,
  And scatters all the dismal shade,
  That hung so heavy round our head.

3 He frees the prisoner from his chain,
  And rends the iron bars in twain;
  Takes off the load of guilt and grief,
  And gives the labouring soul relief.

4 O may the sons of men record
  The wondrous goodness of the Lord!
  How great his works! how kind his ways!
  Let every tongue pronounce his praise.

107.3   F.M.

WITH songs of grateful praise,
    Surround Jehovah's seat;
  His goodness and his ways
    Through all the earth repeat:

His mercy rose, ere time was known,
And from his throne eternal flows.

2 Ye ransomed of the Lord!
   To you the strains belong:
His boundless grace record
   In a triumphal song:
That mercy tell, whose power displayed
Your ransom paid from death and hell.

3 He bade his light arise,
   And sent his gospel forth;
From east to west it flies,
   And fills the south and north:
His sovereign grace its power imparts,
And willing hearts his truth embrace.

4 O then that men would raise
   Their tribute to his name!
Would speak Jehovah's praise,
   His goodness to proclaim;
His wonders show, and deeds of grace,
Which to our race abundant flow.

107.4   C.M.

HOW are thy servants blest, O Lord!
   How sure is their defence!
Eternal wisdom is their guide,
   Their shield Omnipotence.

2 In foreign lands and realms remote,
   Supported by Thy care,
Through burning climes they pass unhurt,
   And breathe in tainted air.

3 Confusion dwells on every face,
    And fear in every heart,
While waves on waves, and gulfs on gulfs
    O'ercome the pilot's art.

4 Yet then from all our fears, O God!
    Thy mercy sets us free;
Whilst in the confidence of prayer
    Our spirit turns to thee.

5 The storm is laid, the winds retire,
    Obedient to thy will:
The sea, that roared at Thy command,
    At thy command is still.

6 In midst of dangers, fears, and death,
    Thy goodness we'll adore;
And praise thee for thy mercies past,
    And humbly hope for more.

7 Our life, while thou preserv'st our life,
    Thy sacrifice shall be;
And death, when death shall be our doom,
    Shall join our souls to Thee.

107.5   H.M.

THANK and praise Jehovah's name,
    For his mercies, firm and sure,
From eternity the same,
Still to endless years endure.

2 Let the ransomed thus rejoice,
    Gathered out of every land,
Happy people of his choice,
Plucked from the destroyer's hand.

3 In the wilderness astray,
  Hither, thither, lost they roam;
  Hungry, fainting by the way,
  Far from refuge, shelter, home.

4 Then unto the Lord they cry;
  He inclines a gracious ear,
  Sends deliverance from on high,
  Rescues them from all their fear.

5 To a pleasant land He brings,
  Where the vine and olive grow;
  Where from flowery hills the springs
  Through luxuriant valleys flow.

6 O that men would praise the Lord
  For his goodness to their race!
  All his works with joy record,
  Sing the wonders of his grace.

107.6   K.M.

O THAT in the congregation,
  Men would bless and praise the Lord!
Young and old, with exultation,
  All his noble deeds record!

2 Rivers into wastes He turneth,
  Bids the watersprings be dry:
  Harvests fail, each pasture mourneth,
  When his rod is lifted high.

3 Wastes again He turns to rivers,
  Feeds with showers the running rills;
  Needy souls He thus delivers,
  And with food the hungry fills.

4 Fields are sown, and vineyards planted,
    Cities mid the waste appear;
Gracious rains and dews are granted,
    Goodness crowns the fruitful year.

5 Still with praise their God confessing,
    They are safe beneath his eye;
Multiplied, enriched with blessing,
    Crowned with mercies from on high.

6 Oft again with sorrows minished,
    When their chiefs forsake the Lord;
Soon his chastening strokes are finished,
    Souls redeemed, and peace restored.

7 Sinners, cease your fatal blindness,
    Saints of God, aloud rejoice!
Own and bless his loving-kindness,
    Tune to praise your grateful voice.

108   C.M.

O GOD, my heart is fully bent
    To magnify thy name:
My tongue, with cheerful songs of praise,
    Shall celebrate thy fame.

2 Awake, my lute! nor thou, my harp,
    Thy sweetest notes delay;
Whilst I, with cheerful hymns of joy,
    Prevent the dawning day.

3 To all the listening tribes, O Lord!
    Thy wonders I will tell;
And to those nations sing thy praise
    That round about us dwell.

4 Because Thy mercy's boundless height
    The highest heaven transcends;
And far beyond the aspiring clouds
    Thy faithful truth extends.

5 Be thou, O God, exalted high
    Above the starry frame;
And let the world, with one consent,
    Confess thy glorious name.

109   C.M.

WHAT grace, O Lord, and beauty shone
    Around thy steps below!
What patient love was seen in all
    Thy life and death of woe!

2 For ever on thy burdened heart
    A weight of sorrow hung;
Yet no ungentle, murmuring word
    Escaped thy silent tongue.

3 Thy foes might hate, despise, revile,
    Thy friends unfaithful prove;
Unwearied in forgiveness still,
    Thy heart was filled with love.

4 O give us hearts to love like Thee!
    Like thee, O Lord, to grieve
Far more for others' sins, than all
    The wrongs that we receive!

5 One with Thyself, may every eye
    In us, thy brethren, see
The gentleness and grace that spring
    From union, Lord, with Thee!

110 Day 23. Psalms 110–115.　D.M.

O CHRIST, thy work completed,
　　That brought thee from the sky,
In glory Thou art seated
　　At God's right hand on high;
For sinners there art pleading,
　　With patience all divine,
And power and love, exceeding
　　All human thought, are Thine.

2 Thy rod of strength and glory
　　From Zion forth shall go,
Thy gospel's blessed story,
　　Heaven's balm for sin and woe:
The powers of hell, conspiring,
　　Resist its course in vain;
Heaven's might and grace, untiring,
　　Its glorious cause maintain.

3 See! new-born souls, in millions,
　　Thy earthly courts adorn,
And shine in Thy pavilions,
　　Like dew-drops of the morn:
Thy mercies banish sadness,
　　Their sins and fears remove;
The sunshine of thy gladness
　　Steeps them with light and love.

4 The Lord hath sworn, and never
　　That mighty oath can fail,
Thou art High Priest for ever,
　　Enthroned within the veil:
Priest, Prophet, King victorious,
　　All praises in thee meet;
Thy foes shall fall inglorious,
　　Crushed low beneath thy feet.

5 God's firm decree is written,
   It shall not long delay;
Hell's might, before thee smitten,
   Shall fail and pass away:
From sin's dark slumber waking,
   All earth thy power shall own;
Shall see heaven's dawn is breaking,
   And bow before thy throne.

110.2   F.M.

ALL hail, victorious Lord!
   At God's right hand above,
Triumphant o'er thy foes,
   Triumphant in thy love:
To Thee our joyful songs we bring,
To Thee we bow, all-conquering King!

2   All hail, exalted Priest!
   To Thee our all we give;
Enthroned above the skies,
   Our homage to receive;
There deign on our behalf to plead,
Yea, there for ever intercede!

3   O haste, victorious Prince,
   That glorious, happy day,
When souls, like drops of dew,
   Shall own thy gentle sway:
O may it bless our longing eyes,
And bear our songs above the skies!

4   All hail, triumphant Lord!
   Eternal be thy reign:
By all the earth adored,
   Thy glorious cause maintain:
Thy name let earth and heaven adore;
Thine be the kingdom evermore.

110.3   12.M.

JESUS, Lord, to thee we sing;
    Thee, our Saviour, Priest, and King!
Who our guilt and woes sustained,
And the cup of vengeance drained:
Now Thou sitt'st enthroned on high,
Crowned with power and majesty;
All thy foes shall prostrate fall,
Every nation hear thy call.

2 As at morning's youthful hour
Dew-drops gem each leaf and flower,
So, O Lord, our sons unborn
Shall thy crowded courts adorn;
Gladly own thee for their King,
Gladly free-will offerings bring;
Till thy spreading empire prove
Boundless as thy wondrous love.

110.4   F.M.

JESUS ascend thy throne,
    And all thy foes dismay;
Where'er thy power is shown,
    Thy people shall obey:
Thy sovereign hand its grace imparts,
And willing hearts adoring stand.

2   Thy grace, disclosed anew,
    A numerous seed shall yield,
As drops of morning dew,
    Bright glistening o'er the field:
Eternal Lord, O haste the day!
Thy power display, and own thy word.

3   At thy right hand, my God!
       I see the Saviour rise:
    He spreads his power abroad,
       Who dares oppose him, dies:
    The Gentile lands shall own his sway,
    And kings obey his high commands.

4   The storms of sorrow rose,
       Through all his paths they stood;
    Around the torrent flows,
       He drank the bitter flood;
    His love alone the cross sustains,
    And thence he gains the eternal throne.

110.5   G.M.

THE Lord to his Anointed said,
   At my right hand I throne thee;
Till, at thy feet in triumph laid,
   Thy foes their ruler own thee:
From Zion's hill the Lord shall send
Thy sceptre, till before thee bend
   Rebellious hearts, adoring.

2 The saints, to greet thy day of might,
      In holy throngs assemble,
   As countless dew-drops in the light
      On leaf and floweret tremble:
   Jehovah's oath and firm decree
   Declares thy endless majesty,
      O King and Priest of Salem!

3 The Lord, at God's right hand, shall bring
      On rulers desolation;
   His arm shall smite each heathen king,
      And judge each rebel nation:

He, on his swift victorious way,
Shall drink the brook, then rise to sway
Earth's conquered realms for ever.

110.6   K4.M.

GREAT High Priest, in glory seated
  On the Father's throne on high,
All thy work of love completed,
  Thou art crowned with majesty:
Holy garments now are Thine,
Grace and beauty most divine.

2 Thou the golden ephod wearest;
  There, engraven deep, remain
Names of souls for whom thou carest,
  Ransomed by thy bitter pain:
Strong to suffer once wast Thou,
Strong to plead in glory now.

3 On Thy breast, in light resplendent,
  See the mystic stones appear:
Pledges these of love transcendent,
  All thy saints to Thee are dear:
Thou dost bear them on thy heart,
Never can thy love depart.

4 Once for sins despised, abhorred,
  Thou hast gained thy full reward;
Now Thou wearest on thy forehead
  Holiness unto the Lord:
Thou art crowned with thorns no more,
Angel hosts thy name adore.

5 Blessed be thy name for ever,
  Great High Priest, eternal King!

Never shall thy people, never
  Cease thy wondrous work to sing :
Heaven and earth, through endless days,
  Shall resound thy matchless praise.

111   C.M.

SONGS of immortal praise belong
  To Thee, almighty God!
Awake, my heart! awake, my tongue,
  To spread his name abroad.

2 How great the works his hand hath wrought!
  How glorious in our sight!
And men in every age have sought
  His wonders with delight.

3 When He from bonds his chosen freed,
  He fixed his covenant sure :
The laws, that from his lips proceed,
  To endless years endure.

4 Nature, and time, and earth, and skies
  Thy heavenly skill proclaim :
What shall we do, to make us wise,
  But learn to read thy name?

5 To fear thy power, to trust thy grace,
  Is our divinest skill :
The wisest he of all our race,
  Who best obeys Thy will.

111.2   C.M.

ETERNAL Lord! thy deeds of might
  Demand our noblest lays :
Let upright souls with joy unite
  To speak thy worthy praise.

2 Great are thy works, and men of grace
    Their wonders still explore :
Thy wisdom, truth, and righteousness
    Endure for evermore.

3 Thy Son, the great Redeemer, came
    To seal thy covenant sure :
Holy and reverend is thy name,
    Thy ways are just and pure.

4 They that would grow divinely wise,
    Must with thy fear begin ;
And all, who thy commandments prize,
    Eternal life shall win.

112   C.M.

BLEST is the man who fears the Lord,
    And loves His holy ways ;
Who gladly hears his holy word,
    And still that word obeys.

2 True wealth, more precious far than gold,
    Shall in his house abound :
His seed shall prosper, love untold
    Shall all his steps surround.

3 In darkest hours a heavenly light
    Shall dawn, his path to guide :
No terrors shall his soul affright,
    With God's own peace supplied.

4 His liberal hands disperse around
    The plenty God hath given ;
And blessings from the poor abound,
    To cheer his path to heaven.

5 O fill us, Lord! with heavenly grace,
   Our homes with peace divine;
And bring us to behold thy face,
   Where all thy glories shine.

112.2   C.M.

HOW blest thy creature is, O Lord!
   When with a single eye
He views the lustre of thy word,
   The Day-spring from on high.

2 Through all the storms, that veil the skies,
   And frown on earthly things,
The Sun of Righteousness he eyes,
   With healing in His wings.

3 Beneath His light the human heart,
   A barren soil no more,
Yields fragrant sweets in every part,
   Where poison lurked before.

4 The soul, a dreary province once
   Of Satan's dark domain,
Feels a new empire formed within,
   And owns a heavenly reign.

5 The glorious orb, with golden beams,
   Doth light and warmth impart,
But, Saviour! 'tis thy light alone
   Can shine upon the heart.

6 Shine ever, Lord, with quickening ray,
   Light, warmth, and love bestow;
Till, in full light of perfect day,
   I all thy glory know!

13.   E3.M.

YE saints and servants of the Lord,
   The triumphs of his name record,
     His sacred name for ever bless:
Where'er the circling sun displays
His rising beams or setting rays,
     Due praise to his great name address.

2 God through the world extends His sway,
   The regions of eternal day
     But shadows of his glory are:
With Him, whose majesty excels,
Who made the heaven in which He dwells,
     Let no created power compare.

3 Though 'tis beneath his state, to view
   In highest heaven what angels do,
     He stoops to gaze on earthly things:
Our mean affairs He deigns to know,
And lifts the sons of want and woe,
     To dwell in palaces of kings.

4 He bids, with life-imparting voice,
   The childless homes of earth rejoice
     With infant smiles and mother's love:
There pious hearts, with glad surprise,
Behold a numerous seed arise,
     And train them for His courts above.

13.2   B.M.

PRAISE ye the Lord! in joyful lays,
   His holy name, ye servants, praise!
His goodness, truth, and love adore
From age to age, and evermore.

2 Where'er the snow-clad mountains rise,
Or valleys sleep 'neath summer skies,
From north to south, from east to west,
Be God's high name for ever blest!

3 His power how vast! his throne how high!
He stoops to view the lofty sky;
Yet down to earth He bends his gaze,
From lowest depths the poor to raise.

4 He lifts the needy from the dust,
Sustains the meek, and guides the just;
And lonely hearts, in their distress,
With new-born love delights to bless.

5 The poor He lifts to thrones on high,
With angel princes of the sky:
His name let all his saints adore,
Praise, laud, and bless him evermore.

113.3   I.M.

HALLELUJAH! raise, O raise
To our God the voice of praise!
All his servants, join to sing
God our Saviour and our King!

2 Blessed be for evermore
That dread name, which we adore:
Round the world His praise be sung,
Through all lands, in every tongue.

3 He can raise the poor to stand
With the princes of the land;
Wealth upon the needy shower,
Set the meanest high in power.

4 He the broken spirit cheers,
　Turns to joy the mourner's tears:
　Great the wonders of his ways,
　Praise His name, for ever praise!

113. 4

O PRAISE the Lord, the God of love!
　Beyond the starry worlds above,
　　His glory far extendeth:
Whom with the Lord can we compare?
He reigns in heaven, his tender care
　　To sons of earth descendeth.

2 He hears the needy when they cry,
　And lifts the poor to thrones on high,
　　Redeemed from fear and sadness;
　To all who want his mercies come,
　And oft he fills the childless home
　　With songs of infant gladness.

3 Ye mourning hearts, his aid implore!
　Ye saints of God, his grace adore:
　　High praise to him be given!
　Let earth, with all the angelic host,
　Praise Father, Son, and Holy Ghost,
　　The God of earth and heaven!

114.　　　　　　　　　A.M.

WHEN Israel forth from Egypt came,
　　Its idol gods in dust o'erthrown,
Before them moved, in cloud and flame,
An awful Guide, a Power unknown.

2 Then gazed the sea, and backward fled;
Affrighted, Jordan slunk away;
Hills leaped, like deer, with sudden dread,
Huge mountains trembled in dismay.

3 What ailed thee, O thou mighty sea?
Ye mountains, why convulsed with fear?
Why, Jordan, back in terror flee?
Why leaped the hills like frighted deer?

4 Tremble, O earth, before the Lord,
The King of kings, who reigns on high;
Rocks gush with fountains at His word,
And nature faints, for God is nigh.

115 A.M.

NOT to ourselves, who are but dust,
   Not to ourselves is glory due,
Eternal God, thou only just!
Thou only gracious, wise, and true!

2 In vain are senseless idols made;
Deaf are their ears, their eyes are blind:
In vain are costly offerings paid,
The vows are scattered to the wind.

3 The God we serve maintains His throne
Above the clouds, beyond the skies:
Through all the earth his will is done,
He knows our sorrows, hears our cries.

4 O Israel, make the Lord thy trust,
Thy help, thy refuge, and thy shield!
His hand shall raise thee from the dust,
His arm a sure protection yield.

5 The dead no more can speak Thy praise
They dwell in silence, and the grave;
But we shall live to sing thy grace,
And tell the world thy power to save.

115.2   C.M.

NOT unto us, but Thee alone,
  Blest Lamb! be glory given;
Here shall thy praises be begun,
  And perfected in heaven.

2 The hosts of spirits now with Thee
  Eternal anthems sing:
To join their worship, Saviour, we
  Our hallelujahs bring.

3 Had we our tongues, like them, inspired,
  Like theirs, our songs should rise;
Like them, we never should be tired,
  But love the sacrifice.

4 Till we the veil of flesh lay down,
  Accept our weaker lays,
And when we stand before thy throne,
  We'll give thee nobler praise.

115.3   A.M.

NOT unto us, almighty Lord!
  But to thyself the glory be:
Created by thine awful word,
We only live to honour Thee.

2 Where is their God? the heathen cry,
And bow to senseless wood and stone:
Our God, our Maker, fills the sky,
And calls ten thousand worlds his own.

3 Vain gods! vain men! the Lord alone
Is Israel's worship, Israel's friend:
O fear his power, his goodness own,
And love him, trust him to the end.

4 Who lean on Him, from strength to strength,
From light to light shall onward move;
Till through the grave they pass at length,
To sing on high his saving love.

116 C.M.

I LOVE the Lord, for he hath heard
   My supplicating voice:
I love the Lord, and in his love
   Will evermore rejoice.

2 Now, O my soul! from all thy woes
   Return to God, thy rest,
Who graciously hath dealt with thee,
   And bountifully blessed.

3 What shall I render to the Lord,
   Whose love is still the same?
Salvation's sacred cup I'll take,
   And call upon his name.

4 For all thy benefits, O Lord,
   To thee I pay my vows;
Now, in the presence of thy saints,
   Here, in thy sacred house.

5 Henceforth my few remaining years,
   Which Thou to me shalt lend,
In thy blest service and thy praise
   Will I for ever spend.

116.2   B.M.

I LOVE the Lord, his gracious ear
Inclined and listened to my prayer;
He heard my supplicating voice,
And bade my fainting soul rejoice.

2 'Twas in the depth of my distress
I called upon the God of grace,
Whose power can death and hell control,
" Lord, I beseech thee, save my soul! "

3 For ever gracious is the Lord,
For ever faithful is his word:
By sweet experience now I prove
His mercy, his unchanging love.

4 For this, when darkest sorrows rise,
To Him will I direct my cries;
And still, through all my future days,
Adore his name, and sing his praise.

116.3   B.M.

REDEEMED from guilt, redeemed from fears,
My soul enlarged, and dried my tears,
What can I do, O Love divine!
What, to repay such gifts as Thine?

2 What can I do, so poor, so weak,
But from thy hands new blessings seek?
A heart to feel thy presence more;
A soul to know Thee, and adore!

3 O teach me at Thy feet to fall,
And yield thee up myself, my all!
Before thy saints my debt to own,
And live and die to Thee alone.

4 Thy Spirit largely, Lord, impart,
   Expand, and raise, and fill my heart;
   So may I hope my life shall be
   Some poor return, O Lord, to thee!

116.4   C.M.

WHAT shall I render to the Lord
   For all his kindness shown?
My feet shall visit thine abode,
   My songs address thy throne.

2 Among the saints, that fill thy house,
   My offerings shall be paid:
There shall my zeal perform the vows
   My soul in anguish made.

3 How much is mercy thy delight,
   Thou ever-blessed God!
How dear thy servants in thy sight!
   How precious is their blood!

4 How happy all thy servants are!
   How great thy grace to me!
My life, which thou hast made thy care,
   Lord, I devote to Thee.

5 Now I am Thine, for ever Thine,
   Nor shall my purpose move:
Thy hands have loosed my bonds of pain,
   And bound me with thy love.

116.5   A.M.

RETURN, my soul, unto thy rest,
   From vain pursuits and maddening cares;
From lonely woes, that wring thy breast,
The world's allurements, Satan's snares.

2 Return unto thy rest, my soul,
From all the wanderings of thy thought;
From sickness unto death, made whole,
Safe through a thousand perils brought.

3 Then to thy rest, my soul, return,
From passions, every hour at strife;
Sin's work and ways and wages spurn,
Lay hold upon eternal life.

4 God is thy rest; with heart inclined
To keep his word, that word believe:
Christ is thy rest; with lowly mind
His light and easy yoke receive.

116.6   S.M.

O CEASE, my wandering soul!
  On restless wings to roam:
All the wide world, to either pole,
  Has not for thee a home:

2 Like Noah's weary dove,
  That soared the world around,
And still no resting-place above
  The cheerless waters found.

3 Behold the ark of God!
  Behold the open door!
O haste to gain that calm abode,
  And rove, my soul, no more!

4 There safe thou shalt abide,
  And sweet shall be thy rest,
Thy deepest longing satisfied,
  In God for ever blest.

117   S.M.

THY name, Almighty Lord!
  Shall sound through distant lands:
Great is thy grace, and sure thy word,
  Thy truth for ever stands.

2   Far be thine honour spread,
    And long thy praise endure;
Till morning light and evening shade
    Shall be exchanged no more.

117.2   H.M.

ALL ye nations, praise the Lord;
  All ye lands, your voices raise:
Heaven and earth, with loud accord,
Praise the Lord, for ever praise.

2 Firm his truth and mercy stand;
Vast his love, a boundless sea;
Like the years of his right hand,
Like his own eternity.

3 Praise him, ye who know his love;
Praise him from the depths beneath;
Praise him in the heights above;
Praise your Maker, all that breathe.

118   C.M.

O PRAISE the Lord! for He is good,
  His mercies ne'er decay:
That his kind favours ever last,
  Let thankful Israel say.

2 Joy fills the dwellings of the just,
　　Whom God hath saved from harm;
　And wondrous things are brought to pass
　　By His almighty arm.

3 The stone the builders once refused
　　Is now the corner-stone:
　This is the wondrous work of God,
　　The work of God alone.

4 This day is God's, let all the lands
　　Exalt their cheerful voice:
　Lord, we beseech thee, save us now,
　　And make us still rejoice.

5 God is the Lord, who shows us light:
　　O draw us near to Thee!
　That hearts and souls, by love constrained,
　　Thy sacrifice may be.

6 Give thanks to God, the mighty Lord,
　　Whose mercies ne'er remove;
　And let the tribute of our praise
　　Be endless as his love.

118.2 　　　　　　　　　　　　C.M.

BEHOLD the sure foundation-stone,
　　Which God in Zion lays,
To build our heavenly hopes upon,
　　And his eternal praise.

2 Chosen of God, to sinners dear,
　　And saints adore the name;
　They trust their whole salvation here,
　　Nor shall they suffer shame.

3 The foolish builders, scribe and priest,
    Reject it with disdain;
Yet on this Rock the Church shall rest,
    And envy rage in vain.

4 What though the gates of hell withstood,
    Yet must this building rise:
'Tis thine own work, almighty God!
    And wondrous in our eyes.

118.3   C.M.

LORD, thou hast heard thy servant's cry,
    And snatched him from the grave:
Now shall he live, for none can die
    If God resolve to save.

2 Thy praise, more constant than before,
    Shall fill his daily breath:
Thy hand, that hath chastised him sore,
    Shall keep him still from death.

3 Open the gates, and we will go,
    Thy mercy to declare
In Zion's courts, thy house below,
    To which the just repair.

4 Among th' assemblies of thy saints
    Our thankful voice we raise;
There we have poured our sad complaints,
    And there we speak Thy praise.

118.4   B.M.

ALL power and grace to God belong,
    He is my strength, and He my song:
He comes, my Saviour, from his throne;
He comes to bring salvation down.

2 I shall not die, my Saviour's care
 Exhausted nature will repair:
 My life prolonged, my health restored,
 His wondrous mercies be adored.

3 His hand, with chastisement severe,
 Weakened my strength, awoke my fear:
 Yet did his love revive my breath,
 And raised me from the shades of death.

4 O may I then, with grateful mind,
 Within his gates admittance find;
 And enter where his altars rise,
 With prayer and praise for sacrifice!

5 O Lord, within thy temple gate,
 Where all thy saints in worship wait,
 I'll praise thee, who hast heard my prayer,
 And own thee my salvation there.

118.5

DAY of light, all days excelling,
 Day our Lord in love hath made,
Let our songs, His mercy telling,
 Speak its joys that never fade:
Light from darkness newly springing,
 Out of grief is joy new born;
Pay your vows, your offerings bringing,
 Bind them to the altar's horn.

2 Lord, this day we bow before thee;
 Evermore thy love to own,
To extol thee and adore thee,
 Be our service at thy throne:

Praise the Lord with glad thanksgiving,
    For his mercies aye endure;
Praise, O praise the Everliving,
    Wise and faithful, just and pure.

119   Days 25 and 26.   Psalm 119.

O FAIREST bowers of Eden!
    The work of God alone,
In loveliness exceeding
    What later years have known;
How soon your beauty vanished,
    Your glory passed away,
When our first parents, banished,
    To death became a prey!

2 But still, for pilgrims weary,
    A garden bright and fair,
O Lord, midst deserts dreary,
    Thy mercy doth prepare:
Thy word hath richer treasure
    Than Pison's golden sand;
A field of sacred pleasure,
    By heavenly wisdom planned.

3 There trees of life are growing,
    With fruits of blessing crowned,
And streams of mercy flowing
    Through all the holy ground:
There precepts pure and holy,
    With promises divine,
To cheer and bless the lowly
    In fragrance sweet combine.

4 O Father, Son, and Spirit!
  Amidst a world of woe,
May we by grace inherit
  This Paradise below;
Till, trained to nobler vision,
  And perfected in love,
We reach, in blest fruition,
  The Paradise above.

119.2   Verses 11—19.   C.M.

BEFORE thy mercy-seat, O Lord!
  Behold, thy servants stand,
To ask the knowledge of Thy word,
  The guidance of Thy hand.

2 Let thy eternal truths, we pray,
    Dwell richly in each heart;
  That from the safe and narrow way
    We never may depart.

3 Lord, from thy word remove the seal,
    Unfold its hidden store:
  O teach us, while we read, to feel
    Thy presence more and more!

4 Help us to see a Saviour's face
    Revealed in every page;
  And let the thought of joys above
    Our inmost souls engage.

5 Thus, while thy word our footsteps guides
    O may we safely go
  To those fair realms, where love provides
    A final rest from woe.

119.3   Verses 9, 130.   C.M.

How shall the young secure their hearts,
  And guard their lives from sin?
Thy word the choicest rules imparts,
  To keep the conscience clean.

2 When once it enters to the mind,
   It spreads such light abroad,
 The meanest souls instruction find,
   And raise their thoughts to God.

3 'Tis like the sun, a heavenly light,
   That guides us all the day;
 And through the dangers of the night
   A lamp to lead our way.

4 Thy word is everlasting truth,
   How pure is every page!
 That holy book shall guide our youth,
   And well support our age.

119.4   Verses 25—32.   C.M.

My soul lies cleaving to the dust:
  Lord, give me life divine!
From vain desires and every lust
  Turn off these eyes of mine.

2 I need the influence of Thy grace,
   To speed me in thy way;
 Lest I should loiter in my race,
   Or turn my feet astray.

3 When sore afflictions press me down,
   I need thy quickening powers:
 Thy word, that I have rested on,
   Shall help my heaviest hours.

4 Are not thy mercies sovereign still,
    And thou a faithful God?
Wilt thou not grant me warmer zeal,
    To run the heavenly road?

5 Doth not my heart thy precepts love,
    And long to see thy face?
And yet how slow my spirits move,
    Without enlivening grace!

6 Then shall I love thy gospel more,
    And ne'er forget thy word,
When I have felt its quickening power
    To draw me near the Lord.

119.5   Verses 33—40, 176.   C.M.

O THAT the Lord would guide my ways
    To keep his statutes still!
O that my God would grant me grace
    To know and do his will!

2 O send thy Spirit down, to write
    Thy law upon my heart!
Nor let my tongue indulge deceit,
    Nor act the liar's part.

3 From vanity turn off mine eyes;
    Let no corrupt design,
Nor covetous desires arise
    Within this soul of mine.

4 Order my footsteps by thy word,
    And make my heart sincere:
Let sin have no dominion, Lord!
    But keep my conscience clear.

5 My soul hath gone too far astray,
   My feet too often slip :
Yet, since I've not forgot thy way,
   Restore thy wandering sheep.

6 Make me to walk in thy commands,
   'Tis a delightful road ;
Nor let my head, nor heart, nor hands
   Offend against my God.

119.6   Verses 64, 73.   C.M.

THY mercies fill the earth, O Lord!
   How good thy works appear !
Open mine eyes to read thy word,
   And see thy wonders there.

2 My heart was fashioned by thy hand,
   My service is thy due :
O make thy servant understand
   The duties he must do.

3 When I confessed my wandering ways,
   Thou heardst my soul complain :
Grant me the teaching of thy grace,
   Or I shall stray again.

4 When I have learned my Father's will,
   I'll teach the world thy ways :
My thankful lips, inspired with zeal,
   Shall loud pronounce thy praise.

119.7   Verses 65—72.   A.M.

FATHER, I bless thy gentle hand :
   How kind was thy chastising rod,
That forced my conscience to a stand,
And brought my wandering soul to God !

2 Foolish and vain, I went astray,
　Ere I had felt thy scourges, Lord!
　I left my Guide, and lost my way;
　But now I love and keep thy word.

3 'Tis good for me to wear the yoke,
　For pride is apt to rise and swell:
　'Tis good to bear my Father's stroke,
　That I may learn his statutes well.

4 Thy hands have made my mortal frame,
　Thy spirit formed my soul within:
　Teach me to know thy wondrous name,
　And guard me safe from death and sin.

5 Then all that love and fear the Lord
　In my salvation shall rejoice;
　For I have hopèd in Thy word,
　And made thy grace my only choice.

119.8　　Verse 94.　　B.M.

O GOD, thy mercy, vast and free,
　Has turned my ransomed soul to Thee!
Still round me let that mercy shine,
And save me, Lord, for I am Thine!

2 Thy truth display, thy power reveal;
　O let me now thy presence feel:
　Grant me the joys of love divine,
　And save me, Lord, for I am Thine!

3 From self, from Satan, and from sin,
　From foes without, and fears within,
　Though all against my soul combine,
　O save me, Lord, for I am Thine!

4 And when in glory I appear,
   Redeemed from sin and every fear,
   Then shall this work of joy be mine,
   To praise the love which made me Thine.

119.9   Verses 89—96.   C.M.

FOR ever, Lord, thy faithful word
   Endures beyond the sky;
Unchanging as the stars, that keep
   Their silent course on high.

2 From age to age thy truth remains,
   A refuge firm and sure:
Thy mighty hand the earth sustains,
   So steadfast to endure.

3 The ocean surge, the silent heaven,
   All air, and earth, and sea,
Obey the laws thy hand hath given,
   They serve and wait on Thee.

4 Lord, I am Thine: thy quickening grace,
   Thy saving mercy send;
I love thy word, I seek thy face,
   And on thy help depend.

5 Alas! in men's proud works below
   Is no perfection found:
From Thee, my God, all blessings flow,
   Thy goodness hath no bound.

119.10   Verses 97—104.   C.M.

O HOW I love Thy holy law!
   'Tis daily my delight;
And thence my meditations draw
   Divine advice by night.

2 How doth thy word my heart engage!
 How well employ my tongue!
And through my earthly pilgrimage
 Yields me a heavenly song.

3 No treasures so enrich the mind;
 Nor shall thy word be sold
For loads of silver, well refined,
 Or heaps of choicest gold.

4 When nature sinks with grief and pain,
 Thy promises of grace,
Like pillars, shall my hope sustain,
 And there I'll write thy praise.

119.11 Verse 105. C.M.

HOW precious is the book divine,
 By inspiration given!
Bright as a lamp its doctrines shine,
 To guide our souls to heaven.

2 Thy word, Redeemer, cheers our hearts
 In this dark vale of tears;
Life, light, and joy it still imparts,
 And quells our rising fears.

3 This lamp, through all the tedious night,
 Shall guide our pilgrim way;
Till we behold the clearer light
 Of everlasting day.

119.12 Verses 105, 130. C.M.

THE Spirit breathes upon the word,
 And brings the truth to sight;
Precepts and promises afford
 A sanctifying light.

2 A glory gilds the sacred page,
   Majestic as the sun :
It gives a light to every age,
   It gives, but borrows none.

3 The hand that gave it still supplies
   The gracious light and heat :
Its truths upon the nations rise ;
   They rise, but never set.

4 Eternal thanks, O Lord, be Thine
   For such a bright display,
As makes a world of darkness shine
   With beams of heavenly day.

5 My soul rejoices to pursue
   The steps of Him I love,
Till glory breaks upon my view
   In brighter worlds above.

119.13   Verses 111, 112.   C.M.

LORD, I have made thy word my choice,
   My lasting heritage :
There shall my noblest powers rejoice,
   My warmest thoughts engage.

2 I'll read the histories of thy love,
   And keep thy laws in sight ;
While through thy promises I rove
   With ever fresh delight.

3 'Tis a broad land of wealth unknown,
   Where springs of life arise,
Seeds of immortal bliss are sown,
   And hidden glory lies.

4 The best relief that mourners have,
   It makes our sorrows blest;
Our fairest hope beyond the grave,
   And our eternal rest.

119.14   Verses 10, 145, 120.   C.M.

WITH my whole heart I seek thy face;
   O let me never stray
From thy commands, O God of grace!
   Nor tread the sinner's way.

2 Thy word I treasure in my heart,
   To keep my conscience clean;
And guard me well in every part,
   From all the snares of sin.

3 My soul with sacred reverence hears
   The threatenings of thy word:
My flesh with holy trembling fears
   The judgments of the Lord.

4 I hope, I long, by day and night,
   For thy salvation still;
O make it, Lord, my chief delight
   To do thy holy will!

119.15   Verses 147—160.   C.M.

TO Thee before the dawning light,
   My gracious God, I pray;
I meditate thy name by night,
   And keep thy law by day.

2 When midnight darkness veils the skies,
   I call thy works to mind:
My thoughts in warm devotion rise,
   And sweet acceptance find.

3 My waking eyes prevent the day,
   To meditate thy word:
My soul with longing melts away,
   To hear thy gospel, Lord!

4 My soul for thy salvation faints;
   When will my troubles end?
Consider, Lord, my sad complaints,
   And full deliverance send.

5 Thy precepts, Lord, how just and pure,
   To wandering sinners given!
Thy words of grace for aye endure,
   And guide our souls to heaven.

119.16   Verse 176.   K5.M.

WILT thou not, O Shepherd true!
   Spare thy sheep, in mercy spare me?
Wilt thou not, as shepherds do,
   In thy bosom gently bear me?
Bear me, where all troubles cease,
Home to folds of joy and peace?

2 See how I have gone astray,
   How earth's wilds do oft mislead me!
Bring me back into the way,
   In thine own green pastures feed me:
Gather me within the fold,
Where thy lambs thy light behold.

3 With thy flock I long to be;
   With the flock, to whom is given
Safe to feed, from danger free,
   In the happy plains of heaven:
Free from fear of sinful stain,
They can never stray again.

4 Lord, I here am sore beset,
   Fears at every step confound me;
Lo, my foes have spread their net,
   And with craft and might surround me:
Not one moment can I be
Safe, O Lord, away from Thee!

5 Jesus, Lord, my Shepherd true,
   From each snare thy sheep deliver;
Help, as tender shepherds do,
   Bring me safe through death's dark river:
Bear me homeward in thy breast,
To thy fold of endless rest.

120   Day 27.   Psalms 120—131.   C.M.

IN my distress to God I cried,
   And bowed before his feet:
O save my soul from lips of pride,
   And tongues that frame deceit!

2 Thou tongue of falsehood, what shall be
   Thy just and sure reward?
Hot burning coals are stored for thee,
   Thy portion from the Lord.

3 Too long with Mesech's tribes, alas!
    A dweller I have been:
In Kedar's tents my days I pass,
    Where only strife is seen.

4 My soul too long hath dwelt with those
    Who hate the name of peace:
I seek it still, and still my foes
    Their violence increase.

5 O bring me through this world of strife,
    To reach the happier shore,
Where death is lost in endless life,
    And storms shall vex no more.

120.2   C.M.

ON God I cried in trouble's hour,
    And never called in vain:
Again afflictions round me lower,
    Lord, hear and help again!

2 A stranger's lot, a pilgrim's fare
    Is all I meet below:
In every sweet I find a snare,
    In every smile a foe.

3 Ah! woe is me, that I must roam
    So long the land of tears!
When shall my spirit reach her home,
    Above all foes and fears?

4 There is a peace that none can break,
    A joy that ne'er shall flee:
When shall I lay me down, and wake
    To these, O Lord, and Thee?

121   B.M.

UP to the hills I lift mine eyes,
   Th' eternal hills beyond the skies:
Thence all her help my soul derives,
There my almighty Refuge lives.

2 He guides our feet, He guards our way;
His morning smiles bless all the day;
He spreads the evening veil, and keeps
The silent hours, while Israel sleeps.

3 Israel, a name divinely blest,
May rise secure, securely rest:
Thy holy Guardian's watchful eyes
Admit no slumber or surprise.

4 No sun shall smite thy head by day;
No moon by night, with sickly ray,
Shall blast thy couch: His heavenly care
Defends thy life from every snare.

5 On thee foul spirits have no power,
And in thy last, departing hour,
Angels, that track the airy road,
Shall bear thy spirit home to God.

121.2   C.M.

TO heaven I lift my waiting eyes;
   There all my hopes are laid:
The Lord, who built the earth and skies,
   Is my perpetual aid.

2 Their feet shall never slide and fall,
   Whom He vouchsafes to keep:
His ears attend the softest call,
   His eyes can never sleep.

3 He will sustain our weakest powers
    With his almighty arm;
And watch our most unguarded hours,
    To save from each alarm.

4 He guards thy soul, He keeps thy breath,
    When thickest dangers come;
Go and return, secure from death,
    Till God command thee home.

121.3   D.M.

TO th' everlasting mountains
    I lift my weary eyes;
O whence for me in trouble
    Shall hope and help arise?
From mountain nor from valley
    Shall help to thee be given:
Thy help is in Jehovah,
    Who made the earth and heaven.

2 Thy foot shall never stumble,
    For He thy way shall keep:
His loving eye beholds thee,
    It hath no need of sleep:
Thy keeper ne'er shall slumber,
    So be not thou afraid:
His presence is around thee
    For solace or for shade.

3 The fierce sun shall not smite thee
    At burning noon of day;
The moon shall not affright thee
    With pale, deceiving ray.

Go and return in safety,
  No evil shalt thou fear:
Jehovah is thy Keeper,
  Thy Help for ever near.

122   C.M.

HOW did my heart rejoice to hear
  My friends devoutly say,
In Zion let us all appear,
  And keep the solemn day!

2 I love her gates, I love her road:
  The church, adorned with grace,
Stands like a palace, built for God,
  To show his milder face.

3 Peace be within the sacred place,
  And joy a constant guest:
With holy gifts and heavenly grace
  Be her attendants blessed.

4 My soul shall pray for Zion still,
  While life or breath remains:
There my best friends, my kindred dwell,
  There God my Saviour reigns.

122.2   S.M.

GLAD was my heart to hear
  My old companions say,
Come, in the house of God appear,
  For 'tis a festal day.

2   Our willing feet shall stand
  Within the temple door;
While young and old, a numerous band,
  Shall throng the sacred floor.

3   Pray for Jerusalem,
      The city of our God :
The Lord from heaven is kind to them
      Who love that dear abode.

4   Within thy walls may peace
      And constant love be found :
Zion ! in all thy palaces
      May heavenly grace abound !

5   For friends and brethren dear
      Our prayer shall never cease :
Oft as they meet for worship here,
      God send his people peace.

122.3   E.M.

THE festal morn, my God, is come,
That calls me to thy honoured home,
    Thy presence to adore :
My feet the summons shall attend,
With willing steps Thy courts ascend,
    And tread the hallowed floor.

2 E'en now, to our transported eyes,
  Fair Zion's towers in prospect rise,
    Within her gates we stand ;
  And, lost in wonder and delight,
  Behold her happy sons unite
    In friendship's fairest band.

3 Be peace by each implored on thee,
  O Salem, while with bended knee
    To Jacob's God we pray !
  How blest, who calls himself thy friend !
  Success his labour shall attend,
    And safety guard his way.

4 To thee, from earth's remotest coast,
Let all the saints, a countless host,
   Their willing tribute bring:
There, crowned with everlasting joy,
In hymns of praise their tongues employ,
   And hail th' immortal King.

123   13.M.

LORD, before thy throne we bend,
Now to Thee our prayers ascend;
Servants, to our Master true,
Lord, we yield thee honour due;
Children, to our God we fly;
Abba, Father, hear our cry!

2 Low before thee, Lord, we bow;
We are weak, but mighty Thou:
Sore distressed, but suppliant still,
Here we wait thy holy will;
Bound to earth, and rooted here,
Till our Saviour God appear.

3 From the heavens, thy dwelling-place,
Hear and grant thy pardoning grace;
In temptation's darkest hour,
Keep us from the tempter's power,
God our Father, still be nigh,
Save and bless us when we cry.

124   S.M.

O SAVE us, heavenly Lord!
   From the dark fowler's snare;
And may the promise of thy word
   Still shield us from despair.

2   When o'er thine Israel roll
      Proud waters of the deep,
    Thy voice their surges will control,
      And bid their fury sleep.

3   O thou eternal Rock!
      We bless thee day by day;
    Thou wilt not leave thy feeble flock
      To powers of hell a prey.

4   Our help is in the King,
      Whom heaven and earth adore;
    And safe beneath his sheltering wing
      We rest for evermore.

125 C.M.

UNSHAKEN as the sacred hills,
  And firm as mountains be,
Firm as a rock the soul shall rest,
  That leans, O Lord, on Thee!

2 Not walls nor hills could guard so well
    Old Salem's happy ground,
  As those eternal arms of love
    Which every saint surround.

3 The wicked may awhile prevail,
    The righteous feel the rod;
  But every stroke shall only bring
    Their spirit near to God.

4 Deal gently, Lord, with souls sincere,
    And lead them safely on
  To the bright gates of Paradise,
    Where Christ, their Lord, is gone.

125.2   S.M.

WHO in the Lord confide,
    And feel his sprinkled blood,
In storms and hurricanes abide
    Firm as the ark of God.

2   Steadfast, and fixed, and sure,
    His Zion cannot move;
His faithful people stand secure,
    Beneath his guardian love.

3   As round his temple hill
    The mountain bulwarks rise,
With patient love He shields them still,
    And ever-watchful eyes.

4   On every side He stands,
    And for his Israel cares:
Safe in his own almighty hands
    Their souls He ever bears.

5   O may we still abide
    In Thee, all gracious Lord!
Till every soul is sanctified,
    And perfectly restored.

6   The men of heart sincere,
    O Saviour! still defend;
And do them good, and save them here,
    And love them to the end.

125.3   K3.M.

ZION stands by hills surrounded,
    Zion, kept by power divine;

All her foes shall be confounded,
    Though the world in arms combine:
      Happy Zion!
What a favoured lot is thine!

2 Every human tie may perish,
    Friend to friend unfaithful prove;
Mothers cease their own to cherish,
    Heaven and earth at last remove:
      But no changes
Can attend Jehovah's love.

3 When thy God may show displeasure,
    'Tis to save, and not destroy:
If he punish, 'tis in measure,
    'Tis to purge from all alloy:
      Be thou patient;
Soon thy grief shall turn to joy.

4 In the furnace God may prove thee,
    Thence to bring thee forth more bright;
He will never cease to love thee,
    Thou art precious in his sight.
      God is with thee,
God thine everlasting light.

126   C.M.

WHEN Zion from her bonds arose,
    'Twas like a joyful dream:
Deep wonder seized her friends and foes,
    So great God's mercies seem.

2 Yes, great and wondrous things the Lord
    Hath wrought in days of old;
And oft from deepest woe restored
    The people of his fold.

3 Once more, O Lord, thy grace display,
    Thy captive Church restore;
Turn Zion's weary night to day,
    And build her as before.

4 Thrice happy they in tears who sow!
    Large shall their harvest be:
Who bear the cross with Christ below
    His triumphs soon shall see.

126.2   E.M.

GREAT Mover of all hearts, whose hand
    Doth all the secret springs command
      Of human thought and will,
Thou, since the world was made, dost bless
Thy saints with fruits of righteousness
      In ceaseless order still.

2 Faith, hope, and love, here weave one chain,
But love supreme shall then remain,
    When life's short day is gone:
O Love, O Truth, O endless Light!
When shall we see thy Sabbath bright,
    With all our labours done?

3 We sow mid perils here, and tears;
He there the joyful harvest bears,
    Who here in grief hath sown:
Blest Three in One, the increase give,
And these thy gifts, by which we live,
    With endless glory crown.

127 C.M.

EXCEPT the Lord do build the house,
 Its walls unbuilt remain:
Unless the Lord the city keep,
 The watchman wakes in vain.

2 In vain we rise ere morning light,
 And lengthen out the day
With cares, that vex the peaceful night,
 And banish sleep away.

3 Only thy blessing, gracious Lord!
 Our feeble souls can keep;
Can prosperous wealth by day afford,
 By night, refreshing sleep.

4 Friends, children, all the smiles that cheer
 The homes of peace and love,
Are Thine, to bless thy servants here,
 And swell their joys above.

127.2 C.M.

EXCEPT the Lord the city keep,
 The watchman will be slain:
Except the Lord do build the house,
 The builders build in vain.

2 But Thou hast crowned my actions, Lord!
 With good success to-day:
This crown, together with myself,
 At thy blest feet I lay.

3 I reap the fruit of God's design,
 By Him it was foreseen:
He thought of this as well as I,
 Or it had never been.

4 I blindly guessed, but He foresaw,
   I wished, He gave command:
I praise and bless his careful eye,
   And his unerring hand.

5 O mighty God, who pleased art
   To bless me in my ways,
Prosper my weak, endeavouring heart,
   Which longs to yield thee praise.

128   C.M.

HOW blest is he who fears the Lord,
   And loves his holy will!
His soul enjoys a sure reward,
   And peace attends him still.

2 Thy wife a fruitful vine shall be,
   With richest clusters graced;
Each child, a green, fair olive tree,
   Around thy table placed.

3 The Lord will out of Zion shower
   Dews of celestial peace;
Thine eyes shall witness, hour by hour,
   His Church's glad increase.

4 Yea, children's children shall be given,
   To cheer thy latest days;
Blessings attend thy path to heaven,
   And fill thy lips with praise.

129   K4.M.

OFT, from youth, have sorrows tried me,
   Now may thankful Israel say;
But Thy help was ne'er denied me,
   Strength was given in trial's day.

Never, Lord, thy promise failed,
Never once my foes prevailed.

2 Though the plowers cruel furrows
   On my back full oft have made;
Though perplexed with sins and sorrows,
   Tempted, desolate, dismayed,
Thou hast saved me from despair,
Rent and broken every snare.

3 Zion, trust thy God for ever!
   Make His arm thy constant stay:
Foes may rage, but harm thee never,
   Soon like grass they pass away;
Clouds and storms shall soon be past,
Peace and joy for ever last.

130   S.M.

FROM lowest depths of woe
   To God I send my cry:
Lord, hear my supplicating voice,
   And graciously reply.

2   Shouldst thou severely judge,
   Who can the trial bear?
But Thou forgivest, lest we despond,
   And quite renounce thy fear.

3   My soul with patience waits
   For Thee, the living Lord;
My hopes are on thy promise built,
   Thy never-failing word.

4   My longing eyes look out
   For thy enlivening ray,
With eager hope, like those who watch
   To spy the dawning day.

5   Let Israel trust in God ;
No bounds his mercy knows,   [whence
The plenteous source and spring, from
Eternal succour flows.

6   Those friendly streams of love
Supplies in want convey :
A healing spring, a spring to cleanse,
And wash our guilt away.

130.2   C.M.

FROM depths of woe to God I cry,
And God my cry will hear :
The Friend of sinners reigns on high,
And suppliants need not fear.

2   I cast me on thy plighted word,
I knock at mercy's gate :
O hear my supplications, Lord !
Receive me, ere too late !

3   As seamen on the stormy main,
As pilgrims on their road,
Look out by night for morn again,
So looks my soul for God.

4   Sweet are the dawnings of his grace,
More sweet the perfect day :
Rise, Sun of righteousness, and chase
Each lingering cloud away.

130.3   C.M.

OUT of the depths of guilt and fear
I cried unto the Lord :
"In mercy lend a gracious ear,
And timely help afford."

2 Shouldst thou, O Lord, severely just,
   Each secret action try,
Who may abide, what child of dust,
   Thy pure, all-searching eye?

3 But thou art plenteous in thy grace,
   And ready to forgive;
That such as humbly seek thy face
   May fear thy name, and live.

4 My longing soul desires thy aid
   More earnestly than they,
Who, tempest-beaten and dismayed,
   Watch for the dawn of day.

5 O Israel, place thy confidence
   And only stay in God!
His mercy is a sure defence
   To such as trust his word.

6 His ready help is always near;
   And they, who seek his face,
Shall be redeemed from guilt and fear
   Through his abounding grace.

130.4   D.M.

WHEN tempests round us gather,
   And waves are raging high,
To thee, our God and Father,
   We lift our plaintive cry:
Behold our lamentation,
   Our restless sighing hear,
And to our supplication
   Incline thy pitying ear,

2 In peril and in sadness
    Thou art our stay, O Lord!
And all our hopes of gladness
    We build upon thy word:
Our souls, this earth despising,
    More long with God to be,
Than rosy morn's arising
    The watchman waits to see.

3 Be God thy strong foundation,
    My soul! and trust him well;
Thy God, with whom salvation
    And boundless mercy dwell:
The bonds of sin that chain thee
    He gently will untie,
Will evermore sustain thee,
    And saving health supply.

130.5   G3.M.

OUT of the depths to thee I cry,
    Hear, Lord, my sad petition!
Be swift, O Lord, to heed; be nigh
    To save me from perdition.
If sin to strict account Thou call,
    Lord, who may stand before thee?
But with thee pardon dwells, that all
    May tremble and adore thee.

2 I wait the Lord's redeeming grace,
    My soul for Him is yearning;
More eagerly than watchmen trace
    The daylight's sweet returning:
O Israel, make the Lord thy stay,
    With him is rich salvation:
His love will put thy sins away,
    And bless his chosen nation.

131   H.M.

LORD, for ever at thy side
  Let my place and portion be;
Strip me of the robe of pride,
Clothe me with humility.

2 Meekly may my soul receive
  All thy Spirit hath revealed:
Thou hast spoken, I believe,
  Though the prophecy were sealed.

3 Quiet as a weaned child,
  Weaned from the mother's breast,
By no subtlety beguiled,
  On thy faithfulness I rest.

4 Saints, rejoicing evermore,
  In the Lord Jehovah trust:
Him in all his ways adore,
  Wise, and wonderful, and just!

131.2   H3.M.

QUIET, Lord, my froward heart,
  Make me teachable and mild;
Upright, simple, free from art,
  Make me as a weaned child,
From distrust and envy free,
Pleased with all that pleases Thee.

2 What Thou shalt to-day provide,
  Let me as a child receive;
What to-morrow may betide
  Calmly to thy wisdom leave:
'Tis enough that Thou wilt care,
Why should I the burden bear?

3 As a little child relies
   On a care beyond his own,
Knows he's neither strong nor wise,
   Fears to stir a step alone,
Let me thus with Thee abide,
Thee, my Father, Guard, and Guide.

4 Thus preserved from Satan's wiles,
   Safe from dangers, free from fears,
May I live upon thy smiles,
   Till the promised hour appears,
When the sons of God shall prove
All their Father's boundless love.

132 Day 28. Psalms 132—138. C.M.

ARISE, O King of grace, arise,
   And enter to thy rest:
Lo! thy Church waits with longing eyes
   Thus to be owned and blessed.

2 Enter with all thy glorious train,
   Thy Spirit and thy word:
All that the ark did once contain
   Could no such grace afford.

3 Here, mighty God, accept our vows,
   Here let thy praise be spread;
Bless the provisions of thy house,
   And fill thy poor with bread.

4 Here let the Son of David reign,
   Let God's Anointed shine;
Justice and truth his court maintain,
   With love and power divine.

5 Here let him hold a lasting throne,
   And as his kingdom grows,
 Fresh honours shall adorn his crown,
   And shame surround his foes.

132.2   A.M.

IN this wide, weary world of care,
  How kindly God to us hath given
A Sabbath-day, a house of prayer,
  Fair emblems of approaching heaven.

2 Here pilgrims view their future home,
  Here find refreshment by the way;
  And here we to thy footstool come,
  And seek thy favour, Lord, to-day.

3 Arise, O Lord, thy Church to bless;
  Shower down thy graces from above:
  O clothe thy priests with righteousness,
  And crown thy saints with light and love.

4 Thy chosen flock, blest Saviour, lead;
  In every heart set up thy shrine:
  The naked clothe, the hungry feed,
  And make us all for ever Thine.

132.3   A.M.

GOD in his temple let us meet,
  Low on our knees before him bend:
There He hath placed his mercy-seat,
There on his Sabbath we attend.

2 Arise unto thy resting-place,
  Thou, and thine ark of strength, O Lord!
  Shine through the veil, we seek thy face;
  Speak, for we hearken to thy word.

3 With righteousness thy priests array;
Joyful thy chosen people be!
Let those who teach, and those who pray,
Let all be holiness to Thee!

133 S.M.

BLEST are the sons of peace,
Whose hearts and hopes are one;
Whose kind desires to serve and please
Through all their actions run.

2 Blest is the pious house,
Where zeal and friendship meet:
Their songs of praise, their mingled vows,
Make their communion sweet.

3 Thus when on Aaron's head
They poured the rich perfume,
The ointment o'er his vesture spread,
And fragrance filled the room.

4 Thus on the heavenly hills
The saints are blest above;
Where joy like morning dew distils,
And all the air is love.

133.2 I3.M.

'TIS a pleasant thing to see
Brethren in the Lord agree,
Children of a God of love
Live as they shall live above,
Acting each a Christian part,
One in lip and one in heart.

2 As the precious ointment, shed
  Once on Aaron's hallowed head,
  Downward through his garments stole,
  Spreading odours o'er the whole,
  So from our High Priest above
  To his Church flows heavenly love.

3 Gently as the dews distil
  Down on Zion's holy hill,
  Dropping gladness, where they fall,
  Brightening and refreshing all,
  Such is Christian union, shed
  Through the members from the head.

4 Where divine affection lives,
  There the Lord his blessing gives;
  There his will on earth is done,
  There his heaven is half begun:
  Lord! our great example prove,
  Teach us all like Thee to love.

133.3   C.M.

HOW sweet, how heavenly is the sight,
    When those who love the Lord
All in each other's peace delight,
    And so fulfil His word!

2 Free us from envy, scorn, and pride,
    Our wishes fix above:
  May each his brother's failings hide,
    And show a brother's love.

3 Let love, in one delightful stream,
    Through every bosom flow:
  And union sweet, and pure esteem,
    In every action glow.

4 This is the golden chain, that binds
    The happy souls above;
And he's an heir of heaven, who finds
    His bosom glow with love!

133.4   F.M.

HOW beautiful the sight
    Of brethren, who agree
In friendship to unite,
    And bonds of charity:
'Tis like the precious ointment, shed
O'er all his robes from Aaron's head.

2   'Tis like the dews, that fill
    The cups of Hermon's flowers;
Or Zion's fruitful hill,
    Bright with the drops of showers,
When mingling odours breathe around,
And glory rests on all the ground.

3   For there the Lord commands
    Blessings, in boundless store,
From his all-bounteous hands,
    Yea, life for evermore:
Thrice happy they, who meet above,
To spend eternity in love.

133.5   C.M.

O HAPPY state on earth to see,
    And blest from God above,
Where brethren meet, and make their home
    The dwelling-place of love!

2 'Tis like the costly odours sweet
    That, poured on Aaron's head,
Down to his beard and bordered vest
    Their gladdening fragrance shed.

3 'Tis like the fruitful sky-born dews,
    On Hermon gathering still,
Descending thence in gentlest showers,
    On Zion's sacred hill.

4 Like rain, it comes with blessing down
    From heaven's unfailing store;
The blessing of the God of peace,
    And life for evermore.

134   13.M.

PRAISE to God on high be given,
    Praise from all in earth and heaven;
Ye that in his presence stand,
Ye that walk by his command,
Saints below, and hosts above,
Praise, O praise the God of love!

2 Praise him at the dawn of light,
Praise him at returning night;
Strings and voices, hands and hearts,
In his praises bear your parts:
Thou that madest earth and sky,
Answering bless us from on high.

134.2   C.M.

YE that obey th' immortal King,
    Attend his holy place;
Bow to the glories of his power,
    And bless his wondrous grace.

2 Lift up your hands by morning light,
    And raise your souls on high;
Raise your admiring thoughts by night
    Above the starry sky.

3 The God, who heaven and earth has made,
    Will bless his Zion still:
To Him be ceaseless worship paid,
    With songs his temple fill.

135   C.M.

AWAKE, our souls! to bless our King
    The sweetest anthems raise;
Our holy gladness, while we sing,
    Increasing with the praise.

2 Great is the Lord, and works unknown
    Are his divine employ;
But still his saints are near his throne,
    His treasure and his joy.

3 Heaven, earth, and seas confess his hand,
    He bids the vapours rise;
Lightnings and storms, at his command,
    Sweep through the sounding skies.

4 O bless the Lord with heart and voice,
    All ye that fear his name;
And let the people of his choice
    Exalt his wondrous fame.

136   I.M.

LET us, with a gladsome mind,
    Praise the Lord, for He is kind;
For his mercies aye endure,
Ever faithful, ever sure.

2 He, with all-commanding might,
   Filled the new-made world with light;
   For his mercies aye endure,
   Ever faithful, ever sure.

3 He the golden-tressèd sun
   Caused his daily course to run;
   For his mercies aye endure,
   Ever faithful, ever sure.

4 And the moon to shine by night,
   Midst her starry sisters bright;
   For his mercies aye endure,
   Ever faithful, ever sure.

5 He his chosen race did bless
   In the wasteful wilderness;
   For his mercies aye endure,
   Ever faithful, ever sure.

6 All things living He doth feed,
   His full hand supplies their need;
   For his mercies aye endure,
   Ever faithful, ever sure.

7 He hath with a piteous eye
   Looked upon our misery;
   For his mercies aye endure,
   Ever faithful, ever sure.

8 Let us, then, with gladsome mind,
   Praise the Lord, for He is kind;
   For his mercies aye endure,
   Ever faithful, ever sure.

136.2
B.M.

GIVE to our God immortal praise,
Mercy and truth are all his ways;
Wonders of grace to God belong,
Repeat his mercies in your song.

2 Give to the Lord of lords renown,
The King of kings with glory crown;
His mercies ever shall endure,
When lords and kings are known no more.

3 He built the earth, He spread the sky,
And fixed the starry hosts on high;
Wonders of grace to God belong,
Repeat his mercies in your song.

4 He fills the sun with morning light,
He bids the moon adorn the night;
His mercies ever shall endure,
When sun and moon shall shine no more.

5 He sent his Son with power to save
From guilt, and darkness, and the grave;
Wonders of grace to God belong,
Repeat his mercies in your song.

6 Through this vain world He guides our feet,
And leads us to his heavenly seat;
His mercies ever shall endure,
When this vain world shall be no more.

136.3
I.M.

O GIVE thanks unto the Lord,
All his mighty deeds record:
Wondrous works to God belong,
Worthy of eternal song.

2 Wise and just are all his ways,
  Great his power beyond our praise:
  Lord, thy mercies, firm and sure,
  Through eternal years endure.

3 Thou hast filled the sun with light,
  Moon and stars, that rule the night:
  Wondrous works to Thee belong,
  Worthy of eternal song.

4 Thou, in time of sorest need,
  Hast our souls from bondage freed;
  For thy mercies, firm and sure,
  Through eternal years endure.

5 Thou dost guide, with loving hand,
  Through the waste to Canaan's land;
  Wondrous works to Thee belong,
  Worthy of eternal song.

6 Thou, in hours of deep distress,
  Still art near, thy saints to bless;
  For thy mercies, firm and sure,
  Through eternal years endure.

7 Thine the springtide and its flowers,
  Thine the dews and gentle showers;
  Wondrous works to Thee belong,
  Worthy of eternal song.

8 Thou dost make the fruitful field
  All its autumn stores to yield;
  For thy mercies, firm and sure,
  Through eternal years endure.

9 Nobler gifts thy love hath given,
Heavenly bread, the wine of heaven;
Wondrous works to Thee belong,
Worthy of eternal song.

10 Praise, O praise him evermore!
Heaven and earth, his name adore!
Him whose mercies, firm and sure,
Through eternal years endure.

136.4   F.M.

TO God, the mighty Lord,
  Your joyful thanks repeat:
To Him due praise afford,
  As good as he is great:
For God does prove our constant Friend,
His boundless love shall never end.

2   To Him, whose wondrous power
    The angel hosts obey,
  Whom earthly kings adore,
    This grateful homage pay:
For God does prove our constant Friend,
His boundless love shall never end.

3   He, in our depth of woes,
    On us with favour thought,
  And from our cruel foes
    In peace and safety brought:
For God doth prove our constant Friend,
His boundless love shall never end.

4   He does the food supply
    On which all creatures live;

To God, who reigns on high,
  Eternal praises give:
For God doth prove our constant Friend,
His boundless love shall never end.

136.5   F.M.

GIVE thanks to God most high,
  The universal Lord;
The sovereign King of kings,
  And be his grace adored:
His power and grace are still the same,
O let his name have endless praise!

2   He saw the nations lie,
  All perishing in sin;
He pitied the sad state
  Our ruined world was in:
Thy mercy, Lord, shall still endure,
And ever sure abides thy word.

3   He sent his only Son,
  To save us from our woe;
From Satan, sin, and death,
  And every hurtful foe:
His power and grace are still the same,
O let his name have endless praise.

4   Give thanks aloud to God,
  To God, the heavenly King;
And let the spacious earth
  His works and glory sing:
Thy mercies, Lord, shall still endure,
And ever sure abides thy word.

136.6   A.M.

O PRAISE the Lord, for He is Love,
   The mighty Lord and King of kings!
O thank the God all gods above,
   From whom eternal mercy springs!

2 O praise him on his glorious throne,
   The mighty Lord and King of kings!
Who doth all wondrous deeds alone,
   From whom eternal mercy springs!

3 He by his wisdom heaven arrayed,
   The mighty Lord and King of kings!
And earth above the waters laid,
   From whom eternal mercy springs.

4 He feeds all tribes that live and move,
   The Lord of lords and King of kings,
Thank him, whose heavenly name is Love,
   From whom eternal mercy springs.

137   A.M.

WHEN we, our wearied limbs to rest,
   Sat down by proud Euphrates' stream,
We wept, with doleful thoughts oppressed,
   And Zion was our mournful theme.

2 Our harps, that when with joy we sung,
   Were wont their tuneful parts to bear,
With silent strings neglected hung
   On willow trees, that withered there.

3 O Salem, once our happy seat!
When I of thee forgetful prove,
Then let my trembling hand forget
The speaking strings with art to move!

4 If I to mention thee forbear,
  Eternal silence seize my tongue;
  Or if I sing one cheerful air,
  Till thy deliverance is my song.

137.2   S.M.

YOUR harps, ye trembling saints,
  Down from the willows take:
Loud to the praise of love divine
  Bid every string awake.

2 Though in a foreign land,
  We are not far from home;
And nearer to our house above
  We every moment come.

3 His grace will to the end
  Stronger and brighter shine:
Nor present things, nor things to come,
  Shall quench the spark divine.

4 When we in darkness walk,
  Nor feel the heavenly flame,
Then is the time to trust our God,
  And rest upon his name.

5 Wait till the shadows flee,
  Wait the appointed hour:
Wait, till the Bridegroom of our souls
  Reveal his love with power.

6 Blest is the man, O God!
  That stays himself on Thee;
Who waits for thy salvation, Lord,
  Shall thy salvation see.

137.3 A.M.

O ZION! when I think on thee,
I wish for pinions like the dove;
And mourn to think that I should be
So distant from the place I love.

2 A captive here, and far from home,
For Zion's sacred walls I sigh:
To Zion all the ransomed come,
And see the Saviour eye to eye.

3 While here, I walk on hostile ground;
The few, that I can call my friends,
Are like myself with fetters bound,
And weariness our steps attends.

4 But soon we hope to see the day,
When Zion's children shall return:
Our sorrows then shall flee away,
And we shall never, never mourn.

137.4 A.M.

HIGH on the bending willows hung,
Why, Israel, sleeps the tuneful string?
Why mute and sad thy silent tongue,
And Zion's song refrains to sing?

2 Awake! thy loudest raptures raise,
Let harp and voice unite their strains;
Thy promised King his sceptre sways,
Thy Lord, thy own Messiah reigns.

3 No more a lonely exile roam,
Nor weep for thoughts of Zion's hill:
O seek in faith a heavenly home!
Let heavenly hopes thy bosom fill.

4 No taunting foes a song require,
  No strangers mock thy captive chain,
  For friends attune the silent lyre,
  Thy brethren ask the holy strain.

5 Then why, on bending willows hung,
  O Israel, sleeps the tuneful string?
  Awake to joy thy ransomed tongue,
  And Zion's songs with rapture sing.

137.   A.M.

CREATOR of the world, to Thee
  An endless rest of joy belongs;
And heavenly choirs are ever free
To sing on high their festive songs.

2 But feeble, tempted mourners here,
  Where pain and sorrow daily come;
  O how can we, in exile drear,
  Sing out, as they, sweet songs of home?

3 O Father, who dost promise still
  That they who mourn shall blessed be,
  Our hearts with godly sorrow fill,
  For sins that keep us far from Thee.

4 But grant us, in our tears, to rest
  With faith upon Thy loving care;
  And soon restore us, with the blest,
  Their songs of praise in heaven to share.

138   B.M.

WITH all my powers of heart and tongue
  I'll praise my Maker in my song:
Angels shall hear the notes I raise,
Approve the song, and join the praise.

2 To God I cried, when trouble rose;
  He heard me, and subdued my foes;
  He did my rising fears control,
  And strength diffused through all my soul.

3 Amidst a thousand snares I stand,
  Upheld and guarded by Thy hand:
  Thy words my fainting soul revive,
  And keep my dying faith alive.

4 I'll sing thy truth and mercy, Lord!
  I'll sing the wonders of thy word:
  Not all thy works and names below
  So much thy power and glory show.

5 Complete, O Lord, thy work of grace,
  Prepare me to behold thy face:
  O let thy mercies ne'er remove
  From souls that taste thy pardoning love!

138.2   C.M.

WITH my whole heart, O heavenly King!
    Thy goodness I'll proclaim;
Before thy angels gladly sing,
    And praise thy holy name.

2 Within thy earthly temples, Lord,
    Our songs shall still abound;
  Thy name is high, Thy faithful word
    With highest honours crowned.

3 To Thee my fainting spirit cried,
    With sins and fears oppressed:
  New strength and grace thy love supplied,
    And soothed my fears to rest.

4 The kings of earth shall hear thy word,
 And sing, with loud acclaim,
How great how glorious is the Lord!
 How wonderful thy name!

5 O perfect, Lord, thy work of grace;
 Our souls with goodness fill;
Nor leave us, till we see thy face
 On heaven's eternal hill.

139 Day 29. Psalms 139—143. B.M.

THOU, Lord, by strictest search hast known
 My rising up and lying down;
My secret thoughts are known to Thee,
Known long before conceived by me.

2 Surrounded by thy power I stand,
 On every side I find thy hand:
O skill, for human reach too high!
Too dazzling bright for mortal eye!

3 O could I so perfidious be,
 To think of once deserting Thee,
Where, Lord, could I thy influence shun,
Or whither from thy presence run?

4 The veil of night is no disguise,
 No screen from thy all-searching eyes:
One glance from Thee, one piercing ray,
Would kindle darkness into day.

5 Search, try, O God, my thoughts and heart,
 Cleanse thou my soul in every part;
O still restore me, when I stray,
 And guide me in thy perfect way!

139.2   B.M.

LORD, thou hast searched and seen me through;
Thine eye commands, with piercing view,
My rising and my resting hours,
My heart and flesh with all their powers.

2 My thoughts, before they are my own,
Are to my God distinctly known:
He knows the words I mean to speak,
Ere from my opening lips they break.

3 Within thy circling power I stand,
On every side I find thy hand:
Awake, asleep, at home, abroad,
I am surrounded still with God.

4 Amazing knowledge, vast and great!
What large extent! what lofty height!
My soul, with all the powers I boast,
Is in the boundless prospect lost.

5 O may these thoughts possess my breast,
Where'er I roam, where'er I rest!
Nor let my weaker passions dare
Consent to sin, for God is there.

139.3   C.M.

IN all my vast concerns with Thee,
In vain my soul would try
To shun thy presence, Lord, or flee
The notice of thine eye.

2 Thine all-surrounding sight surveys
My rising and my rest,
My public walks, my private ways,
And secrets of my breast.

3 O wondrous knowledge, deep and high!
   Where can a creature hide?
Within thy circling arms I lie,
   Beset on every side.

4 So let thy grace surround me still,
   And like a bulwark prove,
To guard my soul from every ill,
   Secured by sovereign love.

139.4   C.M.

LORD, where shall guilty sinners flee,
   Forgotten and unknown?
In hell thy dreadful wrath they see,
   In heaven thy glorious throne.

2 If, winged with beams of morning light,
   I fly beyond the west;
Thy hand, which must support my flight,
   Would soon betray my rest.

3 If o'er my sins I think to draw
   The curtains of the night,
Those flaming eyes, that guard thy law,
   Would turn the shades to night.

4 The beams of noon, the midnight hour,
   Are both alike to Thee!
O may I ne'er provoke the power,
   From which I cannot flee!

139.5   C.M.

IN silent wonder, Lord, I stand,
   And all thy works survey:
We are thy work, Thy wisdom planned
   And built this house of clay.

2 Thou hast possessed my heart and reins,
    And all my infant powers:
Each child of man thy love sustains,
    In life's young morning hours.

3 Air, earth, and sea, the fire, the wind,
    Proclaim thy matchless skill;
We gaze upon ourselves, and find
    Diviner wonders still.

4 Thy awful glories round me shine,
    My flesh proclaims thy praise:
O may I know thy love divine,
    Thy miracles of grace!

139.6   B.M.

THERE'S not a bird, with lonely nest,
    In pathless wood, or mountain crest,
Or meaner thing, which doth not share,
O God! in thy paternal care.

2 Each barren crag, each desert rude,
Holds Thee within its solitude;
And thou dost bless the wanderer there,
Who makes his solitary prayer.

3 In busy mart and crowded street,
No less than in the still retreat,
Thou, Lord, art near, our souls to bless,
With all a parent's tenderness.

4 And every moment still doth bring
Thy blessings on its loaded wing;
Widely they spread through earth and sky
And last to all eternity.

5 O Lord, where'er our lot is cast,
 While life, and thought, and feeling last,
 Through all our years, in every place,
 We'll bless thee for thy boundless grace.

139.7   C.M.

LORD, when I count thy mercies o'er,
 They fill me with surprise:
Not all the sands, that spread the shore,
 To equal numbers rise.

2 My flesh with fear and wonder stands,
 The product of thy skill;
And hourly blessings from thy hands
 Thy thoughts of love reveal.

3 These on my heart by night I keep,
 How kind, how dear to me!
O may the hour that ends my sleep
 Still find my thoughts with Thee!

139.8   C.M.

TRY us, O God, and search the ground
 Of every evil heart:
Whate'er of sin in us is found,
 O bid it all depart!

2 When to the right or left we stray,
 Restore thy helpless sheep:
Bring back our feet into the way,
 And there thy wanderers keep.

3 Complete at length thy work of grace,
 And take us to thy rest;
Among the saints, who see thy face,
 To be for ever blest!

139.9   A3.M.

SEARCHER of hearts! to Thee are known
   The inmost secrets of my breast;
At home, abroad, in crowds, alone,
   Thou seest my rising and my rest;
My thoughts far off, through every maze,
Source, stream, and issue, all my ways!

2 No word, that from my mouth proceeds,
   Evil or good, escapes thine ear;
Witness Thou art to all my deeds,
   Before, behind, for ever near:
Such knowledge is for me too high,
I live beneath my Maker's eye.

3 How precious are thy thoughts of peace,
   O God, to me! how great the sum!
New every morn, they never cease;
   They were, they are, and still to come;
In number and in compass more
Than ocean's sands or ocean's shore.

4 Search me, O God, and know my heart,
   Try me, my secret soul survey;
And warn thy servant to depart
   From every false and evil way:
So shall thy truth my guidance be
To life and immortality!

140   S.M.

PRESERVE me, Lord, from those
   Who meditate my fall;
From flattering friends, and threat'ning foes,
   Preserve me, Lord, from all.

2   The tempter's hate or guile
The feeblest soul may brave,
The lion's rage, or serpent's wile,
With Thee at hand to save.

3   In hours of want and dread
I found in Thee a friend;
Thou cover'dst my defenceless head,
And Thou wilt still defend.

4   Strength of the poor and weak,
Still faithful, good, and true!
Put down the proud, uphold the meek,
And bear thy people through.

141   C.M.

To thee, O Lord, my spirit flies;
  Give ear unto my cry:
Like incense let my prayer arise,
  And reach thy throne on high.

2 Guard thou my lips from words of pride,
  And cleanse my heart within;
Nor let my spirit turn aside,
  Allured by sweets of sin.

3 O may the righteous, when I stray,
  With gentle voice reprove!
Like fragrant spices, day by day,
  Are words of faithful love.

4 When darkest sorrows round them gloom,
  For such my prayer shall rise;
My friends on earth, beyond the tomb
  My partners in the skies.

5 In this dark world of sin and woe,
  I trust, O Lord, in thee!
O let me serve thee here below,
  And soon thy glory see!

141.2   L.M.

LORD, I daily call on Thee,
  Hear my voice, and answer me!
Save me, for in faith I pray;
Take, O take my sins away!

2 Let my prayer as incense rise,
Pure, accepted sacrifice:
Let my life with virtue shine,
Fill my soul with love divine.

3 Keep, O keep my lips and heart;
Let me ne'er from Thee depart:
Holy, happy may I be,
Perfect, O my God, like Thee!

142   S.M.

TO God with earnest cry
  In deep distress I prayed;
I told my griefs, with groan and sigh
  My soul's petition made.

2 When troubles round me lowered,
  My path to Thee was known:
Beset with snares, with fears o'erpowered,
  I wept before thy throne.

3 I looked, and none would lend
  A pitying ear or eye:
All refuge failed, no earthly friend
  In my distress was nigh.

4   To thee, O Lord, to thee
      I pour my secret prayer:
   My refuge and my portion be,
      To save me from despair.

5   Free me from every foe,
      The snares of death remove;
   And let my ransomed spirit know
      The wonders of thy love.

6   Then saints in eager throngs
      Shall hear my lips record,
   In melody of joyful songs,
      The bounties of the Lord.

143
B.M.

HEAR me, O Lord, in my distress,
   With pardoning grace thy servant bless:
By thy severer judgment tried,
No child of earth is justified.

2 My soul is crushed with mighty foes,
   And shades of death around me close:
Faint with its load of guilt and sin,
My heart is desolate within.

3 Sadly I muse on former days,
   Whose hours shone bright with joy and praise,
And stretch to Thee my eager hands,
As thirst for showers the desert sands.

4 O may thy kind and gentle voice
   Each morning bid my heart rejoice!
In Thee I trust! reveal the way,
That leads to realms of heavenly day.

5 Teach me thy will, my fears subdue,
With secret grace my soul renew;
May thy good Spirit guide me still,
And bring me safe to Zion's hill.

6 My foes disperse, my sins destroy,
And bless thy child with holy joy;
Till 'midst thy ransomed host I shine,
Enriched and filled with life divine.

143.2   C.M.

WHENE'ER the morning lights the skies,
Thy beams, O Lord, display;
And let thy loving-kindness rise
To bless the early day.

2 In Thee I trust, thy light afford,
And make thy goodness known:
I lift my soul to thee, O Lord!
In prayer before thy throne.

3 Thou art my God, thy will express,
And teach me to obey;
And let thy Spirit's quick'ning grace
Direct me in thy way.

4 O raise me to the life divine!
My Saviour's name I plead;
And let my soul on Thee recline,
From every danger freed.

5 Let mercy all my foes subdue,
My wandering soul restore;
Nor sense nor sin their arts renew,
To vex thy servant more.

143.3   K.M.

EARLIER than the star of morning,
   Lord, thy mercy still is near :
Guide me, while I seek thy warning,
   In the paths of holy fear.

2 On the wings of prayer ascending,
   Lo! my spirit mounts to Thee :
From my foes my life defending,
   Guard me, shield me, set me free.

3 Earthly love shall ne'er divide me
   From the God whom saints confess :
Let thy loving Spirit guide me
   To the land of righteousness.

4 Life is thine, the life immortal,
   Life from sin and sorrow free :
Open soon the heavenly portal,
   Let me find my rest in Thee.

144   C.M.

FOR ever blessed be the Lord,
   My Saviour and my Shield!
He sends his Spirit with his word,
   To arm me for the field.

2 When sin and death their force unite,
   He makes my soul his care ;
Instructs me to the heavenly fight,
   And guards me through the war.

3 A friend and helper so divine
   Doth my weak courage raise :
He makes the glorious victory mine,
   And His shall be the praise.

145 B.M.

MY God, my King! thy various praise
Shall fill the remnant of my days;
Thy grace employ my humble tongue,
Till death and glory raise the song.

2 The wings of every hour shall bear
Some thankful tribute to thine ear,
And every setting sun shall see
New works of duty done for Thee.

3 Thy truth and justice I'll proclaim,
Thy bounty flows, an endless stream;
Thy mercy swift, thine anger slow,
But dreadful to the stubborn foe.

4 Let distant times and nations raise
The long succession of thy praise;
And unborn ages make the song
The joy and labour of their tongue.

5 But who can speak thy wondrous deeds?
Thy greatness all our thoughts exceeds:
Vast and unsearchable thy ways,
Vast and immortal be thy praise.

145.2 C.M.

LONG as I live I'll bless thy name,
My King, the God of love!
My work and joy shall be the same
In the bright world above.

2 Great is the Lord, his power unknown;
Great let his praises be!
The splendour of thy glorious throne
No mortal eye can see.

3 Thy grace shall dwell upon my tongue,
   And while my lips rejoice,
The men that hear my sacred song
   Shall join their cheerful voice.

4 Fathers to sons shall teach thy name,
   And children learn thy ways;
Ages to come thy truth proclaim,
   And nations sound thy praise.

5 Thy glorious deeds in time of old
   Shall through the world be known;
Thy mighty power, thy love untold,
   Thy searchless wisdom shown.

6 The world is governed by thy hands,
   Thy saints are ruled by love;
And thy eternal kingdom stands,
   Though rocks and hills remove.

145.3   C.M.

SWEET is the memory of thy grace,
   My God, my heavenly King!
Let age to age thy righteousness
   In sounds of glory sing.

2 God reigns on high, but not confines
   His goodness to the skies:
Through the whole earth his bounty shines,
   And every want supplies.

3 With longing eyes thy creatures wait
   On thee for daily food:
Thy liberal hand provides their meat,
   And fills their mouths with good.

4 How kind are thy compassions, Lord!
   How slow thine anger moves!
But soon He sends his pardoning word,
   To cheer the souls He loves.

5 Creatures, with all their endless race,
   Thy power and praise proclaim;
But saints, who taste thy richer grace,
   Delight to bless thy name.

145.4   C 2.M.

1 THE heavenly spheres to thee, O God!
   Attune their ceaseless hymn;
All-wise, all-holy, Thou art praised,
   In song of seraphim:
All worlds, through depths of space un-
   Unite to worship Thee;   [known,
The glory of thy presence fills
   Heaven, air, and earth, and sea.

2 The song of gratitude is sung
   By spring's awakening hours;
And summer offers at thy shrine
   Its earliest, sweetest flowers;
The autumn brings its ripened fruits,
   In rich luxuriance given;
And winter's silver heights reflect
   Thy brightness back to heaven.

3 All nature is thy temple, Lord,
   And beams with light and love;
Its flowers how sweetly bloom below,
   Its stars rejoice above.
But more than all, in souls redeemed
   Thy brightest glories shine;
And saints proclaim, through endless days,
   Thy power and love divine.

146   E 3. M.

I'LL praise my Maker with my breath,
And when my voice is lost in death,
  Praise shall employ my nobler powers:
My days of praise shall ne'er be past,
While life, and thought, and being last,
  Or immortality endures.

2 Happy the man, whose hopes rely
On Israel's God; He made the sky,
  And earth and seas with all their train:
His truth for ever stands secure;
He saves th' oppressed, He feeds the poor,
  And none shall find his promise vain.

3 The Lord pours eyesight on the blind,
The Lord supports the fainting mind;
  He sends the labouring conscience peace:
He helps the stranger in distress,
The widow and the fatherless,
  And grants the prisoner sweet release.

4 I'll praise him, while He lends me breath,
And when my voice is lost in death,
  Praise shall employ my nobler powers:
My days of praise shall ne'er be past,
While life, and thought, and being last,
  Or immortality endures.

146.2   C. M.

O PRAISE the Lord! and thou, my soul,
  For ever bless his name!
His wondrous love, while life shall last,
  My constant praise shall claim.

2 On kings, the greatest sons of men,
    Let none for aid rely:
In dangerous times they cannot save,
    Nor timely aid supply.

3 Thrice happy he, who Jacob's God
    For his protector takes;
Who still with well-placed hope the Lord
    His constant refuge makes;—

4 The Lord, who made both heaven and earth,
    And all that they contain;
Who ne'er will quit his steadfast truth,
    Nor make his promise vain.

5 The God, that doth in Zion dwell,
    Is our eternal King:
From age to age his reign endures,
    Let all His praises sing!

146.3   E.M.

NOW let the Church in strains of praise
    Their tribute to Jehovah raise;
My soul, the triumph join:
Long as I live, I'll praise my King,
Till with immortal powers I sing,
    Where all his glories shine.

2 How blest the man, whose hopes are stayed
    On Him, who heaven and earth has made,
        Whom Israel's sons adore!
He spread the seas, He formed the land,
His truth for ever firm shall stand,
    When time shall be no more.

3 Thy God, O Zion, ever reigns:
  The King of heaven thy cause maintains,
    His throne shall ne'er remove:
  Let all the earth resound his praise!
  His Church a nobler song shall raise,
    In brighter worlds above!

147
C.M.

O PRAISE the Lord! his greatness sing,
    His noble deeds proclaim;
  For 'tis a good and pleasant thing
    To bless his holy name.

2 The Lord will build Jerusalem,
    Though levelled with the ground;
  And Israel's outcast sons restore
    From all the nations round.

3 He heals the humble, contrite soul
    With words of peace divine:
  He counts the stars from pole to pole,
    By his command they shine.

4 Great is the Lord, and great his might;
    His wisdom hath no bound:
  His arm will save the meek, and smite
    Th' ungodly to the ground.

5 He bids the clouds ascend the sky,
    He sends the fruitful rain;
  And deserts, watered from on high,
    In beauty smile again.

6 He loves the souls that love his name,
    Who rest upon his word;
  Then praise thy God, Jerusalem!
    O Zion, praise the Lord!

147.2   C.M.

WITH songs and honours sounding loud
  O praise the Lord on high!
Over the heavens He spreads his cloud,
  And waters veil the sky.

2 He sends the showers of blessing down,
  To cheer the plains below:
He makes the grass the mountains crown,
  And corn in valleys grow.

3 His steady counsels change the face
  Of the declining year:
He bids the sun cut short his race,
  And wintry days appear.

4 He sends his word, and melts the snow;
  The fields no longer mourn:
He calls the warmer gales to blow,
  And bids the spring return.

5 The changing wind, the flying cloud,
  Obey his mighty word;
With songs and honours, sounding loud,
  Praise ye the sovereign Lord!

147.3   B.M.

O KING of earth, of air and sea!
  The hungry ravens cry to thee:
To thee the lions roaring call,
The common Father, kind to all:
Then grant thy servants, Lord, we pray,
Their daily bread from day to day.

2 The roaring lions lack and pine;
But God! thou carest still for Thine:
Thy bounteous hand with food can bless
The bleak and lonely wilderness:
And Thou hast taught us, Lord, to pray
For daily bread from day to day.

3 And oh, when through the wilds we roam,
That part us from our heavenly home;
Do Thou the gracious comfort give,
By which alone the soul may live;
And grant thy servants, Lord, we pray,
Their daily bread from day to day.

148   F.M.

YE boundless realms of joy
   Exalt your Maker's fame:
His praise your song employ,
   Above the starry frame:
Your voices raise, ye cherubim
And seraphim, to sing his praise.

2 Thou moon, that rulest the night,
   And sun, that guidest the day;
Ye glittering stars of light,
   To him your homage pay:
His praise declare, ye heavens above,
And clouds, that move in liquid air.

3 Let them adore the Lord,
   And praise his holy name,
By whose almighty word
   They all from nothing came;
And all shall last from changes free;
His firm decree stands ever fast.

4 His chosen saints, by grace,
 He lifts to thrones on high;
And favours Israel's race,
 Who still to Him are nigh :
O therefore raise your grateful voice,
And still rejoice the Lord to praise.

148.2   13.M.

COME, O come, in sacred lays,
 Sound ye God Almighty's praise :
Hither bring, with one consent,
Heart, and voice, and instrument ;
Let no creature dumb be found,
That hath either voice or sound.

2 Come, ye sons of human race,
In this chorus take your place,
And, amid the mortal throng,
Be ye masters of the song :
High your notes of worship raise,
And your great Creator praise.

3 Angels and celestial powers,
Praise our God, both yours and ours :
Let the praise of God resound,
Still in never ceasing round :
Let your tide of worship be
Vast and boundless as the sea !

4 From the earth's remotest end
Let the voice of praise ascend :
Spreading wide from shore to shore,
Let the ocean fulness roar :
Winds and clouds, as on ye move,
Bear the mighty sound above.

5 So shall He, from heaven's high tower,
On the earth his blessing shower;
And this huge, wide orb we see,
Shall one choir, one temple be:
Come, then, come, in sacred lays,
Sound we God Almighty's praise!

148.3   12.M.

PRAISE the Lord, ye hosts on high!
   Praise him, angels, through the sky:
Sun and moon, and stars of light,
Praise your Maker day and night:
He commanded, and ye all
Rose obedient to his call:
He commandeth, and ye still
Move submissive to his will.

2 Praise the Lord, thou earth below!
Praise him, lightnings, hail, and snow!
Ocean, wide his glory roll!
Waft it, winds, from pole to pole:
Seasons, tell it as ye fly;
Forests deep, and mountains high:
Birds, and creatures great and small,
Praise the Lord, the Lord of all.

3 Let mankind their tribute bring:
Monarchs, own a higher King!
Young and old, his mercies tell;
Men and maids, the chorus swell:
Praise him, saints, above the rest;
Praise him, for ye know him best:
All his love, his grace record;
Praise the universal Lord.

148.4   B.M.

O PRAISE the Lord, ye hosts above!
  Ye spirits, perfected in love!
Sun, moon, and stars, your voices raise,
And sing aloud your Maker's praise.

2 From all the mighty deeps below
  Let ocean's hallelujahs flow;
While lightning, vapour, wind and storm,
Fire, hail, and snow, his will perform.

3 O kings! your Sovereign serve with awe;
  Ye judges, own his righteous law:
Ye princes, worship him with fear;
His power confess, his name revere!

4 By infants let his truth be told,
  His mighty wonders by the old:
Let youths and maidens, in their prime,
Prolong the everlasting chime.

5 How great and wonderful his name!
  Let heaven and earth his power proclaim:
Let all combine, in sweet accord,
To praise the everlasting Lord.

148.5   K2.M.

PRAISE the Lord, whose mighty wonders
  Earth and air and seas display;
Him who high in tempests thunders,
  Him whom countless worlds obey:
In the eastern skies ascending,
  Praise him, glorious orb of day;
Ocean, round the world extending,
  Praise him in thy boundless sway.

2 Pines, that crown the lofty mountains,
   Bow in sign of worship low;
All ye secret springs and fountains,
   Warble praises, as ye flow:
Beasts, through nature's drear dominions,
   Praise him, where the wilds extend;
Praise him, birds, whose soaring pinions
   Up to heaven's high gate ascend.

3 Man below, the lord of nature,
   Angel choirs, in realms above,
Hymning, praise the great Creator,
   Praise th' eternal Fount of love:
Teach us, Lord, to sing thy glory,
   Here rehearsing heavenly lays;
Till we cast our crowns before thee,
   Lost in wonder, love, and praise!

149   K.M.

PRAISE the Lord! ye saints, adore him,
   While in joyful throngs ye meet:
Sons of Israel, come before him,
   Bow with rapture at his feet.

2 Sing, rejoice! away with sadness!
   Harp and timbrel hither bring:
Sons of Zion, filled with gladness,
   Triumph in your Saviour King.

3 Sing, for He beholds with pleasure
   Souls that on his grace rely:
Sing, for beauty without measure
   He will to the meek supply.

4 Lo, He comes! the day is breaking,
 All his saints in glory rise;
From their peaceful slumbers waking,
 Caught to meet him in the skies.

5 They shall judge the guilty nations,
 They shall wield the conqueror's sword;
Armed with might, and trained in patience,
 Chosen warriors of the Lord!

6 Praise the Lord! ye saints, adore him;
 Wait in faith the solemn day:
Sons of Zion, bow before him,
 Grateful songs with reverence pay.

149.2   O.M.

O PRAISE ye the Lord! prepare your glad voice,
His praise in the great assembly to sing:
In our great Creator let Israel rejoice,
And children of Zion be glad in their King!

Let them his great name extol in the dance,
With timbrel and harp his praises express;
Who always takes pleasure his saints to advance,
And with his salvation the humble to bless.

With glory adorned, his people shall sing
To God, who their lives with safety doth shield;
Their mouths filled with praises of him their great King,
A sword of just judgment their right hand shall wield.

The haughty and proud when God shall destroy,
His dreadful decree the meek shall proclaim:
Such honour and triumph his saints shall enjoy;
O therefore for ever exalt his great name.

149.3   L4.M.

Praise ye Jehovah! praise the Lord most
    holy,   [the weak:
Who cheers the contrite, girds with strength
Praise Him, who will with glory crown the
    And with salvation beautify the meek.[lowly,

Praise ye the Lord for all his loving-kindness,
    And all the tender mercies he hath shown:
Praise Him, who pardons all our sins and
    blindness,
    And calls us sons, and takes us for his own.

Praise ye Jehovah! source of every blessing;
    Before his gifts earth's richest boons are dim;
Resting in him, his peace and love possessing,
    All things are ours, for we have all in Him!

Praise ye the Father! God the Lord, who gave
    With full and perfect love, his only Son: [us,
Praise ye the Son, who died himself to save us,
    Praise ye the Spirit! praise the Three in One!

150   I.M.

Praise, O praise the name divine!
    Praise it at the hallowed shrine:
Let the firmament on high
To its Maker's praise reply.

2 Let each tongue, and every chord,
    Praise the name of Jacob's Lord:
Let his acts and power supreme,
To our songs suggest a theme.

3 Be the harp no longer mute,
   Sound the trumpet, touch the lute:
   Wake to life each tuneful string,
   Psaltery, pipe, and timbrel bring.

4 Let the organ, in his praise,
   Learn its loudest notes to raise;
   And the cymbal's varying sound
   From the vaulted roof rebound.

5 All who vital breath enjoy,
   In his praise that breath employ;
   All in one great chorus join,
   Praise, O praise the name divine!

150.2   P.M.

PRAISE the Lord, who reigns above,
   And keeps his courts below;
Praise him for his boundless love,
   And all his greatness show:
Praise him for his noble deeds,
Praise him for his matchless power;
Him, from whom all good proceeds,
   Let earth and heaven adore!

2 Publish, spread to all around
     The great Immanuel's name;
   Let the gospel trumpet sound,
     Him Prince of Peace proclaim:
   Praise him, every tuneful string,
   All the reach of heavenly art;
   All the power of music bring,
     The music of the heart.

3 Him, in whom they move and live,
   Let every creature sing;
Glory to our Saviour give,
   And homage to our King:
Hallowed be thy name beneath,
As in heaven on earth adored;
Praise the Lord in every breath,
   Let all things praise the Lord!

150.3   A.M.

O PRAISE the Lord in that blest place,
  From whence his goodness largely flows;
Praise him in heaven, where He his face
Unveiled in perfect beauty shows.

2 Praise him for all his mighty acts,
   Which He in our behalf has done:
His kindness this return exacts,
   With which our praise should equal run.

3 Let the shrill trumpet's warlike voice
   Make rocks and hills his praise rebound:
Praise him with harp's melodious noise,
   And gentle psaltery's silver sound.

4 Ye saints, who joyful hymns compose,
   On cymbals tune your notes of praise;
While loudly sounding music flows
   In anthems sweet, and solemn lays.

5 Let all, who vital breath enjoy,
   The breath he doth to them afford,
In just returns of praise employ;
   Let every creature praise the Lord.

FINIS.